Dear Brad + Roberta,

I am sorry t.

time to get to you. I greatly

appreciate you wanting it. I certainly

hope you enjoy it. Have a

Great Christmas.

James

Common Sense for Today's America

Common Sense for Today's America

by

JJ McKeever

"A world full of ignorant people is too dangerous to live in."

Garson Kanin, *"Born Yesterday"*

ISBN-10: 0991355024

ISBN-13: 978-0-9913550-2-0

Freeze Time Media

Cover illustration by Jen C. McKeever

To My Mom
With Lots of Love,
You have been so supportive for so long through so much,
my first book is dedicated to you.
(Hey, it only took me 30 some years after college to finally do one.
Hopefully there will be more in the near future!)

Acknowledgments

Putting a book together takes more than the author. First, I want to acknowledge the people who read my daily column. While it is nice to hear from friends and family that they like the way I write and what I have to say, it is very encouraging to hear from strangers who also enjoy my articles. I also appreciate their comments on my opinions. Some agree, some vehemently take me to task, but all of the feedback I receive helps to clarify my thinking and sometimes see a situation in a different light.

I want to thank my daughter-in-law, Jennifer C. McKeever, for designing the cover art for this book. She is a very talented artist and it is a joy to have her in the family.

I want to also thank Di Freeze of Freeze Time Media (www.freezetime-media.com) for the publishing and layout of the book. It is amazing how you can become friends with someone from across the country and you have not had a chance to meet yet! Di's encouragement and knowledge and occasional nagging were important in the development of this project.

A heartfelt thank you goes out to Marc LeVine of ICA Social Media (www.icanewfriend.com) for his work in the promotion of this book. Marc and I met as he came on board of the sinking ship of a start-up company I was working for. His knowledge and expertise showed up too late to help that company, but I learned an awful lot about marketing in this day of social media.

A special note of appreciation to Sandy Youngblood for reading my column every day and letting me know when something did not sound correct. Funny how I do well proofing someone else's work, but can't proofread myself!

Certainly not least is God who I want to thank for providing me wisdom and guidance as I set out on a different path in life.

And finally, I want to thank all of the politicians, government officials, sports figures, church leaders, and pretty much all of our diverse and exciting country that constantly gave me material to work with!

Introduction

I found myself at those middle age years of life where circumstances dictated a change of career. My story is not unlike so many others who suffered at the hands of the recession that plagued America in 2008. I first made a career detour by working for a start-up company as an editorial director and saw that after two years that we were never going to get off the ground. I decided to start my own writing business as a way to supplement my income and to prepare myself for the future. It was nice to actually have some foresight in my planning for a change since AuthorMax (www.authormax.com) became my main source for a livelihood when the start-up went kaput.

I learned that when you have a website, it is important to have a dynamic section that is always changing to increase the likelihood of the site showing up near the top of search results. Thus "Common Sense" was born. I started it to discipline myself to write something new every day (at least Monday through Friday), and it gave me the chance to vent. For a long time I have been getting disgusted with the direction so much of America has been going in. Many times it seems like problems get blown out of proportion just because individuals do not take the time to look clearly at a situation and try to think it through with a little common sense. And as time went on, my "Common Sense" took on a life of its own.

The other major issue that became a central theme is that we have become a country of extremes. Or at least the big mouths of the extremes are too loud and given too much credibility. I believe America is a country that settles more to the center between extreme liberal and conservative outlooks than anything else. While that may not be controversial or contribute to TV ratings, it is the truth. I think it is important to finally have a spokesman for that part of our nation. This group used to be called the "silent majority" and they tend to be the ones who suffer the most from the debates and inaction of our leaders. I want to continue see America grow and progress, not be mired in mud like we seem to have been for the last decade. If I can help direct some constructive conversation to an issue, then I did well.

But beside politics, I like to talk about other aspects of life. Nothing in this country is one dimensional. Politics is a big thing, but so are religion, work, education, and our fun activities like sports and movies. I touch on them all at one time or another. They all greatly affect us and sometimes need a new outlook breathed into them.

This book is a compilation of columns from my first year writing based on the comments I received or the fun factor I had in writing them. The paragraphs in italics at the end of each article are added comments I wrote as I put this book together. Pay attention to the date of each entry so you have an idea of what was going on in the country at that point.

I have always been a fan of this type of writing. Two of my favorite columnists of all time are the late, great Art Buchwald, and the great, still alive Rick Reilly. Art did politics and Rick mainly writes about sports and they both had the talent to make you laugh or cry, but they always made you think. If I can achieve just a fraction of what they did, then I did ok.

JJ McKeever

January 2014

The Day After

November 7, 2012

Now that the election is over we can all breathe a collective sigh of relief. Not because of who won, but because it is done with for another 4 years. Outside of a Donald Trump press conference where have you seen so much money spent and so little said? What's worse is that we are now living in the movie *Groundhog Day*. We wake up and are reliving the same nightmare we had the day before. We have the same President and basically the same House and Senate. If the movie continues we have the same results – nothing getting done – and we are all in trouble.

I would like to alert our government that getting elected or re-elected does not give you a mandate to do exactly as you please. You are there to help make this country a place where its people can hunt for life, liberty and the pursuit of happiness. You do not sit there holding your breath until you turn blue in the face because the other party is trying to do something you don't like. Nobody has a monopoly on good or bad ideas. Look around you – people are struggling to just stay even with life; forget about getting ahead. It is easy to throw around rhetoric about how you are all for the middle class. Now it is time to actually do something that strengthens the country, not tear it apart.

It is not a sin to compromise. The United States of America was founded on compromise. When the founding fathers were doing their thing to tell Great Britain to take a hike, they mothballed the whole slavery issue because that would have gotten in the way of independence. Of course that issue simmered for years. In fact, the one great case where the government ultimately did not compromise in the end was on slavery, and that resulted in a little conflict known as the Civil War.

Could the various economic and social issues facing this government lead to a Civil War? Probably not, but it could result in a great deal of conflict between the government and the people it is supposed to watch out for. We are not far from the situations we see in Europe where mismanagement of government has led to riots and public demonstrations. In fact we are darn near being bankrupt like some of those countries. I mean, we actually are bankrupt if you use the definition of having more debt than income to pay the bills.

Seems like it is time for the government to rise up and impress us. Make decisions that work without the constant bickering that makes every issue sound like a fight to the death. And everyone has to be willing to give a little. On the economic side, some taxes may have to be raised but there better be reductions in the budget at the same time. Some aspects of the county needs to be run like a business. No company can have a 20 year plan to reduce debt like our country comes up with to solve our fiscal crisis. They would be out of business.

I don't think the election made anyone feel relieved in the general population. We are all scared. My cry to the government is my favorite bumper sticker: "Lead, Follow or Get the Hell Out of the Way!"

This was my first column and ended up being a theme that I would repeat again…and again…and… The sad truth is that after a year since I wrote this, nothing has changed. One of the reasons I decided to put a book of columns together is so people can purchase it and present it to their government representatives…and whack them in the head with it in the hope of beating some sense into them!

A Tale of Two Networks

November 8, 2012

Last night I decided to see what the extremes of network TV news had to say about the election. After all, I am the kind of person who enjoys watching the cameras on Jerry Jones when the Dallas Cowboys lose a football game. First I watched MSNBC – primarily parts of *Hardball, Rachel Maddow, and the Ed Show*. I watched pieces of the show because their excessive glee made me look for an air sickness bag. I wish I had such a blind faith in a political party like they do. It was a bit of a consolation knowing the evening ratings for MSNBC were slightly higher than the IQ of a chipmunk so they were not affecting a lot of people.

Then I went over to Fox News. I mainly watched *The O'Reilly Factor* and *Hannity*. For full disclosure here I want to state that I am a registered Republican and fairly conservative. I did like Bill O'Reilly's show. I am not a regular viewer of any of these programs but I thought Bill did a fairly good job of looking at all sides of the election. I especially liked how at the end of his show when he responded to viewer's emails that accused him of not being more anti-Obama. He stuck to his guns about how he perceived his opinions and actions over the course of the election process (the incredibly loooong election process).

And then I watched Hannity…and started looking for my air sickness bags again. I really do not know what is worse: a sore loser or a sore winner. Sean started going off on the tactics the Obama team did in regards to ads, misrepresentation of the facts, the "liberal bias media," etc. This comes under the heading of one of my favorite quotes from the Bible: "Let him without sin throw the first stone." I understand that if news organizations adhered to this principle, a news show would have 30 minutes of commercials and no news. But really…did he watch any of the Republican commercials or review their tactics over the years?

Didn't Bush's team do some really underhanded tactics against John McCain in the 2004 primaries to torpedo his candidacy? Or is it ok to be a jerk when you are doing it within your own party?

Speaking as a Republican and conservative, Republicans do not have far to go to look at one of the major problems they have within their party. As long as their primary spokespeople are the Sean Hannity's and Rush Limbaugh's of the world, there is never going to be an environment where the Republican Party can analyze what they have to do to become relevant. You have to clinically look at all sides of the situation – not hope that by stating your point of view louder than anyone else it will be accepted. If they are really sincere in their beliefs, then they have a responsibility to the lemmings they continually lead over the cliff.

You are never going to have pure unbiased news, especially on television. The 24/7 news channels have created an environment where the media is no longer happy with just reporting the news…they want to be the news. Fine – that is not going to change. But whether you are a Democrat or Republican, go outside your box and get more information on the issues that concern you. And then speak out to your government reps. The last time I looked at our Constitution or any rules that govern a state or local community, those people that are elected are there to listen to us. We all forget that is basically their job! It is the system we have but if we actually try to use it, we may give elected officials a reality check of what they are doing. Time to stop being lazy and having others be our unelected mouthpieces. By the way, nowhere in the Constitution do I see anywhere where a media person or network is my representative.

So began another theme that became part of my writing. I really hate how people are so blinded by being a liberal or conservative that they think their side is always telling the truth. God gave us a brain; we have an obligation to use it. I blame channels like Fox and MSNBC for how they skewer things so much in their own particular direction. But in fairness, if the lemmings are going to suck up the Kool-Aid at the stations' troughs and that is what brings in their ratings, it is how the networks will plan programming. However, just declare yourself an entertainment network as opposed to a news outlet.

2016!!!!!........Enough Already!

November12, 2012

I knew it would happen with the inevitability of Christmas commercials after Halloween: speculation on who would run for President in 2016. Come on…candidates' campaign headquarters aren't cleaned up yet nor has Mitt Romney had a chance to drown his sorrows in his personal fortune. I think we owe it to the folks we just elected or re-elected to actually let them do something before we throw them out. Instead of looking ahead to the next cycle of lambast, the media should do something novel: report the damn news! Let's take as an example the country running towards the proverbial fiscal cliff. Take the time to explain what this means and the options available to the government. And here is something even more incredibly original to do: keep personalities and parties out of the discussion – at least in terms of laying down the facts.

I know things get tied up in politics today. You cannot get away from that. What scares me is how the flagship stations of the Republicans and Democrats (Fox News and MSNBC) use every single issue facing us as a scorecard. Way back in the dark ages when I took a journalism class at college, the emphasis was on reporting in an impartial way what was happening. Great effort was to be exerted in not injecting our own bias into a story. It is a sad day when the place where many people get their news – television – shot that entire concept to hell. The networks I have named are the greatest culprits, but you can see the shadows of it occurring all across network news.

So why should it matter? Because when the news is always wrapped in politics, it makes it harder for people to understand how the country works or what their government officials are trying to do. This breeds ignorance. This country is getting harder and harder to govern because of the sheer size and complexities of issues. The two political parties make it more difficult when they try to paint everything blue and red. But it seems to me that the news media is too lazy to do anything but jump on the bandwagon. Why go to the extra effort of showing both sides of a story if it fits your agenda to only show one?

So in the wake of the 2012 election being over, let's see what is going to happen before we have to listen to the pundits (that is really a Greek word meaning empty-headed) about the next go-around. We have many scandals, natural disasters, economic pitfalls, international incidents, etc. to get through before we need to worry about another election. Let's face it, 2012 decided nothing! It determined the leadership we will have to depend on, but it did nothing to solve the many problems facing the average American.

Think of a canoe going down a river of rapids with rocks and boulders all over the place. Two people are in the boat. Because of the election results, the Democrat is in the back, the Republican in the front. The rear paddler has primary responsibility for steering, but the truth is if they don't work together then the canoe will be dashed to pieces on the rocks. It would probably be best if they learned how to do things as a team for the safety of the boat. When you look at it in that light, it sounds kind of silly if the news is pulling for one paddler or the other, doesn't it? If it is turned into a contest of winning, the country…I mean canoe…is destroyed.

Following politics and happenings in American government has taken on the aura of sports. That is probably not fair to stations like ESPN who probably do a better job of digging into a topic than most major news outlets do these days. No longer is covering government about what is good for the American people; it is about who the winners and losers are between Republicans and Democrats. When that is the emphasis then Americans seem to always be on the losing end.

Where Are the Heroes?

November 13, 2012

In light of all the stories on General Petraeus stepping down as head of the CIA, it can be depressing that a bona fide military hero will forever be cast in a negative light. That part is a shame. Americans need good examples to look up to. There are a lot of problems within this story that we can look at in future columns. We can look at the role of the FBI, the timing of the announcement, who knew what when, etc. And I am not going to throw stones at Petraeus for his affair – that is between him and his wife. One thing I am sure of is that when it comes to the subject of sex, most people in this country are incredibly hypocritical. That is also another topic for the future.

And in spite of my title, I am not going to talk about the absence of heroes in America, but rather the abundance of them! While it is nice to have that Captain America type figure to look up to, it is easy to look locally for those to honor. These past two weeks have been showcases on just how much Americans look out for their own.

On the one hand we have the aftermath of Superstorm Sandy. It is incredible how when one's back is against the wall, people dig down to help their own. In my neck of the woods there has been a tremendous amount of property damage, very-long term power outages, and loss of life. Some of the more inspirational stories I heard included the work of the nurses and doctors in evacuating Bellevue Hospital in NYC. These folks went beyond the call of duty in getting everyone out of there when the storm crippled the power. There was a young man at the shore who heard his neighbors calling for help as the ocean whipped around the street. He got his surfboard out and negotiated 10 feet of water to ferry them back to his house. And there was the unemployed woman whose car broke down as she was trying to get back to her kids in the storm. A couple stopped, picked her up, and then gave her $200 to tie her over without wanting any payback. These are but a few small examples of how people helped others during the catastrophe.

And you want more heroes? You just had to look at the National Football League on Sunday and Monday. I am not talking about the players. The NFL does one of the finest jobs in honoring the military as they showed on Veterans Day. Watching the beginning of the Monday Night game on ESPN, Pittsburgh spotlighted veterans who were there saluting the flag in the pouring rain. There was a gentleman there who was a survivor of Pearl Harbor and a sergeant from Korea and others. Their dignity showed through on TV. This scene was repeated throughout stadiums across the country. Not only do we have our veterans of the military around us, but we have our current crop of military heroes, many who are in harm's way.

The story of General Petreaus is unfortunate, both for him and for our country. But it is no reason to get discouraged. America is full of heroes from the inner city to the prairies to the battlefield. And you know what would be really cool: if you meet a current or former military person, or someone who has done something special, say "thank you." It costs nothing and goes a long way.

It is the average person on the streets that can be the most heroic. In this day and age, if a person can go out day-after-day, work hard and be able to support themselves and/or their family, they are a hero. Heroes come in all shapes and sizes — just look around!

Childhood Memories of the Fiscal Cliff

November 14, 2012

Do you remember being a kid and hearing your parents discussing the household finances? Sometimes these could escalate into arguments that may last days. And most kids get the same feeling when their folks cannot get along – a sick, queasy feeling in the stomach and the sensation that a black cloud is hanging over the home. Plus there is a feeling of helplessness. A child can offer to give back his $2.00 a week allowance, but he knows it is a drop in the bucket. Sometimes there is a family talk on how everyone needs to cut back a little to make ends meet. Circumstances can be as varied as a parent losing a job to a new baby coming into the family.

This is what we have been experiencing with all of the talk of the impending "fiscal cliff" of higher taxes and budget cutbacks looming ahead of the country on December 31. The parents (Congress and the President) are bickering about how to fix the situation. The news media treats it like a sporting event to determine who the winner of the argument is going to be. And us, the American citizens, are huddled in our homes listening to the stubborn parents argue because we know that whatever they decide is going to affect us one way or the other.

To even find ourselves as a country in this situation is a crime. We elect these people to prevent the United States from getting into this situation. First of all, a common sense household creates a budget and works at following it. And a family knows it has to be nimble enough to weather unexpected emergencies and set-backs. When was the last time the President or Senate had an honest-to-goodness budget? I guess their philosophy is that if they had an approved budget, they would actually have to measure up to it. Without anything in writing there is no accountability.

In a home, an event like the water heater breaking is unforeseen and can throw the family budget off. Our national fiscal cliff did not just appear the day after the election. Everyone knew it was coming, but nobody wanted to jeopardize their chances by taking a stand that could alienate the voters. (A lot of this is because elected officials fear to tell people the truth. They should try it. I think they would be surprised that the American people really are not stupid...but that is another column.) Not only did Congress and the President know it was coming – they created it! They failed to have the balls last year and in the previous years to implement a plan to run our country smoothly and economically. Read that phrase again: "run our country." Isn't that their job description?! The deals of 2011 were made to set up this scenario. They hid from actually solving the problem. The party mascots should not be a donkey or elephant...they should both use an ostrich with its head stuck in the ground!

And now the same old speeches are being made about how to solve the problem. It is only a week after the election and the only thing needed to get through the rhetoric is a bigger shovel. It is frightening because whatever is decided is going to affect our "allowance." Not only are individuals at a loss of what to expect but so are all the small, midsize, and large businesses that make up our country. Unlike the government, people and companies need to plan ahead in the hope of reaching their goals. It is just like the really sick feeling inside a kid when the parents' argument reaches nuclear levels. Maybe as a kid we did not have a say, but as an American you can at least tell the people who represent you that they are playing with your life and they better get their head out of the sand (or wherever you think their head is at).

My mind is constantly boggled by the fact that our country operates without a real budget. As a country, we do everything that is counter-intuitive to how a large company or any organization would run. One of the problems when you constantly do not follow any rules or procedures is that things fall apart. Sound familiar?

Black Thursday — Stop the Madness!!

November 16, 2012

The great thing about Thanksgiving is that it is an American holiday that everyone embraces. It does not matter what a person's race, religion, nationality, or political leanings are. It is a time to gather with family and friends to relax and reflect on all that life provides. Actually thanking God here would be a big plus, but that is a different issue. The warmth of the holiday also spills out through people and organizations who try to provide a Thanksgiving meal to folks who are having a tough time. I am sure there will be stories of Thanksgiving reaching those who were displaced by the recent hurricane in the East.

However, there are storm clouds gathering over this genuine American celebration. American greed is now running rampant through the day as retail stores launch their big Christmas sales on Thanksgiving Day. Really?!?!? Now we can end our Turkey Day by watching the late news when the local Wal-Mart or Target open their doors for the "Early Bird" sales and we watch customers rush in like the Running of the Bulls at Pamplona! We get to see people pushing and shoving their way over others who should still be digesting their dinner. We can see first-hand the happy employees who had no choice but to leave their families to be ringmasters of this circus.

And for what? I guess so the stores can start ringing up their Christmas sales 8 − 12 hours earlier than if they opened their doors at 6:00 AM on Friday. I dare anyone to show me a study that shows the same sales generate more income when implemented on Thanksgiving instead of Black Friday. All the stores are doing is ruining one of the few American celebrations we have. And it is for blatant greed on their part. Nothing more, nothing less. It does not help the consumer. It further commer-cializes both Thanksgiving and Christmas in one single meaningless grandstand marketing ploy.

Wal-Mart employees are threatening to strike. I hope they do. I hope the customers realize how ridiculous it is and they strike too. You know what would be really cool? If customers stayed away from all stores that open on Thanksgiving for the whole weekend. The only way to get greed to stand up and listen is by kicking it in the money till.

The truth is that many people are still hurting in this country and most people are watching their dollars. Uncertainty abounds in what the future holds for the United States economy. In the last few years statistics show that people are sticking to a budget when buying for Christmas. When they reach their limit, they are done.

To the retailers of America, you are going to get everyone's Christmas money anyway. What is the difference if you get it Thanksgiving, Black Friday or December 24th? Let's face it — many people shoot their wad and finish shopping the Thanksgiving weekend. Then the retailers beat their chests and cry how nobody is spending in December and then produce really crazy sales. So thanks for ruining Thanksgiving and may your cash registers all burnout on November 22.

I still hate that stores open on Thanksgiving. The idea of the day is to be together with friends and family and to reflect and give thanks for all we have. I really do not see how not being open for a few extra hours is going to completely ruin a store's Christmas sales. That happens because people don't have enough money to spend at Christmas like they used to.

Twinkies, the Job Market, and Fear

November 19, 2012

I always thought that in the event of a nuclear holocaust, the only survivors would be cockroaches and Twinkies. Both are indestructible while having questionable nutritional value with the edge going to the cockroaches. As we have seen in the past week, even Twinkies can be brought to their knees by the way companies are run in America.

According to the the news, Hostess, the company that makes Twinkies and other baked goods, has to file for bankruptcy because it could not settle a strike with one of its unions that the actual bakers work for. The company wanted these employees to take an 8% cut in wages as well as cuts in benefits. The union held firm and the company said it had to lay off all the other workers and shut down operations. So it sounds like a case of a union screwing up another company.

Union bashers would love to showcase their ignorance and trumpet this as an example of their mindlessness. But taking a minute to look at United States labor history and this event should make anyone who brings home a paycheck realize how tenacious their situation is. Back at the turn of the 20th century, the majority of American workers were in terrible work situations. Long days, child labor, no job protection, and the threat of unsafe conditions were a constant. It was only by workers banning together and exerting that power that many job constraints and benefits we take for granted today came into being. Indeed, the entire strength of the middle class that politicians shout out to rebuild today developed from strong union activity after World War II.

The issue here was that the pendulum of power swung too much in favor of the unions. Innovation and profitability of companies became severely threatened because of union demands. This led to an enlightened time of management and unions having to work together to get a company back on the right foundation. The automotive industry is a good blueprint in how to manage this partnership.

However, many companies took advantage of a stagnant economy and high unemployment to tilt the partnership to their favor. The argument became that you either do what we say, take what we give you in pay, and suck up the cuts in your benefits or we will find someone else to take your place. Loyalty to workers became non-existent for many companies. And Hostess became a model of this type of business. For one thing, it is currently owned my two hedge funds. Their only purpose is to make money for those who have invested into the funds. To hell with the products that are made or what is paid to the minions that produce them. This is what too many businesses have deteriorated into: no human being with a pride of ownership. Many bear a stronger resemblance to a bunch of jackals that want to take down the weak of the herd and get as much out of it as possible before discarding the bones.

So instead of just yapping about strengthening a middle class, maybe it is time to actually do something about it. Capitalism is our foundation, but only if there is a sense of actually having a good company at the end of the day. Regulations that force companies to cut back on worker's hours, benefits and well-being are incredibly short-sighted and exactly what is happening. Take a quick look at Hostess. Let's say a baker for them makes $40,000 a year. An 8% cutback would mean that employee is taking home $3200 less AND has to pay more for fewer benefits. Who of us can afford that? And it is easy to scoff and say, "Let them get a part-time job!" Many of us do that. And we wonder why family life suffers, fear runs rampant, and people are on edge about the future.

One more thing on this discussion: I did not see in any news story where the investors of the hedge funds owning Hostess were taking any kind of cut. They will make out fine if they sell the company off. The almost 20,000 employees can sweat out the change. In too much of the corporate world, this is what America has become. Happy Thanksgiving!

Unions came about because the average worker was exploited. Then they went too far in one direction where the unions' demands caused a problem with a company making profits. So things went completely in the other direction where workers are once again exploited. In this example, if you do not pay your workers a fair wage, your own workers cannot afford the Twinkies.

God, Thanksgiving and Lincoln

November 21 & 22, 2012

With the cinematic masterpiece *Lincoln* in theatres, it is timely to remind the nation that it was President Lincoln who decreed the establishment of a day of Thanksgiving. I think it is important to look at an excerpt of the proclamation he signed on October 3, 1863:

"….No human counsel hath devised nor hath any mortal hand worked out these great things. They are the gracious gifts of the Most High God, who, while dealing with us in anger for our sins, hath nevertheless remembered mercy. It has seemed to me fit and proper that they should be solemnly, reverently and gratefully acknowledged as with one heart and one voice by the whole American People. I do therefore invite my fellow citizens in every part of the United States, and also those who are at sea and those who are sojourning in foreign lands, to set apart and observe the last Thursday of November next, as a day of Thanksgiving and Praise to our beneficent Father who dwelleth in the Heavens. And I recommend to them that while offering up the ascriptions justly due to Him for such singular deliverances and blessings, they do also, with humble penitence for our national perverseness and disobedience, commend to His tender care all those who have become widows, orphans, mourners or sufferers in the lamentable civil strife in which we are unavoidably engaged, and fervently implore the interposition of the Almighty Hand to heal the wounds of the nation and to restore it as soon as may be consistent with the Divine purposes to the full enjoyment of peace, harmony, tranquility and Union…."**

Notice how prominent God is mentioned in this statement? Lincoln does not call for thanks to be given to the government or the enlightened human race for all we have, but to God. The proclamation eloquently illustrates all that the Lord has done for this great country and the belief in how He is in Heaven over us. It is a daily lesson we should all be reminded of every day. OK, for some Thanksgiving may be the only time all year you may bow your head in thanks, but it is better than nothing.

There are two lessons here that I believe people should think about. The first is that we do live in a truly blessed nation. The United States, with all of our problems and conflicts, has the greatest combination of natural resources and freedom in the world today. You can make a great case of how God has looked out for this nation. I do not think it is silly to believe we should conduct ourselves in such a way that he will continue to bless us. And this is not an endorsement or indictment of any one religion institution. It is more of an overall call to action to guard against our tendency to get too full of ourselves. History shows that when man thinks he is supreme, disaster usually follows.

The second lesson is the whole church vs. state thing. That amendment to the Constitution came about to guard against the historical problem in Europe of government sticking its fingers into church affairs and vice-versa. It was not meant to strike God out of all conversation. We forget about God and He is going to distance himself from us. If an atheist wants his beliefs respected, then he needs to respect the beliefs of others. He should not be able to run to court and complain about a Nativity display set up on public land because it is against his beliefs. If he wants to set up a "Happy Winter Solstice" banner across from it, fine. That is the right the Constitution gives: freedom to worship, not blocking someone's ability to do so by technicality.

More than ever, I believe people are looking for answers and a moral compass to conducting their life. God has always been there, and always will be. Give Him thanks today, tomorrow and every day. And if you aren't sure about God, don't be afraid to educate yourself. It may open a wonderful new world.

This was my first column where I brought God into the forefront of what I wanted to say. It is a shame that we live in a country where atheists can have their say, but beware if you dare speak of God. And for too many years, our legal system has completely perverted the whole separation of church and state. I would like to feel I can express my beliefs in God without reservation as much as a person who does not believe can express his.

Thanksgiving...and Fear

November 23, 2012

Thanksgiving was everything it is supposed to be. A good time with family and friends intertwined with parades, food, and football. As I marvel at how much food and wine the human body can consume in one day, I also find myself thinking about a conversation that happened last night after dinner. There were a few of us sitting around chatting and it was very enlightening.

First of all, everyone was very thankful for the usual: family, health, and we all actually had jobs. The talk drifted into the state that the country is in when everyone indicated they were extremely thankful the election was over. The consensus was that a lot of money was spent to keep the country in the same state it was in before the election. We once again have a President who has issues as a leader and a Congress that has no clue to what is going on. And this conclusion was reached by people who had quite different jobs: business owners, independent contractors, and typical employees.

The real fear is that the government is doing things without any idea of how it actually affects people. Let's take Obamacare. Full implementation is going to cause companies that can get away with it to cut back on the hours they give employees so they can get under the mandatory 30 hours where they have to provide health care. Several examples were given of business associates where this is their plan. That is a big implementation obstacle that nobody seems to have considered in the frenzy to pass the law.

Folks around the table are tired of hearing how taxes are going to be raised without any real talk about cutting back on the size of the government. Nobody has the guts to lead and spell out for the country the pros and cons of any action. Everything is covered in liberal or conservative bias with no clear communication to everyone. And the media is as guilty as the government since they are so hyped up on *being* the news that they forget to actually report the news. Thus it is hard to get a handle on anything from the Twinkie problem to the Petraeus scandal. There seems to be a lot of shouting going on about issues that affect all of us without any real information.

And Congress received the brunt of the abuse in the discussion. People would like to see their reps actually come into town and talk to people *before* re-election time. Tip O'Neill said, "All politics is local" and maybe our representatives should think of that concept. It would be a good idea if politicians really understood what the people go through that they are supposed to serve. Like how hard it is to keep home and family together. Like how many jobs are terrible because it is difficult to get a living wage and some basic benefits. Like how families have to make decisions between food and medicine if sickness is in the family. And like how business owners want to sell out because they cannot deal with the wishy-washiness of our leaders.

I am not making this conversation up. Franklin Roosevelt famously said, "We have nothing to fear, but fear itself.."He is correct but the truth is that the reality is getting harder and harder to put out of your mind. A lot of our nation has trouble with the goal of living comfortably – not extravagantly – but just with some peace of mind. And our leaders' inaction is creating a lot of anxious moments in families. Everyone was very thankful that we still live in the greatest country, but the seams are starting to give way and we all wonder where we will be a year from now.

That fear FDR talked about is becoming a cancer. And we all know how hard cancer is to cure. I am constantly amazed how often our government officials are so out of touch with what Americans are going through. All you have to do is look around and talk to family and friends and you can see and hear how much folks are so unsure about the future. Granted, man plans and God laughs, but we all like to have some sense of what to expect in the future with things like taxes, health benefits, social security, etc.

Post Thanksgiving Thoughts

November 26, 2012

After giving thanks to God for family, friends, and everything I have in life, here are some tongue-in-cheek thanks (in no particular order). I proudly state that I am also thankful that:

- the Jets lost Thanksgiving night so that Rex Ryan and his big mouth may be sent packing
- there are no more election ads on TV
- Republicans and Democrats are sparring over how to avoid the fiscal cliff (this movie is getting old)
- television has more singing and dancing contests than you can shake a stick at (I honestly cannot keep them straight anymore – I solve the problem by not watching any)
- the country has so many unemployed and underemployed people and still nothing is getting done (good leadership, Obama – what, the election is over and we don't worry about it anymore?)
- the retailers screwed up one of the last real holidays in America with their blatant greed by opening on Thanksgiving
- we will be hearing from these retailers in another week how their sales are shrinking because they already took everyone's money in the first four days of the holiday sales season
- Congress has remained virtually unchanged – it is good to know ahead of time that absolutely nothing constructive will get done in the next year
- Disney bought the Star Wars franchise – it is fun listening to geeks beat their chest and say how George Lucas' vision will be tarnished. Here is a news bulletin: George had a great idea, acted on it and made fun movies that made him scads of cash and then he sold the franchise. That is an American success story. And Disney has a pretty

good rep in making good movies.

- Colleges keep raising their tuition – I think our nation's universities should be commended on devising a business model to charge a consumer outlandish prices that has no bearing on the actual education the student receives

- Donald Trump is still around – he should be the poster child on how not to act if you get wealthy

- the National Hockey League is on lockout/strike – somebody has to explain to me why the sports league that has so much trouble attracting a following goes out of its way every 5 years to cancel the season

- the entertainment media talks about the Kardashians so much –watching this self-absorbed dysfunctional family should make anyone glad they have a constructive purpose in life

- President Obama neglected to thank God (again) in his Thanksgiving message. For someone who professes to be a Christian but would rather suck up to the atheists of the world – well, let's just say that the last election won't be his final judgment

- the Dallas Cowboys have lost so much this season. Is there anyone who does not enjoy watching the TV camera on Jerry Jones when they lose?

- our economy has created a boom for the "independent contractor." Now an employer can hire the workers he needs and not have to worry about paying them well, offering benefits, taking care of his taxes and social security, etc. Nothing like fear and depression to spur others to wield power over those who are really hurting.

One thing I wish I could really be thankful for is that some steps are being taken to help so many people that are hurting. It does not seem to be happening yet, but we can continue to hope and pray. I am still thankful for the Jets and the Cowboys sucking though!

This type of column is fun because there is so much material to work with. Sometimes I put great thought into writing and sometimes I just want to get the laugh! It is nice when I hear that something I write makes someone laugh or chuckle. And since I wrote this it is evident that the New York Jets and Dallas Cowboys really do not have a clue how to be a professional football team.

You Can Teach Children, but the Government...

November 27, 2012

While I was walking through the mall the other day dodging Christmas shoppers, I had a flashback to 20 years ago. The scene was another suburban mall and I was herding my 4 young kids around. I distinctly remember taking a time out and sitting down with them to rest. One of my children asked if we could go to the toy store to buy something. I explained Daddy had only so much money to spend and we could not do that today. Then one of my sons said in all innocence, "Just go to the bank machine and take some more money out." Bang! We had our first economic lesson as I explained to them that you had to make money in order to put it in the bank so it was there when you needed it.

You know what happened? They got the concept and we moved on. In every walk of life, whether personal or business, fiscal responsibility is essential for meeting goals. Why is this treated as a joke in the United States government?

In all the talk of the "fiscal cliff," the fact that the government is once again nearing its debt limit has not been widely talked about. Guess what America? The government only has $154 billion left before it maxes out its $16.394 trillion credit limit. I cannot comprehend that amount. It's even more than the number of reality shows on TV. You can't print up enough Monopoly money to cover the debt. So what does Congress and the President do? They wave the government magic wand and increase the national credit limit. Just try and get your credit card limit increased if you already owe big bucks!

I know this problem won't get fixed overnight, but for the love of the country, start doing something real about it. The other day Treasury Secretary Timothy Geithner said that Congress should stop placing legal limits on the amount of money the government can borrow and effectively lift the debt limit to infinity. You have got to be kidding me!

That would be like putting an alcoholic in the Jack Daniels factory. Instead of hard decisions, the government just changes the fiscal rules. I bet everyone wishes they could do that with their mortgage company or for their car loan, etc. I often wonder if anyone in government could effectively manage a lemonade stand, let alone the country.

I think – and hope – the American people are looking past that instant gratification moment government mistakes for decision-making. This is a message we have to get out to our illustrious elected officials. Don't do something that sounds good; take action that is effective. I do not want to hear about another agreement that will reduce the national deficit by $10 trillion dollars in 20 years. First of all, nobody believes it will happen. It sounds like Rex Ryan proclaiming the Jets will be in the Super Bowl. Second of all, it sounds like how the old Soviet Union unveiled 5 year plans that never went anywhere.

Start modestly. Let's have one year where the United States breaks even. It won't reduce the deficit but at least it won't be added to. That would be something wonderful to build on. And it is going to take some new tax increases AND spending cuts. What the government wastes in a year by being inefficient could probably fund the state of New Jersey. It is way past time for Congress and the President to take responsibility as the stewards of our country. They take an oath to serve the United States, not a certain political party or lobbyist. If we stay on the present course, the country's credit rating will be on par with Ethiopia and our grandkids are going to know this country by another name: Greece!

The smoke and mirrors and BS we put up with as the government tries to explain what they are doing...or not doing...gets very tiresome. Sometimes I think the President and Congress believe we are stupid and cannot see through their lies. Maybe if they treat us with respect, we will start doing the same to them!

Travel the Friendly Skies!

November 29, 2012

There was an article out yesterday listing the Top 10 airlines in the world. Guess what? There was not one American company on the list. For anyone who travels even a little bit, this comes as no surprise. Traveling by air in this country is one of the most depressing experiences known to mankind. From the airlines to the terminals to airport parking, air travel - which used to be exciting and even fun at times - is approached with all of the anticipation of a root canal.

Let's look at the airlines. Usually the flying experience has all the ambiance of a cattle car with tray tables. If these companies could get away with it, we would be standing on flights hanging onto a safety bar for a two hour trip. God forbid if you cannot get a bite to eat at the airport if your flight lands just in time to jump on your connecting flight, because you will starve. Or you pay $5.00 for cheese and crackers and another $3.00 for a mini-bottle of water. Taking a flight is like planning a day at the beach. You have to bring your own food and drink or go without or pay a lot of money for garbage. (Of course you have to buy it at the airport after you go through security or it will be confiscated by the TSA Nazis. More on them in a minute.)

Finding a direct flight anywhere is getting harder and harder. The truth is that in some cases it is actually quicker and cheaper to drive to your destination. When you factor in connecting flights, layovers, getting to the airport, waiting at the airport and the potential for delays and unforeseen hassles, it may be best to just say "the hell with it" and take a car. And a car does not charge you per bag for your luggage. Baggage fees are getting ridiculous. I wish airlines would just factor them into the cost of the ticket and hide the expense like they used to do. It all ends up the same price but psychologically the traveler is not so upset about getting screwed. I guess the other option is if you are going someplace for a week, it would be worth shipping your clothes via UPS or FedEx!

Next problem you deal with are the airports. Airports near major cities tend to be old, out-of-date, crowded, and traffic to them could be a plague out of the Bible. A Sam's Club store is more warm and friendly than airports. It's one thing if you have someone drop you off, but if you take your own car and park, a small loan is necessary to pay the bill. I often wonder what people coming from other countries think when they land at one of our international airports for the first time. Here they are, finally seeing America, and they say, "Yuck. The pilot must have landed in the wrong place. This must be Bulgaria."

And to really get you in the travelling mood, you have to go through security before you get to your plane. I am beginning to think it would be a lot easier if all flights were nude. Frightening maybe, but it would be easier. I have seen TSA agents have an almost sadistic glee at throwing stuff that does not meet their criteria in the trash. Many are good people but some excel at being jerks. I know security is needed, but some of the things you go through — especially if you are one of the random folks they select — are terribly humiliating and invasive. Plus there is no consistency. Procedures and rules can vary from one airport to another. Something that you could carry on a flight in Chicago may be thrown out in Cleveland. And a heads-up to the airlines and airport bosses: like it or not these TSA employees are the faces of air travel. You may have no control of them, but they reflect on you.

The point is that this is an industry that America used to lead in and could be proud of. Now it seems that most American airlines are either in a state of bankruptcy or they nickel and dime you to death for the sake of their solvency. There does not seem to be any pride any more by these companies or a desire to treat the customer as a person. Sometimes people will pay a little more if they feel like they are getting their money's worth. I think the only hope is inventing Star Trek's transporter system. It would be nice to thumb our noses at the airlines, airports, and the TSA storm troopers as we say, "Beam me to my destination!"

Air travel in our country is a joke: airports with the ambience of a warehouse, scheduled flights that are as sure of a thing as buying a lotto ticket, and security that rarely gets anything good said about it. I still enjoy travelling to new places, but the actual trip is now something to survive rather than enjoyed. Once again, the customers get the short end of the buying experience.

Born in the USA...We Are #1...I Mean 16th!!

November 30, 2012

The Economic Intelligence Unit is a renowned research group that announced yesterday their "Where to Be Born in 2013" index. This predicts the countries that offer the greatest possibility of a newborn having "a healthy, safe, and prosperous life." The last time this was done was in 1988 and the United States ranked Number 1. We have not only lost the top spot, we have tumbled out of the Top 10. At #16, I think that those that run the country should hang their heads in shame.

We are still the world's biggest economy and the only borderline super-power that exists, but how does that help the children who are being born in the upcoming year? One of the leading reasons leading to the drop in the polls is the fact that "babies will inherit the large debts of the boomer generation." How ironic, and telling, that the circus consuming Washington and the media right now is focused on the debt and financial crisis of running the country.

Let's do a quick history lesson here. The Revolution happened because the "Founding Fathers" believed we had something here worth fighting for that would benefit future generations. Lincoln persevered throughout the Civil War to keep the country together because he believed it was the best for all present and future Americans. The United States joined two world wars to safeguard our way of life so it would be around for years to come. For over two hundred years, leaders put their honor and lives on the line to keep the country going but always with an eye to the future.

Unfortunately, we now live in an instant gratification world. You can find almost anything you want with a click of the button, and if you have money or credit, it will be on your doorstep within days. I think the economic slump of the last 4 years has been good in the sense that it woke folks up about how they handle their finances. Yes, they can click and buy. But a lot more thought seems to be given to such decisions these days. Unemployment, under-employment, credit crunch, and other circumstances have given many a greater respect for money, accumulating savings, and having a plan when you need to purchase something major. This is how common sense people learn from mistakes and hardships.

Then we have the people in Washington who do not learn. They thrive on instant gratification. It is the Charlie Brown motto: "Why do today what can be put off till tomorrow." $16 trillion in debt? Just raise the debt limit, someone else can figure out how to pay it. Medicare too expensive? We'll come up with a 20-year plan; who cares what happens between now and then. Attempt to make the government a little smaller and less expensive? No, then I may not get elected and that is certainly more important than what is good for the country.

Understand why we are 16th? We send people to Washington who do not care about the future generation anymore. This has been going on for a good twenty years now. Our children and grandchildren are going to be hard pressed to get up to the same standard of living as we have. And it is a struggle now for many. You cannot keep your head in the sand forever. Write letters and emails to your reps and say enough is enough. I want my children and grandchildren to thrive. I do not think it is right when half of every dollar they make will go to paying costs of the country incurred **before** they were born!!

Arrogant boasting about what we used to be does not guarantee the future. Like a sports team, America needs to be a balancing act of keeping a good team on the field while constantly looking to the future. Way too often the country wants to look to what we had in the past. It is a paradox, but to get to the success of the past, you have to plan for the future. And that is something our leadership is pretty woeful at doing.

Football, Guns and Bob Costas

December 3, 2012

Football fans and nonfans had to be shocked as the story unfolded over the weekend of how Jovan Belcher, a defensive back for the Kansas City Chiefs, shot and killed his girlfriend in front of the girl's mother. Then Belcher drove to the Chiefs' training facility and killed himself in front of his coach and general manager. Your hearts and prayers have to go out to the girl's family, the Chiefs, and for the 3-month old daughter of the couple that was left behind. This is a tragedy that touched many.

So during halftime of NBC's Sunday Night Football game, announcer Bob Costas took the time he always has at the intermission to quote extensively from a piece by Fox Sports columnist Jason Whitlock. After praising the column, Costas said: "In the coming days, Jovan Belcher's actions and their possible connection to football will be analyzed. Who knows? But here, wrote Jason Whitlock, is what I believe. If Jovan Belcher didn't possess a gun, he and Kasandra Perkins would both be alive today."

And what is all over the media today: How dare Costas speak out against guns during the game! It is not the time or the place. What right does he have to speak out? Who wants to have a football game mucked up by talking about this? Etc, etc, etc....

I want to make clear I am not writing about guns here. That opinion will come out in a future column. What I do want to talk about is the hypocrisy that pervades this country and the mentality of some sports' fans.

I applaud Bob Costas for taking the forum he had available and for speaking his mind. Too often people in the media are pigeonholed into certain niches and they are not supposed to speak outside of that defined area. Costas over the years has proven himself smart, articulate, and not afraid to give his opinion even if it may not be the "company line." A Chris Matthews or Sean Hannity could give his opinion on the matter and people will think it is part of their job. But heaven forbid if a simple "sportscaster" had something to say about such a tragedy.

I doubt Costas did not think through the ramifications of what he did. I have no idea if he will be called on the carpet by NBC, but he probably figured that was a possibility. And he went ahead and talked about it anyway. That takes guts. Not a lot of media people or politicians are accused of that these days. A theme that runs through much of American literature, movies and TV shows is that if an individual sees something wrong, he goes about trying to correct it. So here we have an actual example of it, and people are up in arms.

Guns are protected by the Constitution. So is free speech. Whether I agree with Costas or not, it does not matter — I will defend his right to say it. That is also true of Rachel Maddow, Bill O'Reilly, Rush Limbaugh or even (gasp) Ed Schultz (from The Ed Show) on MSNBC.

And as for sports fans who decry that a football telecast is no place for talk of this kind — get a life! As much as I miss them, long gone are the days when sports are a place of pure escapism from the trials of living. Any newspaper section, magazine, or TV station devoted to sports is full of talk on labor negotiations, drug abuse, arrest reports, and other matters from the dark side. Once again in our country, we have a murder-suicide that affects many, many people. You cannot sweep it under the rug, nor should it be. Whether your team won or lost yesterday should not over shadow the things going on in your country. I saw 2 other stories about murder-suicides in the news this morning. Not as high profile as a professional football player, but equally tragic.

Let's not kill the messenger of the obvious here. Bob Costas will at least get a dialogue started and maybe some people will start thinking. I do not know what demons were at work on Jevon Belcher, but anything that can be done to lessen the chances of another instance of this tragedy happening is fine in my book.

It is disheartening how myopic people can be. So many folks do not want one part of their life to touch another part. Guess what? Life does not work like that. It is especially true in this day and age when the speed of everything seems to cause seemingly unconnected moments of life to intertwine. I would love it if I could find an activity that lets me forget about all the problems of the world, but that just does not seem to ever happen. So for those that complain about people like Mr. Costas — get over it!

Random Acts of Kindness

December 4, 2012

"When you did it to these my brothers you were doing it to me! When you refused to help the least of these my brothers, you were refusing to help me" (Matthew 25:40-45).

A stranger in NJ giving out hundred dollar bills to people in need, a cop in NY buying boots for a homeless man, and a lady buying the bundle of gifts a family had on layaway at a Wal-Mart are just some outstanding examples of people helping others. These are the stories we always hear about this time of the year as we get closer to Christmas and the Holiday Season. And hopefully they do warm the heart and give you an incentive to act when you run into someone that needs help.

It doesn't have to be anything big either. It could be something as simple as taking a meal to a neighborhood family that has fallen on hard times. Donating a Christmas present through your church or work to someone who would not get anything is great and should not stop. Making a little effort to reach out in person to someone or a group will do wonders for them and you. In this electronic age that puts a premium on speed and a mask to hide behind, a little personal contact will put life into perspective. It is sort of like being in the movie, instead of just sitting back and watching it.

The truth is that there are many people out there hurting. It could be the person who sits next to you every day at work or the woman in front of you at the coffee line. It is obviously the ones who flock to our social service centers for help, but it could also be the happy-looking family at church. It does not matter. Listen. Talk to people. Put "you" aside for a moment and decide if there is anything, no matter how little, that can make someone else's life better. It might even be someone in your own family who just needs to hear that you love them.

Things are going to get worse before they get better in our country. Election time is over so if you are hoping to cash in on promises made by your candidate, I hope you have the patience of Job. All indications are that employment and the economy for the average person is not going to get much better in the near future, and may actually backslide, depending on what Washington decides on finances in the next few weeks.

Our current leaders (I use the term loosely) seem to have the motto, "When the going gets tough, we don't do anything!" But over our history Americans have stuck with, "When the going gets tough, the tough get going." For all of the internal strife we have suffered through at times, Americans tend to watch out for their fellow Americans. Maybe our colors and nationalities are at an all-time mix, but we are still in this together. And it is the little things that eventually add up to one large positive.

So keep your eyes open. We can all do something nice for someone. Such an act has a way of multiplying its effects in manners we cannot even fathom. As Americans we have to watch out for each other – the government is not going to pull it off. It is what we are supposed to do as people. It is what God wants from us. Therefore, the best gift you may get this Christmas season is what you give. Go for it.

There are many good things that people do for others during the Christmas season and quite often throughout the year. This has always been the unsung strength of America: people helping people. I didn't think it hurt to remind folks to keep the giving spirit in mind. I also have discovered for myself how looks can be deceiving. Often there are people we would never guess who are in difficulty who need our help the most. As our national safety net programs are either over-flowing or being phased out, there is no shortage of people needing help.

Republicans, Double-Talk, and Disability

December 5, 2012

I think everyone likes to be associated with an organization they can be proud of. Something they feel reflects their own values and beliefs. This can be a church, social group, service club, political organization, etc. As a Republican it is getting difficult to understand the motivations of the party. And to illustrate this point, we will drive away from the fiscal cliff (thank God) to something that happened yesterday: the rejection of the United Nation's Convention on the Rights of Persons with Disabilities (CRPD).

This was struck down in the Senate with 38 Republicans casting "no" votes. The 61-38 vote fell five short of the two-thirds majority needed to ratify a treaty. This treaty was championed by Senators from both sides of the aisle and endorsed by those who are intimate with the problems of dealing with disabilities. The reason given for the rejection is that Republicans objected to taking up a treaty during the lame-duck session of the Congress and warned that the treaty could pose a threat to U.S. national sovereignty.

Let's look at the lame-duck issue. Who the hell are they kidding? The U.S. Senate has hardly done anything constructive during the previous 11 months of the year. This is the "most exclusive club in America." They cannot even come up with a budget for the country. If they were the Board of Directors of a company, they would all be ousted and people who want to do the job would be in their place.

Speaking on the national sovereignty issue we can look at two quotes by former Senator and Presidential candidate Rick Santorum. He has a child with disabilities and he wrote in an article today:

"The reason I have so strongly opposed CRPD is also simple. Karen and I have experienced first-hand as we care for our little blessing, Bella, that parents and caregivers care most deeply and are best equipped to care for the disabled. Not international bureaucrats."

A couple paragraphs down he continues:

"However, the United States passing this treaty would do nothing to force any foreign government to change their laws or to spend resources on the disabled. That is for those governments to decide."

Are you confused? I am. Which is it: the treaty will control what parents can do for their kids or is it at the discretion of each country's government? You cannot have something both ways. Too often lately politicians use the slogan: "If I cannot dazzle with brilliance, I will baffle with bulls___!"

I see nothing wrong with being part of a group in the United Nations that advocates rights to the disabled throughout the world. The treaty states that nations should strive to assure that the disabled enjoy the same rights and fundamental freedoms as their fellow citizens. Not every country is going to listen, but there are plenty who try to get in line with good ideas. The UN may stink at preventing war, but they are really pretty good at this type of stuff. And you know what much of the treaty is based on: the American Disabilities Act which this country has been operating on for 20 years now.

I am concerned that the Republican Party is turning into something purely reactionary: "If a Democrat is for it, we are against it." Here the United States is not yet a part of something all of our long-time allies have already ratified. Here is a concept we should be proud of, and the world-wide perception is that we do not agree with it or we don't play well with others. And if the arguments are presented like Santorum's, there is going to be a lot of head scratching. You cannot debate something when the argument is illogical.

I cannot wait to write something where the Senate actually does something. Of course I am not the conservative Heritage Action for America group. They advocated a "no" vote on the treaty and told senators it would be a black mark on their scorecard. I guess that is the definition of a constituent these days and the only people Congress actually listens to. Not us. Not the people. Sad.

Maybe I am not as politically astute as I think I am, but the actions of the

United States Senate on this issue still baffles me. I do not know how voting for this treaty is a bad thing. As for the Heritage Action for America Group, the NRA, and all of those other so-called "watchdogs," the fact is simple. They are not watching out for America. They are only looking out for their own self-interest. It is entertaining how they can make the politicians WE vote into office jump through their hoops.

Santa Over Washington

December 6, 2012

North Pole – Santa is reviewing lists on his laptop. He is getting more agitated as he goes through different documents. Finally in frustration he yells for his Chief of Staff.

"Blinky, get in here!"

A harried, middle-aged elf scampers into the office holding his iPad. "What's wrong, boss?"

"In 18 days we have to take off and deliver all over the world. I am checking my "naughty and nice list" and cannot find the one for the Washington government offices. Where is it?"

Blinky's fingers dance on his tablet. "We are having some problems with that one. People there keep saying one thing and doing another and it is hard to figure out who has been good this year."

Santa sits back, eats a chocolate chip cookie, and hits a few keys on his computer. "I cannot wait forever. Let's review a few and maybe we can get a handle on it. The sleigh doesn't pack itself, you know. What do you have on President Obama?"

After entering some info, Blinky looks at his screen. "Well, he won re-election without saying anything of substance and really doesn't have much success in leading the government. Hasn't been good or bad – he's just there."

"That is not a great endorsement for making a Christmas stop," said Santa. "What about Congress?"

"Which branch?" asked Blinky.

"House of Representatives to start."

"Republicans or Democrats?"

"Does it really matter, Blinky?"

Again Blinky checks his iPad. "Not really. They fight with each other, cannot seem to agree on anything and have consistently put their country between a rock and a hard place. I don't think the House leader and the President are on each other's Christmas card list. Think of how the warehouse elves acted when we ran out of hot chocolate last month."

Santa winched. "That was ugly. Taking a walk around the block up here without my fur coat was more fun than getting them to lighten up and get back to work...Ok, how about Harry Reid and Mitch McConnell, the leaders in the Senate. What's their story this year?"

Blinky looked down, hit a few more keys, frowned, shook his iPad and said, "Nothing."

"Your computer is down?" asked Santa.

"No. I mean they didn't do anything. The entire Senate accomplished nothing this past year. Zilch. Nada. Permanent coffee break. Thank the Lord, they don't work here. We wouldn't be delivering anything till Easter!"

With a sigh Santa asked, "Supreme Court?"

"Allowed Obamacare to pass on a technicality. That's like winning the Super Bowl on a penalty."

"Come on, there has to be something good there," exclaimed Santa. "How about that General Petraeus fella? He was a war hero and head of the CIA."

"Had an affair, resigned in disgrace." Blinky was slowly shaking his head. "I am hard pressed to find anyone who would fly to the head of the "nice" list that works there."

"Obviously, they have a different definition for work than we do, Blinky. I wouldn't have them clean the reindeer stables. We'd be up to our knees in..."

"So, Santa," Blinky quickly interrupted, "what do you want me to do here? Schedule a coal drop for these folks."

"No, Blinky, the sleigh isn't that big. Tell the logistics department to re-file the flight plan. We'll skip the government offices there in Washington this year. Besides, when I eat the milk and cookies they leave out, I have to declare it on my income taxes."

This one was just fun to write! I am a great believer that we have to sit back and laugh every now and then...or we would be spending all of our time crying!

In Dog Years I'd Be...Dead!

December 11, 2012

So explained the birthday "card" my daughter texted me this morning. It is fortunate that we share a good sense of humor so she will still get her Christmas present this year. It also brought home why the post office is losing money. "Texting a birthday card" was not even in our vocabulary a short while ago.

With one exception, birthdays for me have never been a time to get depressed. It is one year closer to the afterlife, but only God knows when that will be. Ironically, it was my 25th birthday where I felt down. For some reason it went through my mind that I have lived a quarter of a century and wondered what I had done with my life. Now I would love to be that age again...especially with what I know now!

So excuse the nostalgia, but here are some things that are now absent from life that I yearn for at times:

- Having only one telephone in the house and that's it. If a person really wants you, they will call back. No message, cell phone, text, etc. Gone also will be that anxiety we feel when we cannot get a hold of someone.

- No 24/7 news stations. Sometimes it seems they just throw kerosene on the fire and make the news worse than it is. We are all stressed out enough.

- Acknowledging God in this country. If He was good enough for the Founding Fathers, there is no reason to let the ignorant demand we hide Him.

- Government that can actually make some decisions and not be constantly fighting amongst themselves.

- A television season that starts in September where the shows stay in the same timeslot for more than two weeks.

- Jobs where average people can make a decent living.
- Getting on an airplane without being strip searched.
- Movies with original plots and not retreads.
- 55 cents a gallon for gas!
- $1.15 for a gallon of milk.
- Professional sports playoffs that do not go on as long as the season.
- Election coverage is one or two months before November, not the entire year.
- Johnny Carson.
- Thursday football only happens on Thanksgiving.
- Nobody knows who or what a "Kardashian" is.
- College football has their bowl games on New Year's Day and the season is done.
- People say "Merry Christmas."
- More folks go to church or synagogue or mosque or whatever their appropriate house of worship is.
- News media is fairly unbiased – not today's rampant cheerleader for their favorite side.
- Privacy exists.
- A $370 billion national debt instead of $14 trillion (ok – that is just sick).
- Kids go outside and play with their friends. No video game addiction or depending on sports leagues to determine when you play.
- People with a sense of humor. Folks are just a little uptight worrying about political correctness.
- Howard Cosell.
- I would say I wish all of the bands and rock stars I enjoyed as a teen were still around…but they are. Some should be in wheel chairs and out to pasture, but they hang in there.
- Free beaches at the Jersey shore (or what is left of the Jersey shore).
- And a NY Met team that I can actually see in the World Series!

I get a lot of grief for being a Mets fan, but that is true of all Mets fans. I know this column pines for a simpler life, but we all yearn for that at times. For all of the technology we have added to our lives, it seems to have added more complexity and tension to life. The idea that technology would make life easier gets turned on its head all the time. I think everyone needs to get out and enjoy the world and smell the roses once in a while – not just look at them on the computer or smartphone screen.

Snail Mail? — That Should Be the Worker's Mascot

December 13, 2012

When was the last time you tried to do something at the post office? I went yesterday. And what I am going to talk about here is not particular to now or one location. This relates to something I have seen for 30 years all over the country. Talk about an institutional culture!

I had to get a package shipped out. I was not able to use the self-serve kiosk because of what I needed done. I was the seventh back in line when I got there. It was 20 minutes before I finally talked to a clerk. And in that time the line got longer behind me. Even in Wal-Mart they try to open up a new cashier if it gets that long.

And what is going on behind the counter? They chit-chat with the customers and amongst themselves. There is no urgency. I am all for customer service and being personable with people, but when you have a line of customers (some trying to balance 3 or 4 packages) you try to hurry up things. And I swear they move in slow motion. They take a package and shuffle along to the back with it and then shuffle back up to the counter. It is like watching the replay in a football game – except they are moving in real time!

Everybody was getting impatient. A guy 2 people behind me ordered a pizza and asked them to bring it to the post office! There are many customer- oriented stores and services that would not tolerate this type of treatment of their clients. I can just imagine an efficiency expert coming in and the type of changes they would advocate!

There are two points to this. One is that this is so typical of a governmental agency. I know the post office is not government owned anymore and is some type of privately-owned hybrid. But the mentality is pure government. They still act like they are a monopoly and the only game in town. They collect a pay check so why care about the customer! This is the same attitude you get when dealing with way too many government offices.

The second point is the postal service really needs to start looking at themselves when crying about going bankrupt. I know part of it is some pension financing through the government that is way out of control. But if they really are a company, they better start acting like one that is in competition with the internet, FedEx and UPS. You should not have to stand in line forever to get something simple done. It would be easier to take if you felt like they were trying to move quickly. But the "I don't give a damn attitude" floated through the air for everyone to feel.

Ben Franklin was our first Postmaster General. With his work ethic, I do not think workers 200 years ago moved this slowly. As I said in the beginning, this style has been in post offices everywhere I have lived for as long as I can remember. Instead of crying to Congress for more money, the postal service should first look to itself and clean up their act. I would miss checking my mailbox every day, but if mail ceased to exist, I would get over it with time. We have heard how workers at the post office have gone "postal." I am surprised it did not start with the customers!

Since I wrote this I have been back to the post office. Nothing has changed. If post office workers had a mascot, it would be a sloth. Do you know what our country would be like if organizations and government departments had to go through a review of how they operate? If they had to act on recommendations, they would all save money and be efficient! I just get tired of expecting shoddy service at the post office and never being disappointed.

Elementary School Tragedy

December 14, 2012

The news rarely affects me. What is going on in Connecticut right now with so many children and adults dead is just sickening. There are so many questions without answers and we probably never will find out anything. And my heart feels heavy.

Maybe it is because I remember having 4 kids that age in school. This time of year their biggest concern was how quickly Christmas can get here. Not worry about coming home alive! What are the rest of the kids and their parents going to go through now and for the rest of their lives?

Maybe it is because a couple of my now adult children are teachers. An honorable profession where they are actually trying to help so many kids and teens prepare for their future. Dealing with kids, parents and school administrators is tough enough. Now you have to worry about your life?! Last year my one daughter experienced a school lockdown as a guy was seen with a rifle outside of the school. Nothing came of it but it was a long, stressful day for her and everyone else in the school. It was also tough on those of us outside the school as we waited for a text message saying everything was ok.

Maybe it is because there has been way too much of this lately. There was a mall shooting early in the week and now this. Experts can profile these sickos all they want, but it keeps happening. Yeah, they usually end up dead in the end but why take so many innocents with you? Suicide is a sad event but if you are that mad in the head, just take yourself out – not others.

Maybe it is because it is another indication of how the world seems to be stressing at the seams. Are people reaching their breaking point? Are there folks that need help and don't know how to get it or were ignored?

Too many questions. No answers. No solutions.

Pray for the survivors. Pray for the parents, friends and relatives that were killed. Pray for the school. Pray for the town. Pray for all of us.

If God was ever needed in the world, it is now.

Hug your kids!

One of the sad things today is that there is always something new happening in our country or world and we soon forget the horrific events that happen. But it never ends for the families involved or the communities that they happen in. It is so important to try and always remember the human element in all of these catastrophes. They are real, they hurt, and they can happen to us or those we love tomorrow.

Now What?

December 17, 2012

There is so much to reflect on in the aftermath of the elementary school shooting in Newtown, CT.

First, kudos to President Obama and the speech he gave from the town last night. For one of the few times I felt like I was hearing from a real person. As a Christian, it was gratifying to hear so many references to God, scriptures and publicly talking about the spiritual nature of life. The President has said he is a Christian and it was good for him to talk from that perspective. Isn't it funny how as people we can be so proud of our accomplishments and intellectual ability, but when the chips are down we turn toward God? One of the side lessons here is that He is whom we should be turning to all of the time, not just when the situation is tragic.

Second, is the outpouring of grief, prayers and love from around the country that has occurred over the weekend. Our country may be decisive in politics but Americans do come together when one of their own has been harmed. We are powerless to bring back any of those killed, but reading on the internet and listening on TV you can discover how our country unites. Sports is one of our nation's biggest past-times and it is moving what the NFL and NBA did as leagues before games to acknowledge the pain and grief everyone is feeling. Even more of a statement came from individual players and coaches in on-field tributes or through interviews where they expressed their feelings. These people who are on such a stage showed how human they are too.

Third, is how some politicians and media people who have advocated the right to own guns in the past, have come out and said enough is enough. Common sense has to start prevailing in how we approach gun control in the USA. I am fine if people have a handgun for protection or rifles for hunting, but it is time to disallow semi-automatic weapons and for people to have an arsenal in their basement. I listened to Joe Scarborough on "Morning Joe" on MSNBC early today, and he gave such a moving essay on this very matter. As a 4-term congressman he always received high marks from the NRA. He has acknowledged that it is past time to look at our policies.

Last night, President Obama called for action and others will be following suit. The country is not about to outlaw guns. That will never happen. But it is time to specify what people can and cannot have. It is true that "guns don't kill people, people kill people." However, if people don't have access to guns that shoot 60 rounds a second, it will cut down on the results when somebody does something completely evil.

In closing I give you the other side of the coin and how people think. On Fox News on Sunday, Congressman Louie Gohmert from Texas said that elementary school principals should be armed and have access to assault rifles in order to kill potential shooters. He theorized that if the principal at Sandy Hook Elementary School had an M-4 rifle in her office, then she would have been able to shoot Adam Lanza before he proceeded to kill 20 students and six adults at the Newtown, Connecticut school. "I wish to God she had had an M-4 in her office, locked up so when she heard gunfire, she pulls it out and she didn't have to lunge heroically with nothing in her hands and takes him out and takes his head off before he can kill those precious kids," he said.

Sometimes we have madmen running our country. Let's pray he is a minority, and level-headed people can have intelligent discussions about limiting certain guns. Tragedy cannot be prevented, but God help those who have the responsibility to do something and now go hide.

Not a lot has been done in this country where guns are concerned. They are as plentiful as peanuts and almost as easy to buy. I am not a gun control nut by any means, but the ease of being able to purchase one through legal means is ridiculous. And I reckon it is almost as easy going through backdoor channels to get one. We never learn. The next horrible act like Sandy Hook will also provide the same gnashing of teeth and wails to the heavens. We are just so totally stupid at times.

We Have to Be First, to Hell with the Facts

December 18, 2012

Friday's shooting at the school in Newtown, CT helped emphasize one of the big problems I have with the 24/7 news media. In their rush to be first with the news, they seem to be applying the spaghetti principle: throw a lot of stuff against the wall and whatever sticks, we will keep.

In any tragedy of this magnitude there is going to be a lot of information flying around. It seems that the news outlets have decided to take a course of action to report everything whether it is true or not. I have come to realize that people still believed that things reported during the initial flurry of information on Friday are the facts. Some of these were that the killer's mother was in the school and killed at the time, he killed his father beforehand, and that there was a related murder in New Jersey. All of which were not true. Unfortunately, he did kill his mother but that was at home before he invaded the school.

This is just irresponsible journalism. I know I am old-fashioned here, but in journalism in the old days it was emphasized to verify your facts before reporting them. With the proliferation of news channels, internet news services and all of the social media outlets, this seems to have gone by the wayside. Everyone wants to be first. We are a society that caters to instant gratification and in almost all cases, that is a bad thing. If the purpose of the news is to help folks know and understand what is going on, then making an effort to get things close to right in the beginning would be a big help.

It's like housebreaking a dog. If you adopt an older dog who was not trained well, then you have to "unlearn" all of his bad habits before he will get the idea of what he is supposed to do. It is a more difficult process than starting with a puppy. The news works the same way. Our mind is going to absorb what we hear first on any subject. It becomes that much harder to comprehend later news reports when they contradict what originally was said.

Then we have the reporters giving their own interpretation of events. I can take that to a degree if they are knowledgeable on the topic at hand – but that is rarely the case. If you have a parent whose kid was in that school and you are listening to the news while you are trying to find out about your child – then that report better be full of correct information and not speculation.

The media is supposed to report what is going on, but more and more it wants **TO BE** the news. This especially happens in government and political reporting as we have news channels that actually choose sides. I guess that is fine as long as they are upfront about it and don't say things like "fair and balanced" reporting.

We shouldn't have to take the news with a grain of salt, but we do.

The New York Times slogan is "All the news that's fit to print." It seems like most news outlets now use "any news to fill up space or time."

One of the public services offered by The Daily Show with Jon Stewart and The Colbert Report is how they constantly show the idiocy of the major news outlets – especially the 24/7 cable news channels. I love watching the news when something big happens and one talking head asks another talking head to speculate on the events. An explosion may have happened in a building 10 minutes ago and there are no facts yet, but that doesn't prevent the one from coming up with an answer. You know he or she is pulling it out of their ass and that is usually proven as facts come to light. It happens so much, but the media just does not seem to learn.

TIME Honors Obama. Really?!?

December 19, 2012

Time magazine announced that their "Person of the Year" for 2012 is President Obama. I wonder what is next for him? Obama leaves office in 2016 and thinks about becoming an actor and is automatically awarded an Oscar? He suggests a play for the Chicago Bears and becomes "Coach of the Year?" After all, this is a man who won the Nobel Peace prize in 2009 for "for his extraordinary efforts to strengthen international diplomacy and cooperation between peoples.."At that point in time all he did was be a senator for a couple of years and campaigned and won the presidency. This is like me winning the Pulitzer Prize for writing this little column.

So you know where I come from, I am basically a conservative-minded person when it comes to government. To use a term from the first President Bush, I am a "compassionate conservative." We cannot abandon all the people in need in this country, but neither can we bankrupt the country in doing it. Our leaders have to make hard choices to success-fully run our country for the long-term. This is a lost art among our current government.

I do not hate President Obama. You have to respect the office. I give him great credit for being the first black person to become President. And he persevered to win a second term in a train wreck of an election process. But I do not believe he won based on the work he did in his first term. As most elections are these days, he won because he was the perceived "lesser of two evils" in the minds of most of the Ameri-can people. Or to use another cliché "better the devil you know, than the devil you don't." (And, yes, I find it very disturbing that I had to use sayings with the words "evil" and "devil" in them to describe our electoral process!)

My complaint is that he receives these accolades by being a leader who is style over substance. My opinion is that there is not a great body of work here to even rate him. TIME had some other finalists that have had a bigger impact on the world at large. I get the feeling this is another indication that the marketing of the Obama "brand" is truly the winner here. It's like falling for an advertisement of a new cleaning product that gets the stains off of everything, and it cannot eliminate a pencil mark from your table.

I like Obama as a person. Like Bill Clinton and George Bush, he is best when dealing with people on a personal level. He was good when visiting NJ after superstorm Sandy and I thought he was outstanding talking at Newtown, CT the other night in response to the horrible school tragedy there. I would love to have a beer with him and maybe find out how he really thinks. But as a leader, I do not have confidence in him at this point. The country seems to be continually dealing with the same domestic and international problems over and over again. I am afraid it will be easy when we do get to the next round of national elections for the campaign managers. They will be able to recycle all the ads from 2012 and just change the names because the issues will be the same!

History is the final judge of any President. Someone who maintained the status quo and not moved the country forward will at best be judged "OK." As for TIME, they rank right up there with Fox or MSNBC as a media entity whose political leanings are as subtle as a Kardashian's need for attention.

I still scratch my head over the Obama perception. It is not like everything he touches turns to gold. Quite the opposite in fact. It will be interesting how his body of work will be perceived when his second term is over. I was a kid in the sixties, but it seems like the divisions and frustrations of people today are on par with that era. It is for far different reasons, but this is the most divisive I have seen in America in my lifetime. And President Obama has only widened the divides, not brought people together.

Damn! The World Didn't End

December 21, 2012

It looks like the Mayan "end of world" prophecy did not come to pass. My take on it is that the guy who was carving the huge stone calendar that all of this was based on hung up his chisel one day and said, "I've had it. They can figure the rest out themselves." From a Biblical point of view, we aren't supposed to know the day or hour when it's time to shut out the lights and put up the "We're Closed" sign.

So since the world is going to continue for a while, what does that mean? I am grateful to keep seeing family and friends, but here are some things I was looking forward to doing without:

- 60 minute TV shows containing 15 minutes of commercials (thank God for DVR to skip them)
- Childish squabbling from Washington
- More reality shows coming our way
- Listening to Rex Ryan of the Jets (hopefully that will end in January for good)
- IRS
- Coming to work
- More "best of 2012" lists
- "Trends in 2013" lists
- Too much unemployment
- Listening to pundits on news shows
- Watching the Mets not get to the playoffs again
- Election coverage
- A country in massive debt
- No original movie ideas from Hollywood
- E-mail

- Facebook
- Politicians who say stupid things about gun control (read today's news)
- Politicians
- Drug advertisements where the cure sounds worse than the ailment
- Paying so much for everything for the "privilege" of living in NJ
- Stupid commercials
- Listening to Phil Simms on football game (I used to like him but he has turned into Joe Theisman –he never shuts up.)
- Waiting for a penalty flag to fall on every friggin pass play in the NFL
- Every local weather forecast on local news sounds like Armageddon
- Arguing with Siri on my iphone (does anyone else do this or do I just need help?)
- Ignorant people
- Paying for parking at a sporting event or amusement park when you already had to take out a loan to afford the tickets
- Tolls on NJ highways and to get into NYC – anywhere else it would be called "extortion"
- Calories
- Rap music
- My cable bill (see note on "extortion" above)
- Honey Boo Boo
- Kardashians (you know I would get that in)
- Ads for things that have to do with bodily functions associated with the bedroom and bathroom
- And ever hearing the term "fiscal cliff" again

Nope – all of that is still part of everyday life. As I write this a year after the original column I marvel at how none of that has changed in a year's time. Sigh.

Humbug to the Scrooges

December 26, 2012

The day after Christmas is usually a time to reflect...or rest. I choose reflection today. Christmas Eve and Christmas Day for me were very nice times to be with family from all sides of my life. Circumstances brought everyone together for the holiday which has not happened in a while. And it made me realize that when you get past the news stories on what stores are making money (or not) and the prejudices of other people towards Christmas, the whole thing really works.

I will start with the last first. I work with someone of another culture whose concept of Christmas is that it is an American commercial invention for people to buy presents for others. Here is someone who can give Scrooge and the Grinch a run for their money in what they think Christmas is. If I created an ignorance scale, he would be off the chart. First of all, the foundation and beginning of Christmas is the birth of Jesus Christ in the Christian belief system. Losing sight of that is the subject for another column, but the point here is that occasion has evolved into one celebrating family and friends. Many people in the USA, regardless of faith and heritage, use the time to get together with the ones they love. People journey from all over to get together with others. And what could be better than that? If in this face-paced world we need an excuse other than a wedding or funeral to get people together, then so be it!! If the travel industry makes money on it, well that is how life works. Even Mary and Joseph probably had to rent the donkey in their journey to Bethlehem (I always wonder if they had to pay for collision insurance?).

As for presents, almost everyone likes to get a present. But I think it is also true that everyone enjoys giving presents! When a person gives some thought and time in finding the right gift for someone, there is happiness in the joy you see on the recipient's face when they open it. The most present-happy people at Christmas time are kids. And look how they glow when the present they bought or made for a parent is opened with all the appropriate "ooohs" and "aahhs." Some people say if their kid wants something, they just get it for them during the course of the year. The truth is that not many families have that luxury. They have to save and plan to provide a nice Christmas for the family.

As for the stores, I personally hope the most successful ones were the ones that stayed closed on Thanksgiving (see previous column from November). The others can burn in bankruptcy hell for all I care. Their greed in hours being opened has passed ridiculous. (I hear some Macy stores were open for 48 hours straight the weekend before Christmas. I wonder how profitable that was for them? Was it really worth it to their bottom-line and the poor employees that worked? Were there a lot of customers milling around or people with nowhere to go and no money?) Bottom line is that the store is there to make money and that is part of the season. Of course the media constantly fuels the frenzy with reports on how good or bad the situation is. For me, the only mall I visited was while killing time to go see a movie and I did 90% of my shopping online.

So you got to take the good with the bad. And at Christmas, the good far surpasses the negative. Christmas, and the time up to New Year's is the chance to see people and to catch your breath before another year starts. Embrace it. Have fun. Smile and laugh. Eat, drink and be merry (and hit the gym and diet plans on January 2). If you "Bah, Humbug" this, get a life!

I marvel at how some people take delight in shooting down Christmas. These are folks with issues who probably have a hard time being happy. I like the old adage "If you don't have something good to say, shut-up!" This is especially true at Christmas. We should have Christmas police who shove a candy cane in the mouth of any nay-sayers at this time of the year.

Starbucks Plays Mom

December 27, 2012

Did you see the story on how Starbucks stores in the D.C. area will write "Come Together" on all of their coffee cups from now through December 28, in the hopes that it will encourage lawmakers to reach a "fiscal cliff" deal? Starbucks CEO Howard Schultz wrote in a blog post on the company's website that "Rather than be bystanders, we have an opportunity — and I believe a responsibility — to use our company's scale for good by sending a respectful and optimistic message to our elected officials to come together and reach common ground on this important issue."

First of all, kudos to Schultz. This is not the first time the CEO has used the size and prestige of Starbucks to promote a common sense point to the government. Back in August, Schultz called on his fellow CEOs -- and other would-be donors -- to boycott all campaign contributions to either party until the nation's elected leaders put aside their political posturing and find some common ground on long-term fiscal issues. Here is someone who doesn't hide behind the office door. And he does not advocate something that is conservative or liberal. It is to encourage the government to do what it is supposed to.

And that is the point here. What Schultz is having his stores in Washington do is akin to your Mom putting notes in your lunchbox when you went to school. Little expressions of encouragement like "Do Your Best" or "Remember to study for your spelling test." When you are 10 years old, little things like that do make a difference. Your Mom wants to keep you on track and remind you that you are not alone and that you also have some responsibilities.

So if you take that analogy, what Mr. Schultz is doing is absolutely correct. That is because he is trying to encourage grown adults who are acting like 10 year olds that they have a responsibility. I have not written about the fiscal cliff in a while because I am sick of it. The debate over this has been going on almost as long as the last presidential election. And they both illustrate the same point – our country's leadership leaves much to be desired. It is like the movie "Groundhog Day" where it is the same story over and over again. Nobody can do any planning while the powers-that-be hold the country hostage over their ideals. A business cannot make plans for 2013 when it does not know the tax structure. The same is true of a family trying to figure out how much money they will have to live on.

The party mascots are appropriate. A donkey is also known as a jackass and an elephant gives the impression of a slow, plodding beast. As for President Obama, all he has shown to me is that he can win an election. He cannot promote change nor has a clue how to maneuver through Washington. Read a book! Learn how people like FDR, Lyndon Johnson and Ronald Reagan actually brought change about. If he has some good ideas he would like to see happen in his last 4 years of office, it is time to be a leader and get this problem solved. If he fails here, kiss your agenda goodbye. Solving the fiscal cliff won't cure our ills, but maybe, just maybe the government can then move on to do something constructive.

So, hurray for Howard Schultz and Starbucks. They are speaking for the people. The ironic thing is, Howard probably wouldn't hire anyone in government to run one of his stores. They would not know how to function. He likes his stores to be run well with the customer coming first.

The best thing from this Starbucks story is that the CEO acted on what many in the USA believe: That the government is not doing its job. He brought this home in a way that would embarrass the average person who is involved in government. However, it just seems that our representatives don't care. They get so fat and comfortable in their jobs that they forget about the people who voted them into office. We have to remember it is in our power to put them out to pasture.

Guns, Bullets, and Textbooks

December 28, 2012

It has been two weeks now since the terrible shooting tragedy of children and teachers in Newtown, Ct. My heart aches as I think how those families felt during Christmas and this entire holiday season. Will they ever have a carefree time again at the end of a year?

It can be argued that the one who killed everyone there was a coward for hiding behind a gun and taking other people's lives instead of facing up to the fact he had deep issues he needed help with. The same can be said of the murderer who shot up an Oregon Mall earlier in December. And the creep who killed people in a theatre in Colorado in the summer. I would add to this list of cowards the NRA.

The National Rifle Association absolutely hid when this catastrophe in Connecticut occurred. They even took the step of taking down their Facebook page. It was over a week before they got their story straight enough to come out in public about the incident. The bottom line was that the guns weren't to blame; it was the movies and videos that young people are exposed to that led to the massacre. Was it the NRA's fault this has happened? No, but please take some responsibility for your actions that account for the availability of such assault weapons that were used in Newtown.

For full disclosure, I am all for the Second Amendment and the right to bear arms. I was a certified NRA instructor for a while, and enjoyed target shooting and teaching the correct way for a person to handle a gun. The NRA in these matters is all about safety. All I am asking here is that they look at some of their policies from that safety point of view. Instead, they and their more ignorant members issue statistics like this:

- Tobacco causes 430,700 US deaths per year
- Alcohol causes 110,640 US deaths per year

- Adverse reactions to prescription drugs causes 32,000 US deaths per year
- Suicide causes 30,575 US deaths per year

12,644 homicides in the US involve firewarms. Assuming assault rifles are used 1.8% of the time that is 162 deaths. You are 18 times more likely to be stabbed, bludgeoned, or beaten to death than shot with an assault rifle!

I am sure these statistics gladdens the hearts of the family who just lost a child.

Now let us look at the gun murder rate scorecard of similar industrial nations we are allies with (data is from 2009):

- Japan – 7
- England – 63
- Germany – 381
- Canada – 179

They have much tougher gun control laws than we do, and the results show. If there are not that many guns around, then there are less to be used in killings.

It is ok to have a gun in the home for protection and rifles & shotguns for hunting or target shooting, but only if safely guarded and used properly. People do not need arsenals in their house that consist of assault guns and automatic weapons. If I were the NRA, I would push that every gun had to be properly registered and sold with a proper waiting period and background check. I would get the loopholes closed for gun shows that make a mockery of any purchase requirements. Furthermore, I would push that any gun owner had to go through an NRA safety course in order to buy a firearm. This would be a boon for business for the NRA. The public perception of them would greatly change instead of hearing the reactionary rhetoric they always seem to spew at times like this.

There are tons of illegal guns out there, but they can slowly be weeded out over time. This won't happen overnight but it is past time for the NRA to grow a set of balls and be responsible.

My last note is on the politicians and gun nuts who say that teachers should be armed. Are you out of your f&%$#@g mind?!?!? I have two daughters who teach and I don't think a SWAT certificate should be added to their education requirements. It is hard enough to teach kids today. You want them to do this? Ok, some schools may start putting police full time at school but they are properly trained for this sort of thing. It is bad enough the schools my daughters work at have to do lock-down drills the way we used to have fire drills, but that is the way things are.

Once again it is ignorant people who cannot take responsibility for wrong practices and policies over the years. Let's think people. Lives are at stake!

The leadership of the NRA consists of out-of-touch morons. They all rationalize probably better than they can shoot a gun. It would be nice if a little common sense came into play – especially after something horrific happens. But it shows that money is power and sticking to principles is more important than doing what is right.

Washington: M*A*S*H vs. Mayo Clinic

January 2, 2013

So Washington is patting itself on the back that it averted the "fiscal cliff." The citizens of the country are supposed to be happy about that? It seems to me an immediate financial crisis was averted, but that is about it. Leadership came into play from two unlikely sources, but President Obama, Speaker of the House Boehner, and House Majority Leader Harry Reid were the holy trinity of ineffectiveness. Instead, Vice-President Biden and Mitch McConnell, the Republican Senate Minority Leader, were able to get a deal together in the Senate that led to yesterday's legislation. Is anyone getting tired of looking up to our supposed leadership and finding people who could not successfully lead a pack of Cub Scouts?

We have low opinions of politicians, but by definition a politician is a person who is involved in influencing public policy and decision making. So we don't even have skilled politicians running our government... we have inept ones! I know how we as your average Americans view things, but I would love to hear a member of Congress or the White House candidly talk about their perception of their leadership. Since nobody in Washington has courage to speak their mind, I can only guess what we would hear. I would assume a great deal of frustration and anger simmers below the surface in both places.

The thing I wish the President and Congress would actually do is fix the problems, not just put band-aids on them. We have a wounded patient here called America, and they act more like a M*A*S*H unit than a hospital. If you watched the show or movie you know that Mobile Army Surgical Hospitals were established in the Korean War as close to the fighting as possible to treat wounded soldiers. The surgeons referred to what they do as "meatball surgery" since their mission was to fix the wounded up as quickly as possible so they could get to a hospital for long-term care. Nothing fancy was done. The goal was getting them to survive so they could receive better treatment at a more advanced facility.

In Washington these days, we seem to have the government version of "meatball surgery." The government seems much more comfortable slapping a quick fix on the problem. However, unlike M*A*S*H units, the government has no advanced facility to send the problem onto. All they seem to be doing lately is doing first aid and wait for the same problem to come around to them again.

After all, the President and Congress set the stage for the fiscal cliff. It wasn't like they woke up on Christmas morning, slapped their forehead and said, "Oh my God, we are going to be in big trouble in a week's time!" For some reason they seem to like waiting for the absolute last minute to fix something. And when they do finally take the vote, we are all left with the feeling that we need to take a shower!

It happened again this time. All this "solution" did was raise some taxes on the rich, extended unemployment benefits, and made all Americans lose a little more out of their paychecks when you get your first one this year. The only real "winner" was the financial markets who aren't going to tank today or tomorrow and may keep the U.S. out of another recession. But spending is still out of control, the country's debt is beyond comprehension, and a road map for a fiscally strong America is put on the back burner.

It seems like the best we can do is continue to tell our representatives and the White House we are sick of all of this. Feel free to use this column to get the point across. As Abraham Lincoln said we are a **government of the people, by the people, and for the people."** We need to remind our representatives of that…and not just at election time.

It was tough for Hawkeye and the crew in M*A*S*H. But they did have one thing in their favor…the Korean War did have an ending and they could go home. America is our home, and being managed by the unmanageable!

I am no prophet, but what I said here was the truth. Nothing was fixed and it led to more battles during 2013 including a government shutdown. I would actually find it refreshing to hear anyone in government say, "We spend too much money, we do not have enough coming in, and we have no bloody idea how to fix it!" At least the truth is more palpable than the ongoing BS we get from both parties.

Give 'Em Hell, Governor Christie

January 3, 2013

Maybe it is because I live in New Jersey and I certainly understand the attitude here. For better or worse, many folks are in your face and are not afraid to hold back on their opinions. Sometimes it is for the good, but for other people it just showcases their ignorance. It has been so refreshing for the past 3 years to have a governor who is comfortable and secure enough to speak his mind on the issues that confront our state. Nothing illustrates this better than Gov. Chris Christie blasting members of his own Republican party in Washington.

In a State House news conference yesterday, Christie blasted Republican U.S. House Speaker John Boehner of Ohio for delaying a vote on a $60 billion aid package for Superstorm Sandy recovery. Christie accused House Republicans of focusing on internal politics and "palace intrigue" instead of voting on the bill, which would financially assist states hit by the Oct. 29 storm. Sandy severely impacted New York, New Jersey and Connecticut. "There's only one group to blame for the continued suffering of these innocent victims, the House majority and their speaker, John Boehner," Christie said.

Some Republicans have accused Christie of being unfaithful to the party. Maybe they should take a lesson from the Governor. Because Governor Christie is doing something entirely foreign to Washington politicians: **he is putting people over party!** God, what a concept… looking out for the folks put in your care whether they voted for you or not. I cannot get over the feeling that as soon as so many elected officials get to Washington, they forget who their allegiance is too. We are a representative government where those we put into office are supposed to be concerned for the welfare of everyone in their state (Senate) or their section of the state (House of Representatives). Their priority is not supposed to be an allegiance to the party. I loved Christie's reference to "palace intrigue" because that is most of the BS that is reported from

Washington. In fairness to the media, that is all that there is to report on, because nothing of substance is ever accomplished.

Look, I know in some places people get elected because of the party they belong to. Party politics is a well-oiled machine in many areas. Voters get on the bandwagon because they are too lazy to look into what candidates are really about. That will only change as we get more and more disgusted with how our country is being run. While I hate the cliché, we really need more people like Chris Christie to "step outside the box" on the state and national scene. We need more people in government to work from their own convictions rather than blowing in the wind with poll numbers or party pressure.

Sometimes it only takes one person crying out in the wilderness. Governor Christie carries a lot of weight in the Republican Party. (Sorry Governor, I really do not mean that as a pun). It is going to take someone of his reputation to speak up and maybe get some people to wake up. As I have mentioned in previous columns I am a Republican and am tired of being embarrassed by them. People in NJ were clobbered by Sandy and Congress' inaction to loosen up some funds to help is immoral.

Oh yeah, I forgot, they were too busy being childish with the Democrats and the President to act on an emergency! Whether you agree with him or not, Governor Christie is the type of person we need more of to get our country back on track: a leader. During the next round of elections, take the time to evaluate your representatives on a leadership basis. That should clean house!

I love how some Republicans refer to Governor Christie as a RINO – Republican in Name Only. When did political parties exist to promote purity of purpose instead of an effective philosophy to run the government? So many of the far right get hung up on this concept and hate that someone like Christie found it necessary to work with the President when a catastrophe hit the state. These "purity Republicans" hurt the perception others have of the party. And now Governor Christie may have shot himself in the political foot as his involvement in closing lanes on the George Washington Bridge is under investigation. If not him, I still look for someone to take the extremists of the party head on.

Read Dr. Jim to Your Kids

January 8, 2013

Today's column is a little different. I want to talk about literacy and I am doing it from a viewpoint of a parent. I have run into so many people lately who say they don't like to read. In young people this translates into trouble navigating through school. For adults it is difficulty in doing their job or getting a better one. While it is true some people have learning disabilities that make reading difficult, for many people it comes down to not being exposed to books at an early age. I am not talking about elementary school here. I am talking about when they are much younger and exploring the world. A good rule of thumb is if you are starting to say "No" to the child, it is time to begin reading to them!

This is not a paid endorsement but I recently came across a series of stories that I found enchanting. They are called the *Dr. Jim Stories* which takes the reader, whether adult or child, into the wonderful world of a veterinarian with a magical stethoscope who uses it to hear what the animals are saying. Conceived and written by Scott Nicol and beautifully illustrated by David Youngblood these stories go back to the innocence and fun of the Dr. Seuss books I had when I was a kid. You can find Dr. Jim on his own Facebook page: Facebook - Dr. Jim.

Parents and grandparents have to remember that children are born with an insatiable curiosity. That curiosity can be channeled into a love for the written word as easily as TV shows and video games if harnessed early. The others are easier to do because you sit them in front of a television or computer screen. And as parents we all do that from time to time out of desperation. But nothing beats the bonding of an adult and child like having them on your lap and reading to them. Books like Dr. Jim bring a world to life. A young one may focus on the pictures in the beginning, but his or her little brain comprehends the shapes and sounds of the words that are also on the page. Almost like magic you will find that boy or girl taking that book and going through it on their own.

Reading the Dr Jim stories sent me in my own "wayback machine" (ok, I watched Rocky and Bullwinkle a lot). Thanks to my Mom and Dad I discovered very young the fun of reading. Besides Dr. Jim there are many books still out there like *Dr. Seuss* or *Curious George* that can fire a youngster's imagination. The benefits from reading early are too numerous to mention. By no means do I think I am exceptional in this regard, but reading early makes everything easier. Maybe during school there were certain subjects I did not care for, but doing the reading on them was easy. I cannot imagine what it would be like if I had to study something I hated and I also had a difficult time reading. That carried over in to the adult working world where I had to learn about so much on many different topics…and it still goes on. And reading is still one of the best ways for me to relax whether I am reading fiction or trying to learn more about something that interests me.

So if you are looking for something good to start you and your child with, give Dr. Jim a try. And remember, kids love to imitate their parents. Reading to kids and them seeing you read your books is going to condition them that this is a pretty cool thing.

We can provide our children with food, clothing, shelter, money, education, etc., but the joy of reading is something that will serve them well long after we are gone.

I am appalled at how little adults read and can comprehend. When I am helping someone with his or her website copy, I advocate keeping things short and to the point, or the business will lose potential customers. One reason Twitter became so popular is that people liked communicating in 140 characters or less – that is all they can handle. We lament the fact that our school children are behind other countries. Having a strong foundation of reading will go a long way to improving our kids' education experience.

Les Miserables in Washington — Part 1

January 9, 2013

I love reading stories about our President that starts out:

"Just two weeks before his second inauguration, President Barack Obama is acting as if he believes he has a big mandate for his next term. The latest sign: his decision to defy a concerted campaign against his choice for defense secretary. The Democratic president, re-elected in November, unveiled a more combative approach during the end-of-year 'fiscal cliff' taxes and spending drama, exploiting disarray in Republican ranks that underscored Washington's legislative dysfunction." (Matt Spetalnick | Reuters)

Where have I heard this before? Oh yeah — from President George Bush after the 2004 election when he thought his "mandate" gave him the ok to try and privatize at least part of social security. Regardless of whether it was a good idea or not, I think the first time people heard of it were after he won re-election! It certainly wasn't a central issue to the campaign. And how did the rest of his term go after his self-appointed mandate? By the end he could not get Congress to approve his choice for dogcatcher.

And guess what, Mr. Obama, George's margin of victory in the popular vote was 51% to 48%; almost identical to your 50% to 48%. I am not a math major but to me it looks like neither of those figures is a blow-out. They are more like a football game won on a last second field goal than any team showing domination.

So what does this macho attitude of yours mean: we are in for 4 more years of hell in Washington and nothing getting done! Like the world displayed in the wonderful book, play, and movie *Les Miserables*, we are going to have more instances in this country of people struggling just to survive on a day-to-day basis. Not in the poverty that we see in much of the movie (though that certainly does exist), but in the average family trying to figure out if they have enough money for the basics with a little extra for fun and some luxuries…you know, the American dream.

It is bad enough we all started off the year with more coming out of our paychecks (for those lucky enough to have paychecks) but now you also say you are not going to take any of the Republican guff on spending cuts in the government?!?! I don't believe your "mandate" is to keep doing Washington's version of Einstein's definition of insanity: "continue to do the same thing and expect a different result."

Yes, you won. Congratulations! And you don't have to worry about being re-elected so you do not have that pressure on you. But think, man! Only slightly more than half the nation wanted you so that means you might want to consider governing more toward the middle. If you want to be brave, don't just feel like you can stand up to the Republicans, but stand against your own party when needed. Both parties have extremists in their leadership. Try to bring the country back together. That is the mark of a true leader. You are the President. You can be the man. You want to be known as a politician who could only win elections or as someone who brought the country together?

Your choice. The common people – which are everyone outside of the Washington beltway - are pretty disgusted with the rhetoric and nothing getting done. People may not be ready to raise the barricades but as one of the lines of a song from *Les Miserables* goes:

"When's it gonna end?

When we gonna live?

Something's gotta happen now

Or something's gonna give"

I still feel like something is going to give because we have so many in office that forget most Americans are somewhere in the middle of any conservative or liberal philosophy. As long as our leaders keep arguing out on the extreme edges, an awful lot of Americans are struggling. And because of government action – or inaction – the struggling is getting worse and worse.

Les Miserables in Washington — Part 2

January 10, 2013

I believe in equal opportunity critiques. Yesterday, was the President… today is Congress. There will be a Part 3 tomorrow, but it won't be on the Supreme Court. After allowing Obamacare on a technicality, my impression of them as the last hope in American government died. That is not an opinion of Obamacare, it is a reflection on one justice going out of his way to find a loophole to save it. I did not know that was in their job description.

Anyway, I want to bring your attention to a section of an article published this week and these poll results:

"Good news, Congress! You're more popular than telemarketers, the deadly ebola virus, gonorrhea, the Kardashians, Lindsay Lohan, communism, disgraced Democratic former Sen. John Edwards, playground bullies and meth labs.

Bad news, Congress! Americans still have a higher opinion of head lice, colonoscopies, cockroaches, Nickelback, the NFL replacement refs, and Donald Trump."

This poll was conducted by Public Policy Polling. They found that Congress had an approval rating of 9% with 85% of participants disapproving of the legislative body. And as they say, the margin of error is plus or minus 3.4%. So at best the Senate and House have an approval of a whopping 12.4% of the American people, or it is actually 88.4% of the population who think they stink. And all you have to do is bring up the topic with any group of Americans from any socio-economic, race or religious group and you find that the poll is pretty darn accurate.

I understand the concept of the attitude: "I am going to do the best job possible, and I don't care what others think." It is a proud attitude and usually harbored by people who were fired or who could not get a business off the ground. After all, "pride goes before the fall."

The truth is Congress is set up in such a way that all a lawmaker has to do is appeal to the electorate of his state (or section of the state) and has enough votes to beat his opponent. And one of the many problems of our two party system is that the choice to voters is very limited. Think about it: how many times do you go into a voting booth and enthusiastically vote for someone? Do you do that or is it a case of deciding the lesser of two evils? Or worse…is your attitude one of "I've been a Republican (or Democrat) all my life and by God I am voting that way again this year"…and that person is an idiot!

So we send some good people to Congress, but a lot of idiots and dysfunctional ones too. The funny thing about dysfunctional people is that it seems to be contagious. They seem to make the group they are in totally dysfunctional. And one of the biggest dysfunctions in Congress is that instead of loyalty to the USA and the people they serve, the members profess loyalty to their party and those in charge of the party. It is like a plague on Congress that has been growing steadily over the past 12 years. It paralyzes getting anything accomplished.

It is ok to have different philosophies of how the government should be run. That prevents any extremism by one side or the other. But that means compromise is needed. Compromise is not a bad word. You cannot take your ball and go home if you don't get your way. It means you get a solution where the majority of people can play and get something out of the game.

I don't know when it changed but the United States government got along for more than 200 years with compromise. If the Continental Congress didn't compromise in 1776 the "Declaration of Independence" would have been the "Declaration of We Are Really Mad at the King and Want Him to Stop."

So to the new Congress and Senate I beg you to not turn Washington into the movie "Groundhog Day" where these two years are identical to the last two. It is more important to do the right thing, then to be "right." The country depends on it. And Lord help us, but at the least you should do better in the polling than Donald Trump!

The government's inability to compromise on the simplest of issues is frightening. That makes the bigger decisions seem downright impossible.

Obviously, I had just seen the newest film version of Les Miserables before this and the frustration by so many people in that movie made me think of America's frustration with Congress. Because like the movie, we have many people who are hurting since the government has not done a lot recently to promote the economy and job growth throughout the country.

Les Miserables in Washington — Part 3

January 11, 2013

If anyone follows my column on a daily basis (and if you do, please encourage your friends to "discover" me) you know this is the third piece of my own Les Miserables. And that is not a tribute to the length of the movie or play, but an acknowledgement that it describes Washington where so much is wrong lately. Not to mention, no one there really seems to care about the rest of America outside the city limits. One of the powerful themes of Les Miserables is that the struggles of individuals and people as a whole are full of personal drama and real suffering...and nobody from on high (except God) seems to give a damn.

So far, I have talked about the President and Congress. Today I want to focus on the Republican Party as my third and final problem I see in Washington. (To the Democrats: don't get smug – the only reason I am not talking about you is that I tend to identify myself as a conservative who tries to be very middle of the road, so my own party is an embarrassment lately. You have more than your share of extreme wackos too. They also need to get a grip on reality.)

I saw this in the Washington Post the other day: **"The moderate *Republican Main Street Partnership* is dropping "Republican" from its name. The group is now known as "The Main Street Partnership" and hopes to recruit centrist Democrats. 'The goal is to try and fill the void that is the middle,' the group's new president, former Ohio congressman Steven LaTourette said. 'The American political system is like a doughnut: You've got sides, but you don't have anything in the middle and it would be my goal to work with Republicans and Democrats who want to find the path forward to getting things done and compromise.' "**

I find this more than symbolic. Here is an organization that is trying to get people working towards the middle of two ends and the word

"Republican" has been dropped because it now signifies extremism. And what boggles my mind is that the leaders of the party in Washington do absolutely nothing to counteract this image and try to bring the group back towards the center. Instead of throwing a blanket on the fire, they throw kerosene. Then they whine and lament about why they do not win Presidential elections, why people aren't joining their party, and why they cannot appeal to more diverse ethnicities in this country. I listen to the pundits and read what others say about it and the only thing I can come up with is a psychological technical term: stupidity.

I have followed politics since my seventh grade history class had us reading current events and discussing issues. The Republicans always seemed a little more conservative and had more common sense than the other party. The Dems seemed to be more socialistic in giving things to all people no matter what. It seemed like a good partnership. The country did develop more and more programs to help those in need but not to the extent of bankruptcy. Checks and balances worked. I guess being more conservative in nature I identified more with the Republicans. But I never voted blindly by party. I always liked, and still do, listen to all the candidates.

The United States is facing so many issues, that the Republican Party could be a leader. There is a vacuum at the top in leadership. President Obama pontificates, he doesn't lead. Democratic leadership in the House and Senate say the same things over and over and hold their breath if they don't get their way. And this is what gets me – the Republicans act the same way. Basic rule of kindergarten: you cannot get your way all the time and life is no fun and you get nothing done if you don't play and work together. We need a leader to rise up and have enough confidence in him or herself and do what is right. There are too many paper tigers in the Republican Party and opportunity continues to slip away.

I am at the point to just going back and saying I am an independent (as I did for years). Maybe that is what all voters should be so we aren't biased by labels or parties. And nobody can tell me I want to do that just because I do not want to be associated with losers. After all I am a New York Met fan and I still root for them and wear their hat and T-shirt around!

The national conversation within the Republican Party can be down-

right scary. Too often, the extreme fringe seems to throw its weight around in a disproportionate way and makes it the party of "No." I am ok with telling the democrats "no" to something but you better have a viable alternative. And that is where I find the fringe leaders of the Republicans lacking. Can you imagine if they were suddenly in power across all levels of government? I envision them looking at each other and saying "Now what?"

Do You Have Change for a Trillion?

January 15, 2013

It is so easy to write about what goes on in our nation's capital. That is because if you went to a TV producer with an idea for a television series or movie based on what is happening in Washington, you would be told that it is so far from reality, that nobody would watch it.

This is the case of the trillion dollar coin.

Thanks to an odd loophole in current law, the U.S. Treasury is technically allowed to mint as many coins made of platinum as it wants and can assign them whatever value it pleases. Under this scenario, the U.S. Mint would produce (say) three trillion-dollar platinum coins. The president orders the coins to be deposited at the Federal Reserve. The Fed then moves this money into Treasury's accounts. And just like that, Treasury suddenly has an extra $3 trillion to pay off its obligations for the next year — without needing to issue new debt. The ceiling is no longer an issue.

The funny thing about this is that it is treated as a serious consideration by some far-left liberals in the capital. They believe it is a way to keep the Republicans from demanding real budget cuts in exchange for raising our debt ceiling (which is roughly somewhere between the moon and Mars right now).

Can you picture the scene down at the Federal Reserve office:

Clerk: "Good Morning, may I help you?'

Treasury Intern: "Yes, my boss sent me down here to pay off our account."

Clerk: "And your boss is…"

Intern: "Ultimately, I guess the President of the United States."

Clerk: "Wow! I never got a check from him. What are you paying off?"

Intern (pulling out a document roughly the size of a 24- roll package of toilet paper): "This year's debt. I suggest you just go to the last page of that thing and you will see we owe $2.8 trillion for last year."

Clerk: "And you are going to pay that with a check? I have no idea how long I have to hold something like that to clear."

Intern: "No, I am using these." The intern lays out three coins.

Clerk (looking closely): "Bus tokens?"

Intern (in surprise): "Oh, sorry. Wrong pocket." He reaches into his pants pocket and brings out 3 more coins.

Clerk: "Trillion Dollar coins! What the hell I am supposed to do with them?"

Intern: "Put them in your cash register and write me a receipt. Oh, and I need change."

Clerk: "Change! That is like $200 billion in change. Where am I going to get that kind of money?"

Intern: "Do what we do. Contact the Hasbro Company. You know… the ones that make the Monopoly game. They made our coins. Where else can you go when you want to make stuff up?"

Here is a case where I am afraid humor will turn into truth. There is no answer for the country's massive debt. I am afraid this type of solution will actually happen! It can just be made to vanish. Wish I could do that with my debt!

NRA—The National Rationality Association

January 16, 2013

The national gun debate is exploding all over the news, internet and television like we knew it would. Vice President Biden had his conference and sent recommendations up to President Obama who will make public what he wants to do today. Then we have the National Rifle Association and its incredibly dim marketing department whose screaming is out of sync with America and another tiring example of extremism in this country.

Early indications are that the President is going to push for universal background checks on anyone purchasing a gun, a ban on assault style weapons and excessive magazines for guns, and enforcing the rules which already exist that have gone by the wayside. I don't know, but all of these ideas seem like really good ones to me. If a nut job is going to go off and shoot up a mall or a school, then anything that will limit his options on obtaining a weapon seems smart. He may eventually find one, but if it doesn't shoot 30 bullets a second, there is a chance of reducing the casualties these idiots cause.

Once again as a disclaimer I want to state I have been a member of the NRA and taught rifle shooting to young people. It is fun and gives the opportunity for potential gun owners to understand gun safety right away. I am all for the Second Amendment – as long as it is in the context of having a gun in the house for protection or for hunting purposes. I do not think it pertains to an individual owning a machine gun, bazooka, or anything else that will destroy a herd of deer in 5 seconds.

Since the tragedy in Sandy Hook the NRA, under the stellar leadership of their CEO Wayne LaPierre, has blamed shootings like that on Hollywood and video games, advocated armed guards in every school, released a target shooting app a month after the school shootings, created ads backing their point with images of President Obama's kids (tacky and low), and put many politicians who make use of NRA support in a precarious position. It makes me wonder if they have Joseph Goebbels in charge of public relations.

No pun intended, but I hope the NRA shoots itself in the foot here. They can be a good organization where the safety and positive aspects of firearms is concerned. They could be a hero here! But they sound more like the shrill for every redneck survivalist group out there who are stocking up on their arsenal in case they have to declare war on the U.S. government.

First of all, NRA stands for National *Rifle* Association. What I remember about guns is that an assault weapon capable of shooting off a 30 round magazine in a few seconds does not easily fall under the "rifle" category. Second, the items Obama is going to push for are common sense. It is not gun control. It is a practical application of the Second Amendment for the right to bear arms. As for the scare tactic of this being the first step to severely curtailing guns in America: get real. It will never happen. It is simply that: a scare tactic to make the more ignorant people cry and scream that the government is bad and trying to run their lives. When it comes to health and safety – that is one of the things governments are created for.

And if the bullying tactics of the NRA are going to influence the politicians, I guess sooner or later voters will wake up and say they had enough. More and more, government leaders are perceived as wimps and they go out of their way to prove it. To our "leaders": Maybe the NRA gives you money, but it would be nice if some of you took an honest stand and did what was right for the country, not your pocketbooks. You really want to defend the Constitution? Then defend what was intended – not some perversion that has been created over time by a group that has more money than brains.

There are so many examples of organizations that have gone far beyond their original purpose. The NRA is a stellar example of that. I do not think it was founded on the principle of being a bully with scads of money to throw around and intimidate politicians. But it has and it is nobody's fault but the politicians who have the spine of a jellyfish and Americans who cannot seem to think for themselves. It seems every major problem in the USA is treated with hysteria which prevents any clear thinking getting done. And once again, the NRA pretty much won this battle.

Bread and Circuses

January 22, 2013

Ok, the inauguration is over. It is sort of like the first day of school. There is lots of excitement with the expectations of the year to come. Then on the second day you are given a pop quiz to see what you remembered from the previous school year. Reality sets in and you get into the mindset of bearing down for all the work ahead.

As someone who gets more and more cynical about our government doing anything constructive, I wonder what the mindset is in Washington today. Does the President really think he will get everything passed that he talked about yesterday? Is he willing to work with Congress to give a little on his end so they will come around to some of his points? Or did his "mandate" go to his head and he thinks that because he is President he will automatically get what he wants? That worked well in his first 4 years. (If you heard my voice, you would hear dripping sarcasm.)

I guess the beauty of a second term is that a President is playing with house money. He does not have to worry about being re-elected and can move forward on his agenda with a little more abandon. He cannot control the outside factors of the economy, natural disasters, scandals, etc., but he has a little freer reign.

Unfortunately, of all the Presidents I have lived through in my lifetime, their second terms did not go so well. I think they all thought they had this mandate and then did not navigate the political waters very smartly. Whether they ran into an unfriendly Congress, a scandal in their Administration, or lost interest, the second time around did not go all that smooth. The scary thing here is that President Obama's first term was choppy at best.

And who know what the members of the House or Senate are thinking. They already are worrying about 2014 and the midterm elections. That means a lot of grandstanding, heel digging, and stubbornness will be on stage. You know - pretty much how it has been for the last 6-8 years. (I am fair – that is a dig at both parties who have had control of the House.) Immediate gratification and self-interest will trump long-term stability for the United States once again.

In reality President Obama has about 2 years to do something significant. By then he will be treated as a lame-duck by both sides of the aisle as everyone begins to battle for 2016. In my most optimistic moods I believe the best will be keeping the status quo. When I think about the history I have lived through it looks this way:

- 1960's – the radical 60's. A lot of concern for making things right: civil rights, Vietnam, etc.

- 1970's – the apathetic decade. Hangover effect from the 60's and Watergate made everyone look at the government in a new way.

- 1980's & 90's – the "me" decades. Still going on today, and it is where the focus was on how much an individual could get out of anything and everything.

- 2000's – the disaster decade. 9/11, economic meltdown, political stubbornness reaches a new level and the 24/7 media wants to be the news and not just report it.

- 2010's - ??????? So far, it is the do-nothing decade at an unprecedented scale.

This decade is teetering on a seesaw. Which way are we going to let it go?

As I write now at the beginning of 2014, it looks like "do-nothing" is clearly winning. 2013 had the most inept government progress ever. While watching the workings of the US government is entertaining, it is a lesson in how not to get anything done. As I write my columns most days I marvel at so much needing to be acted on…but political posturing and self-aggrandizing seems so much more important to our politicians.

Memo and the Media: Jump Ball

February 6, 2013

Gosh, it is fun to see the usual news personalities contort themselves like a gymnast as they deal with the recent Justice Department white paper. You know, the one obtained by NBC News, which says the government can order the killing of Americans if they are believed to be senior Al Qaeda members, even if they are not actively plotting attacks.

I am not going to debate the memo here. I can see the national security side of the issue with it, but I have a feeling it stretches the President's Constitutional powers. A lawyer is probably needed but I see no reason to dirty up my column by bringing one of them here.

What I have marveled at is how this news story illustrates the total bias of some major news networks to either the left or the right. Many of the people on MSNBC or FoxNews are not real news people anymore. They are more like a high school debate club. By that I mean, you divide a club into two teams and they have to each debate a particular side of an issue. Then they have to switch gears and be a proponent of the other side. It is an interesting exercise that sharpens argumentative skills and helps refine one's ability to BS better than your opponent.

We are seeing a national case here of debate teams switching their arguments. In general, the liberal side of the media would jump all over the rights of Americans being violated here but Obama is their man. The right would push the need to defend America but cannot stand the President. They all probably wish that George Bush was still President and made this decision – then everyone would be in their comfort zone! Now they are forced to support something that goes against their grain.

If the more radical media outlets who lean in one direction were real news companies, they will take a lesson from this. Report the news… don't feel like you have to always put your own spin on it. I know they are now targeting specific audiences and any rational person knows who is good at news and who is full of it. But so many Americans take what certain people say as gospel truth. I am glad a situation finally arose that shows the fakes for who they are. They are usually the ones with the bigger paychecks and with a personal following. They are only performers on the stage. And this instance shows just how slimy and manipulative they can be in bending a story around to their own way of thinking.

I was pleasantly surprised, though, about a couple of people from MSNBC and FoxNews this week. In his evening program on MSNBC, Ed Schultz (who I can't stand) spoke against the program. "I'm troubled by it," Schultz said. "It doesn't meet the moral or constitutional standard that we expect of any administration ... we're losing the moral high ground by doing this."

And on another subject, I loved the way The National Rifle Association's Wayne LaPierre was pummeled by "Fox News Sunday" host Chris Wallace. You would think that if anyone would be in the NRA's corner, it would be Fox.

It is nice to see a little integrity in the news media. I wish I was not so surprised about it when it does happen.

When I look at the three major 24/7 news channels, I see Fox (Republican/conservative), MSNBC (Democrat/liberal), and CNN (inept). I see media people who try to be black and white in an increasingly gray world. It is encouraging when folks on these stations take baby-steps and actually go against the company line. Because the truth is that either side of the political spectrum is going to make mistakes. To think everything your side does is perfect is being truly disillusional. If Fox and MSNBC actually continue that trend, they may be mistaken for real news agencies.

States Protecting Us from the Feds
This Is What We Are Coming To!

February 7, 2013

Going through the news yesterday I saw this piece from the *Topeka Capital – Journal:*

"Kansas Securities Commissioner Aaron Jack says he wants government to "retreat to its proper role" with a first-in-the-nation constitutional amendment he's pushing. The proposed amendment to the state's constitution is meant to protect holders of private property from the nationalization of businesses by the federal government."

I found this disturbing. Is the fear of our own national government so high that a state feels compelled to pass a law to protect its citizens from its actions? Whether this law passes in Kansas or not, it could very well set a domino effect of other states doing the same thing. I have to admit that I have not taken seriously the idea of the United States government exerting such control over our lives that laws have to be formulated to slow them down. Somewhere in this premise is a really good book or movie. The question is: will it be a work of fiction or a documentary?

This brings me to two thoughts. The first is the idea of the federal government nationalizing businesses. In one way this is not so far-fetched when you look at how they became major stakeholders in such companies as General Motors when they bailed them out a few years back. But it smacks of socialism, communism, and all the other evilisms out there. I believe history is a wonderful teacher. When times are so bad that the people look to the government as the last hope, the government then does anything they want. And it never lasts very long because one rule of absolute power is that it cannot be sustained. Leaders will inevitably screw it up, some other faction will take over and you go into a rebuilding phase that takes decades. Great examples are Russia for the last 100 years and Germany in the first half of the 20th century. If our leaders do not start performing and get our country on a real financial footing, how will people react if we go bankrupt like a Greece? You can paint many dim pictures and all of them will be plausible.

The other thought is one of Franklin Roosevelt's most famous lines: "We have nothing to fear, but fear itself." Fear is like a cancer that grows and grows and continues to feed on itself. You do not think clearly when afraid. Stupid things happen when obsessed by fear. We are continually bombarded by words of gloom and doom about what the government is doing and not doing and how they are negatively affecting our lives. And the people saying this are not the survivalists with the guns and year's supply of food in their bunker; it is our own elected officials and the media. Does that mean it is true or they are just too lazy to do anything about it? Whatever the case, it begins to become a self-fulfilling prophecy where the distrust continues to spread like a wildfire. And that wildfire can lead to actions that do cut into our pursuit of life, liberty, and happiness.

I first laughed off about what Kansas wants to do. But the more I think about it, it is better to be prepared for what the enemy can do, even if they don't do it. On the other hand, the federal government should not be the "enemy" - so do your part by telling your elected officeholders in the government to do their job or they will be on the unemployment line after the next election. That is a fear they understand!

As someone who loves history, I have to admit that I forget that many internal battles in our country's history had to do with state rights vs. the federal government. People were afraid of the United States government becoming too big for its britches. Due to events of the 20th century − world wars, Great Depression, economic volatility, terrorism, etc. − that is exactly what transpired. The federal government has such a central role − and stranglehold − on everything that matters. Unfortunately, the folks in charge are not up to the task of shepherding us through it all. More and more we should be asking: what is the role of national and state governments?

Big Bird More Trustworthy Than Sean Hannity

February 8, 2013

Ok, so I had some fun with the headline. With more people using the internet than the money owed in the national debt, it is hard to get noticed on Twitter or Facebook or all those other things that have replaced human contact in the 21st century. So you try to get a reader's attention. The point is that the Public Policy Polling's annual television survey came out yesterday. The results were mixed. Fox News came out number 1 as the most *and* least trusted news network. Other highlights were that the Comedy Channel scored higher than CNN in the trustworthy department and PBS beat out everybody. The old standbys of my youth: CBS, ABC and NBC were in the middle of the pack. PBS was the only network whose "trust" percentage was higher than their "don't trust" percentage.

Fox News was down 8 points from last year's high of 49% as the most trusted network. My guess is that people got turned off from the results of the presidential election when Fox was forecasting Mitt Romney as the winner for weeks ahead of time and through the actual night time returns. I think Dick Morris is still in a corner somewhere trying to make the numbers come up in Romney's favor. In the cutthroat world of network news Fox was a laughing stock. Their evening ratings have cooled as less people are drinking the Sean Hannity Kool Aid – which is the best thing that can happen for conservatives and the Republican Party.

I could not easily find any hard figures on how many people watch PBS news. I think folks have a very high opinion of Big Bird and the Sesame Street gang as well as the many quality television programs and performances PBS carries on their stations. They figure if a network goes so much beyond the usual manure that is on the rest of TV, then their news must be just as good. I think we have a case of where the company's "brand" elevates the perception of everything. Nothing wrong with that I reckon. I just am not sure if it gives an accurate reading on the news department's trustworthiness. But kudos to them. When only one out of eight networks scores over 50% on the positive side, then they should be applauded.

The biggest joke here (no pun intended) is that Comedy Central scored higher in trustworthiness than CNN! CNN is the first station to pioneer the 24/7 news network (for that alone they should be shot). Comedy Central has 2 shows that *satire* the news: The Daily Show with Jon Stewart and The Colbert Report. I watch both and even went to a taping of the Daily Show last year. They are funny and make fun of everyone! They probably are the most balanced of the news shows because they look at all sides of an issue – and stick closest to the one that will provide the most jokes. CNN is a serious news network! This is like a Double AA team beating the Yankees. (I would love to have used the Mets in my example, but well…you know.) Can you imagine CNN's office today? Not only is CNN not as trustworthy as Comedy Central, they don't even get any laughs (at least not on purpose).

All this means is that you have to take everything we are handed in the news with a grain of salt. Don't sit there and take everything you see on television news at face value. If you see a story that gets your blood going, take the time to go on the internet and look at it from all angles. There are a lot of good journalists out there. Don't drink anyone's Kool Aid because that is what you have always done for so long. Listen, think, research and evaluate. The more you actually know, the bigger difference you can make.

If you did not know by now, I loathe people like Sean Hannity and Rush Limbaugh. Somewhere in their ego-inflated desire for riches, they look at themselves as the gatekeepers of all conservative philosophy. If it doesn't fit their needs, then it must be wrong. I am sure that if they found out they could make the same coin shilling for the liberals, these blow hard carpetbaggers would switch sides. And I hate how people take communion at their altar and blissfully allow themselves to be brainwashed. How can you have constructive dialogue to fix what ails us when the leading mouthpieces are buffoons?

Thank God Pelosi Does Not Teach Family Budgeting

February 11, 2013

I have touched on my frustration on how Republicans in Washington approach developing our national finances. With them I mostly agree with what they want to do because I am financially conservative…my beef with them is how they articulate the message, fight the battle, and constantly put their collective feet in their mouth.

I have wanted to write a little on how the Democrats think. I should have known I could depend on Nancy Pelosi to showcase her ignorance in order to make a point here. I cringed every time she had something to say as Speaker of the House. (In fairness, Boehner has the same effect on me lately.) There are a lot of strong women in politics I admire. Ms. Pelosi is not one of them. And yesterday Pelosi said on "Fox News Sunday" with Chris Wallace that "It's almost a false argument to say we have a spending problem. We have a budget deficit problem that we have to address," Pelosi said. "We have to make a judgment about how do we get growth with jobs — that's where the real revenue comes from," Pelosi said. "You don't get it by cutting ... into education, cutting back on education in science and investments in the National Institute of Health, food safety, you name it. So, it isn't as much of a spending problem as it is about priorities. And that's what a budget is — setting priorities."

Her one point that is true here is that a budget is about setting priorities. But guess what, sweetheart, when a business or organization plans its budget, a great deal of consideration is given to where to cut expenses. You see, if a company, or nonprofit, or even a family is trying to develop a budget, it is usually approached with realistic expectations. Part of those expectations is that the income does have some type of limitations. You cannot keep spending over and above what you figure you are going to bring in because you can keep going out and borrow an infinite amount of money. The real world does not work like that!

And that is the scariest point here for me. Here we have a person who has been in Congress forever and at one point was next in line to be President if something happened to both the President and Vice President. She is still considered one of the leaders of the Democratic Party and she basically advocates a position of "let's keep spending and just raise taxes to keep the status quo."

When I want to go to Fantasyland I take a vacation to Disney World. It is heartbreaking when somebody like Pelosi cannot get their ideology out of the way as they spout nonsense. Look around, women! The people you and your party vow to defend are already hurting. The policies decided at the most recent fiscal cliff cluster%$*& has reached into the pockets of everybody. And don't get on your bandwagon of we have to tax the rich more. A lot of work needs to be done to straighten out the tax code, but stop using the rich as a scapegoat because Washington is afraid of making hard decisions. And that is what it comes down to – a bunch of cowards in office who do not want to do their jobs. And that is both sides of the aisle!

I can take a little hardship if there is a light at the end of the tunnel. But until the people rise up from both parties and stop drinking their party's Kool Aid, and tells their representatives some facts about life, they are going to blindly nod their heads at their leaders like Nancy Pelosi or President Obama or John Boehner, and we will keep spiraling downward. I always thought the job of the government was to protect us and create a framework that makes the pursuit of life, liberty and happiness a real possibility...and not a work of fiction.

I guess you can say I get upset at political rhetoric. It is like a rushing river flowing out of Washington that cannot be dammed up. It is constantly reported, we are sick of it, but we keep listening to it. I guess politicians speeches feed our illusion that they are working on our behalf in Washington. If they stop talking, that means we are in real trouble, because then that illusion is also taken away. Then we have nothing.

Watch the State of the Union
...or Sort My Sock Drawer?

February 12, 2013

The news shows and internet are abuzz with President Obama's State of the Union Address tonight. I am not sure why. The address is as much a formula as any sitcom or drama already on TV. The big difference is that the TV shows are entertaining and can sometimes give you a surprise. Here's my prediction of what you will see tonight:

- Democrats will rise up and cheer when Obama comes into the room.
- Republicans will give tepid applause as if a gun is pointed at their heads.
- Vice President Biden will look like the cat that ate the canary while sitting behind the President.
- Speaker of the House John Boehner will look like he is experiencing internal cramping.
- President Obama will indicate people in the audience to illustrate pieces of his speech.
- Democrats will give periodic standing ovations during the address.
- Commentators will keep track of the number of standing ovations as if keeping score.
- Employment, job creation, and small business support will be talked about.
- Employment, job creation, and small business support will be talked about next year also with no measurable improvement from this year.
- The cameras will show various celebrities in the audience.
- The cameras will show various politicians who look glazed over, asleep or playing "Words With Friends."
- If you are watching, you will think you are in the movie "Groundhog Day" because you heard all of this before.

- Politicians who receive big bucks from the NRA will try to scurry under their chairs when the talk of gun control comes up.
- There will be talk of how both parties should work together more.
- President Obama will point out his way is the best way which negates the preceding point.
- Michelle Obama will look great.
- After the address, the various network pundits will tell us what we think we heard.
- Commentators like Chris Matthews will need a cold shower because they are so excited over Obama.
- Conservative commentators will forecast gloom and doom for the country.
- Republican Senator Marco Rubio will give his party's rebuttal to the State of the Union. This is like the interview of the losing team in the Super Bowl. Nobody cares.

The best we can hope for is that the teleprompter blows a fuse and President Obama has to ad lib his way through tonight. That might make it fun. Or in a show of solidarity the Republicans all rise and exit the room when the President comes in. Or Obama gives Joe Biden ten minutes to warm up the crowd before he starts talking – that could make for some memorable quotes. I think a nice touch would be John Boehner holding up a John 3:16 sign from his position behind the President like you see at baseball games. Because while listening to the rhetoric to be broadcast tonight, even an atheist will realize God is our only hope.

I realize now my opening paragraph was off the mark. There are some really great dramas and comedies on TV today and comparing them to the State of the Union address was unfair on my part. To them – I humbly apologize.

Wal-Mart: Barometer of Where We Are At

February 19, 2013

You may have seen the story where some leaked emails among Wal-Mart executives were made public. One of them was from Jerry Murray, vice president of finance and logistics. His email read, "In case you haven't seen a sales report these days, February sales are a total disaster." This came on top of a February 1 email sent by senior vice president of Wal-Mart U.S. Replenishment Cameron Geiger. In the message he states, "Where are all the customers? And where's their money?"

I take these messages with a tiny grain of salt. For one thing there is a hangover effect after Christmas where people are just tired of shopping and out of money. Plus there is more competition than ever before for Wal-Mart to deal with: dollar stores, Target, online shopping, etc.

I believe once you take that into account though, Wal-Mart's troubles are a good indication of big problems here in the USA. Wal-Mart has made its business by being a low cost retail store catering to an economic class that covers the spectrum from low income to middle class. I am not a big fan of buying my clothes there, but I do go there for a lot of paper products, household items, and bathroom supplies. They are cheaper than many places and the selection is not bad. I do not have a Super-walmart near me that has a full blown food section, but I know many people who are near one that do most of their grocery shopping there.

What it comes down to is that the general public in our country is struggling as we have been for years and it is not getting better. Maybe the unemployment figures and other numbers the government throws our way shows an improvement, but the fact is they can be manipulated to meet the need of whoever is using them.

You know what would be really cool? Have a Wal-Mart Day throughout the nation. All congressmen, senators and the President would have to go to a Wal-Mart and talk to the customers. Throw in the local and state reps too. These would be the rules: Ask people questions. Listen to them. Try to refrain from making excuses and starting a campaign speech how you are doing all that you can to fix things but the other party just won't allow you to do it. Take your aids with you and all they do is record what people are saying and feeling and what they are scared about. I really believe that if this was done for 3 hours in a day, the government would have an accurate picture of how families are struggling and what their concerns are.

President Obama said in his weekly address Saturday that a "thriving middle class" is the "true engine" of America's economic growth. He is right. And I pick on him here, but this is the same thing said by every politician from either party. And that is all they do, they talk about it. Like it or not, America is a class society. And the elite are not necessarily the rich. If someone made a fortune from hard work and smarts, God bless them. Hopefully, they give something back to society and treat their employees fairly. No, the real elite have become the politicians and government. They need to stop hiding behind their desks and lobbing verbal bombs through the media and see what life is like in the real world. There is a lot of hope for our country, but only if our government gets back to basics.

Many, many people struggle to make ends meet. A lot have jobs that 30 years ago would have comfortably paid the bills, but do not cut it anymore. It is a sad day when business for Wal-Mart is down because people cannot afford to shop there.

Back in the dark ages when I went to college, the Soviet Union was big and I took classes on Russian history and politics. What struck me is how socialism was supposed to be a great equalizer among people, but the reality is that it did make two classes: the government and the people. And the government was by far the top dog. You look at our country and we seem to have three classes: the rich, the elected government, and everyone else. "Everyone else" used to be wealthy, middle, and poor but those distinctions seem to be rapidly fading. I really believe our elected leaders need periodic reality checks and I think "Wal-Mart Day" should be enacted.

Social Media Fog

February 21, 2013

Are there other people as confused as I about the merits and work involved with taking advantage of social media? I know from some work I do you can easily find several new articles a day that tout why a business – whether it be a company or an individual – should promote themselves with social media. It seems like everybody has gotten on board from the Fortune 500 companies to mom-and-pop stores and to politicians at every level.

I am convinced it is something that has to be embraced. I know from promoting my site and this column on things like Twitter and LinkedIn that it works. But I also know I am only touching the surface of what I should be doing. On the other hand, if I tried to do everything I have been told about social media and used every available platform, it would turn into a full-time job itself.

Maybe others feel this way but I also feel like it is a cyberspace crap shoot. You do all of this stuff in the hope that people see your material at the time you put it out there. You may market your product through Twitter for example, but you have to do it enough in the hope that the right person sees your tweet at the time they are checking theirs. To counteract this you need a platform where you can program your tweets to go out every so often. The same thing happens in search results. Google has made itself the 700 pound gorilla in the room because you have to bow down to their technology. It almost seems like you can sell your product (at least the first time) even if it is garbage as long as you get all the SEO (search engine optimization) terms correct so a search brings you to the top of the list.

I have always found the internet to be a 2-edged sword. Obviously you wouldn't be able to read these words if it weren't for the internet. On the other hand, this column is like a drop of water in the Pacific Ocean of all of the material out there. I just read that if Facebook was a country, it would be the third largest in the world behind China and India! So if you are taking a photo of what you had for breakfast, that's how many people just don't care!!

But seriously, where is all of this taking us? Marketing and advertising operate on creating an illusion of need. Social media has enabled that to increase tenfold. Companies and politicians now bombard us with conflicting facts and figures at an alarming rate. You can certainly reach more people than ever before in the blink of an eye. By the same token you can also spread more disinformation quicker and to more people.

I am all for technology. But I hope there is a retro-response to all of this where people seek out real friendships, business contacts, and a social network that means a bunch of people in the same building enjoying some event or activity. I have seen it in both the business world and people's personal lives where these digital links to others have become a scorecard. For a business, just because you have 10,000 followers on Twitter may mean you have interesting tweets – but it does not mean a damn thing if nobody is buying from you. And how many of your 500 friends on Facebook will be there for you if you run into difficulty in life?

Social media only has a real meaning if you make the person on the other end mean something with a little old-fashioned contact and interaction. It is not the end all in itself.

It is a great paradox of our modern life that we can be wired into more people than possible in the past, and have less real human contact than ever before. This is a shame and hurts us. I notice in political discussions on things like LinkedIn that the coldness towards people in real difficulties is overwhelming. All of us need to spend more time beyond our keyboards and in the real world dealing with people. It would change some perceptions we seem to harbor that makes it difficult to band together as Americans.

The Poor Elite

February 22, 2013

It was not that long ago that a college degree meant a boost to a young person's career start. Now it seems like a long dark trail to debt and dead ends. There are degrees you can earn that are an exception to this problem, but unemployment for college grads is at an all-time high.

To compound this problem there was an article yesterday in the NY Times. Titled "It Takes a B.A. to Find a Job as a File Clerk" it starts out by saying, "The college degree is becoming the new high school diploma: the new minimum requirement, albeit an expensive one, for getting even the lowest-level job." It illustrates this issue by talking about a law firm where "the firm hires only people with a bachelor's degree, even for jobs that do not require college-level skills. This prerequisite applies to everyone, including the receptionist, paralegals, administrative assistants, and file clerks. Even the office "runner" — the in-house courier who, for $10 an hour, ferries documents back and forth between the courthouse and the office — went to a four-year school."

I think the biggest crime constantly perpetrated by the President and Congress is how they look at the unemployment percentage as the final word on the problem. At 8% our unemployment situation is terrible, but usually all of the hard facts and how it really affects people is ignored. And that is because the problem is so much worse than any percentage of the population that is out of work.

For today, I just want to look at this college degree problem. For the average college graduate these days, they leave their school with a degree and debt equivalent of buying a house. After being out of school for 6 months the loan payments begin. And as the NY Times shows, many places are hiring grads for $10-12 an hour. That is not going to pay the school loans or a car payment or the general food, shelter and clothing expenses. Many parents are longing to give the empty nest syndrome a try, but their chicks are not able to fly for themselves. The entire business model of a university often has student's tuition paying far beyond the actual cost of their education. These colleges are multi-million and billion dollar *nonprofits* operating on the backs of those who are mortgaging their futures. As with so many problems our government tries to solve, they rarely get after the institutions' runaway costs. (Healthcare is another great example of this.)

And this has a trickle-down effect of huge proportions. Because the pool of the unemployed has become so big, companies can now up their standards and decide they will only hire college grads. So they pay them what they used to pay a high school graduate and what becomes of that high school grad? They are sent lower on the pecking scale of the economy. This all starts looking like a snowball rolling downhill in a cartoon: it gets bigger and bigger and takes everything in its path down with it.

I believe in education. I also believe college is not for everyone. But some type of training is needed these days for the vast majority of young people to try to get a good foothold for their future. There is nothing wrong with being good with your hands and getting into carpentry, manufacturing, or auto mechanics. (I think it is harder to find someone who is good with cars than it is to find a decent doctor!) But these skills need to be nurtured and taught too!

We live in an age where our kids have a less than even chance to live better than their parents did. Kind of cheapens that "life, liberty, and pursuit of happiness" line. It seems like all of the energy in Washington is a struggle to maintain the status quo. And since the status quo gets more expensive, then we are actually going backwards while trying to stay the same. Going through college does not make you elite anymore, just poor. It is a glaring example that while the unemployment rate has gone down over the last couple of years, so many of us are underemployed. I fear for the future.

I still fear for the future. For years there was an enthusiasm in America to try and get ahead. Now it is a hope of just trying to stay even. It is hard to get out of bed when you live with that day in, and day out. Yes, we need a national agenda to move the country forward. And move it forward for real — not just pretend. We also have to realize that our colleges are in existence to make money and to stay alive. Education is secondary.

Sequels Work Better in Hollywood Than Washington

February 25, 2013

After taking a week off of not writing directly about Washington's woes, I guess it is time to start up again. And after staying up till midnight watching the Academy Awards, it dawned on me that none of the films up for an Oscar was a sequel. Sequels make big bucks in Hollywood, but rarely show up for the awards. The only two exceptions I can think of in my lifetime are "Godfather II" and the third movie in the Lord of the Ring Trilogy. But the Oscar for "Return of the King" was probably given in recognition of all 3 movies.

I didn't ignore the news from Washington all last week – I just did not feel like getting further depressed by writing about it. But front and center is the government's own version of a sequel. This one is titled "The Sequester." This is the follow-up to everyone's favorite drama – "Fiscal Cliff." And like all good sequels, the new one is almost exactly like the old one:

- Same actors involved
- Similar plot
- Artificial disaster looming which was created by the characters in both cases
- More blame being passed back and forth on which party and office came up with the idea
- A time clock counting down to the new doomsday

This is further proof that no matter what Congress and the President come up with, it can be shot down in the future. The "sequester" was an artificial means to implement spending cuts on March 1 if no formal budget was agreed on. It was a method to drive around a roadblock that was grinding financial discussions to a halt last year. It is truly a case of the government living up to its motto: "Let's not do today, which we can put off till tomorrow." And as usual, when tomorrow gets here, everybody digs their heels in and tries to renege on the decision. Worse yet, nobody takes responsibility of actually coming up with the plan when it was first implemented.

Then we get to the part that the Obama administrations seems to excel in: spreading gloom and doom stories about what happens when the mandated cuts actually take effect. What happened: they woke up one morning last week and realized exactly how the "sequester" would affect the running of the country? Come on! I like to give the American people credit on not being as stupid as our government propaganda seems to believe. It is getting really old being exposed to constant delay tactics, listening to the blame game, and nothing getting done.

Sequels of certain movies fade away when they stop making money or get too dumb for people to watch. Washington is now in that spot. Most of us as Americans are not making money anymore. We work our ass off just to try and stay even, let alone trying to get ahead. And our leaders are becoming more cartoonish everyday with their sound bites of old, retread dialogue. So America, when the next round of elections rears its ugly head, we deserve a new movie. It is time to stop being lazy and pay attention to worthy candidates that can be the new director, producer, actors, and writers of a country we can be proud of! Enough going to the same old, tired plot because that is all we are offered. Hollywood listens to ticket sales. In government terms – that is your vote and voice to our elected reps. Turn them loose!

I realize that if I can accomplish two little things with my writing it is that I want people to think about what is going on with their government and to realize their vote does count. Even if people do not agree with me, I want them to look at what is going on from all sides, and then make a decision to act on it – either actively through contacting their reps, or at least through voting. I guess I am still idealistic that we are truly a nation "of the people." As long as that concept is there, we can still move forward.

The Patient Is in Trouble

March 1, 2013

If you took America's vital signs today you would stick the country in the critical care ward. Look at these three snippets of stories that I saw on the internet this morning:

"Looking to buy a new car, truck or crossover? You may find it more difficult to stretch the household budget than you expected, according to a new study that finds median-income families in only one major U.S. city actually can afford the typical new vehicle."

"The budget ax is about to fall, and there's little lawmakers in Washington are doing to stop it. Despite a parade of dire warnings from the White House, an $85 billion package of deep automatic spending cuts appears poised to take effect at the stroke of midnight on Friday."

"The jobless rate for Millennials (or the 80 million Americans born between 1980 and 2000) continues to increase, reaching the alarming rate of 13.1% in January. Millennials now have the highest generational unemployment in the United States. The Pew Center calls Millennials the "boomerang generation," because nearly 40% of all Americans between the ages of 18-34 still live at home with their parents; numbers this high haven't been seen in over 70 years. And the boomerang trend is expected to continue or even worsen."

The intelligence world is not full of James Bonds. Many intelligence analysts would pour over stories like this from other countries and ascertain their health, future prognosis, etc. Here are stories I found while drinking my morning coffee and it makes me fear for our future. Why do I detect vibes of desperation in many of my friends and associates but folks inside that magical beltway of Washington are so out of touch?

Scanning these three stories in the space of 5 minutes, my anxiety about our future receives confirmation. Much of 20th century America was built on the automobile: business, lifestyle, ability to commute and travel all over, etc. Being able to purchase a car was almost a rite of passage and it was not a reach for the average family to own something new. My income level would be considered "middle class" by today's charts. I would love a new car but realistically I am looking at a better used car. With so many folks unemployed and more importantly, *underemployed,* making ends meet - let alone buying a new car - is another piece of the American Dream going by the wayside. You know that extra 2% many Americans had taken out of their paychecks at the beginning of the year due to the fiscal cliff discussions? That is about all of a buffer many families had. You do not have to be an economist (or a politician) to realize that when income remains stagnant or goes down and expenses soar, we're in trouble.

With the budget cuts taking effect tonight due to the sequester, not a lot is getting done about it except a lot of blame of who had the idea of doing things this way in the first place. I do not find that very reassuring or constructive. Maybe the cries of outrage from people this harms in a substantial way, will get our leaders doing their jobs.

I touched on the problems of these Millennials last week when talking about the crisis school loans cause college students. Some kind of training or college after high school is needed for any hope of a decent job. Most young people know they are going to go into debt when going to school, but the expectation is that they will secure a decent job in order to live on their own and pay back their loans. The problem with this equation is the lack of jobs to move into. And many companies are taking total advantage of the huge employment pool by paying substandard wages.

I know I harp on the same theme a lot, but the bottom line is our national leaders (and often the state too) are doing nothing to really address the problems we have. They pay a lot of lip service, but no action. Style over substance never wins in the long run. Legend has it that Nero played the fiddle as Rome burned around him. We seem to have a lot of the same type of musicians in office. Once again, I encourage people to tell their reps what life is really like. Even with their selective deafness, it has to sink in if enough talk. Otherwise we will keep on a downward spiral and we won't have Nero, but we will have the Dance Band on the *Titanic*.

I have to admit I loved the song by the late, great Harry Chapin: "Dance Band on the Titanic". As I think on what I wrote here, I made a mistake. The Titanic band was made up of brave men who chose to try and keep passengers' spirits up as the ship was sinking. Washington is full of cowards where self-interest is the main motivation for most of our leaders – not trying to govern in a proper way.

White House Becomes Wal-Mart Superstore

March 5, 2013

When I first read that President Barack Obama nominated Wal-Mart Foundation director Sylvia Mathews Burwell for budget director, my brain went into joke mode. Just think, all government workers would be fired or have to be willing to wear blue vests while working for minimum wage. We would have a rollback in prices on everything from National Park fees to the price of weapons to our allies. A veteran or disabled person would give you a friendly greeting as you go into any office (not a bad thing at all) and you can get any government service at a discount price if you are willing to go to their building at 10:00 PM on Thanksgiving evening. Trust me…there were more yucks!

But then I got to thinking, maybe this is exactly what we need. The Wall Street Journal describes the director position for the Office of Management and Budget as a "key policy-making slot that has broad influence on tax and spending proposals." And Ms. Matthews certainly sounds qualified for the position as she has worked in the Treasury Department before. I know this is not why she was chosen, but if the government was approached more like a business in its operations, we would probably get on the right road to good management.

Think about it. Just throw out all of the rhetoric and arguments we hear about raising taxes vs. cutting spending. If the government took real, concrete steps to reduce waste and be more efficient, then we would have an accurate baseline to make some intelligent decisions.

When there is a problem in the country, the government throws money at it. And whether it works or not, that solution becomes embedded in the government and continues to receive funding verging on infinity. It doesn't matter if the program works or not. And if such a program comes under the axe, screams go up about how it will put people out of work. To me the definition of a welfare state is not when we have a welfare program, it is where the government employs people for no viable return on their money.

If a business tries something new, it is usually done under a strict timeline with expected goals to be reached. If it does not do well, it is cut or has changes made to it before it takes the whole company down. A successful company constantly works at reducing waste and streamlining their operations. The U.S. government's approach to solving a problem is more akin to the growth of mold. They start a department and office and before you know it, it has spread far beyond the original intent. The additional spores do not really do anything but they are fed and nourished by the same entity that created them. And the government does not have the will or discipline to clean house and wipe out the mold.

I cannot even begin to guess how much waste could be cleaned out of our county's bureaucracy. I doubt it would wipe out our deficit, but I believe it would put a big dent into it. And to me waste includes loopholes in the tax code that you can drive a tank through. It is not necessary to become a bigger government as the Democrats seem to want or smaller as the Republicans clamor for. It is to be an efficient government. It would then be big enough to do its job and small enough to be fiscally responsible. But it takes guts and courage and a real desire to do best for the USA to accomplish this. And from the President to all of Congress, this leadership is lacking.

So best of luck to Ms. Mathews if she is confirmed. Unfortunately, both sides of the aisle have disregarded the budget director's advice in the past. Maybe she will have the guts to say "No, you cannot do that" when it is warranted. The discipline of a business mind regarding the country's budget is needed more than ever as opposed to a politician's conception of reality.

Wow — I actually compared our government to the growth of mold. As I read back on my description, the more I like it. Washington is notorious for things getting bigger than originally planned. It seems that is what they are best at because so little planning goes into any new idea or program. The irresponsibility of the men and women in charge boggles the mind. This past year had the launching of Obamacare as a case study of poor planning. I cannot wait to see the mold spores that come off that thing as time goes on.

Record Stock Market, Record Disconnect

March 6, 2013

It was great to hear the stock market reached new heights yesterday. It made the rich richer, boosted my mini-401K, helped pension funds all over, and generally signaled good things for all investment portfolios of individuals, business, and government funds. I am good with all of that. I believe in capitalism.

However, the orgasmic delight of newscasters and the smarmy grins of folks on the trading floor are so out of place. Yes, the stock market seems to have fully recovered from tanking 5 years ago. But America certainly has not. Most Americans are not even back to where they were in 2008, let alone ahead. Because the truth is that the stock market used to be a fairly accurate gauge of how things were going in our country. That model needs to be thrown out once and for all.

Maybe the cut-off date for the stock market barometer is about the year 2000. Before that, when the market did well, it meant that American companies were successful. This in turn meant companies hired more Americans to keep up with an increased demand, new products, etc. That just is not the case anymore. These are still American companies but two things have happened to drastically alter the landscape.

One is that every nation is shaped by the worldwide economy more than ever before. It is a fact and we are never going to return to anything else. Worldwide means successful companies sell their stuff all over. In order to increase profits, factories and distribution centers are moved close to the markets the company sells in. This makes everything cheaper to produce and distribute and profits go up, thus increasing the value of the company and its stock. As other countries' economies catch up with us (or we slide down to their level) jobs will return here as soon as it makes sense for a company's profit margin. Capitalism does not allow you to become protectionist of keeping jobs in this country. So having the stock go through the roof has no relation to new jobs here — at least not to the extent it used to.

The second change in company management that affects stocks is the overall clamor demanding that a company does well by its shareholders. It has nothing to do with the community the company is in, its country, or its employees. In fact employees are usually the first to go if a company has to keep the dividend that goes to shareholders. More and more you have the paradoxical relationship that a successful company, in the sense of its stock, is bleeding out employees at a consistent rate. I am sure the ex-workers celebrate when the stock goes up a few more points.

Too often the media focuses on things that just do not matter anymore. It is also a paradox that with news outlets wanting to get the jump on the competition in the 24/7 news cycle, they don't take the time on really reporting on the here and now. I heard and read enough stories yesterday and today telling me how great this news is, that I want to scream. To me the bigger story here is how these companies have used the economy to get rid of and/or underpay people to increase their profit margins. With the way wages have gone down it gets harder for people to buy these products in this country and have the modest standard of living that was taken for granted in the middle class ranks.

The employment situation in the United States reminds me of the shape it was in at the turn of the century — the 20th century! The bosses held all the cards. Guess what? There was an incredible amount of violence from 1900 till the Second World War as our nation tried to get to a middle ground where profits were made but workers were paid decently. Sooner or later we get to the "I am mad as hell and not going to take it anymore." Something has to give as we spiral in the wrong direction. Just once, it would be nice if the powers that be in America — government and business — learn from history before it is repeated.

That last line about learning from history…it never happens. The stock market continued to set records right to the end of 2013 and everything else about the economy was kind of gray. Employment, wages, and opportunity were rather stagnant. At some point the stock market bubble will burst (again, check history — it always does) and there will be wailing and gnashing of teeth in the news media. More and more I realize so many of our talking heads couldn't manage a real job if they had to. They just seem to lack practical smarts.

Cable Companies Need Competition

March 7, 2013

Yesterday I mentioned that our labor practices are beginning to resemble how companies were run in 1900. It does not paint a pretty picture of the reality many workers face today. I am going to head into the "Way Back Machine" again (that is a tribute to Rocky & Bullwinkle and Mr. Peabody, not the internet archive) and visit how monopolies were looked at in American history.

They were pretty much despised. (OK – we aren't doing a lot of hardcore analysis today.) Oil, railroads, steel and every other big company were brought to their knees in court and ordered to break up their strangle-holds on their industry. It was rightly argued that competition was good for capitalism and the consumer. We saw this in later years with the break-up of the telephone company, and Microsoft always seems to be in court fighting the monopoly label. Sometimes these companies broke up, and sometimes they just appeared to with smoke and mirrors. The truth is that competition does bring about choice and lower prices, and sometimes even better service.

Which brings me to your local TV cable company. Bruce Springsteen had a line in his song "Badlands" that should be written on every cable TV building: "Poor man wanna be rich, rich man wanna be king, and a king ain't satisfied, till he rules everything." Your local cable provider wants to be your "one place to get everything" shop. It seems that in most areas of the country you have one or maybe two cable companies that can provide TV, computer, and landline phone. You are at their mercy if you want good technology plugged into your house. Yes, there are options with satellite TV and alternate feeds for an internet connection. The only reason I have a landline phone is because it came with my package – I use my cell for almost everything. But the complete services most cable companies have are technologically advanced and make life easier.

The issue is that with how cable territory is awarded, competition in any given area is limited. It is time to change some things. For one thing, territory should be opened for as many players as possible to get in. I think if you had 6 cable companies competing for business in a well-populated area, rates for everything will drop by half. I hope the internet-based companies make more of a foray into the television field. I admit I am weighing just cutting my channels back to the basics and relying more on Hulu and Netflix for television watching. The thing that stops me is that I would miss ESPN and certain news channels. ESPN on my iPad is convenient in a pinch, but not something I would want to watch long-term.

Competition may also bring about a pick-and-choose capability to the channels you want. Springsteen had another song with the title "57 Channels and Nothing On." With inflation that now stands at 5,700 channels and nothing on. There are probably about 12 channels I consistently go to on my TV. I could care less about the others. But to get some that I like, I have to pick certain packages my cable provider groups together. And I am not talking about things like HBO or other pay channels. If I just had my 12 favorites (at a cheaper price) I would be a happy camper. I think this would be a real possibility if internet companies and the FCC and the entertainment gurus get their act together.

Yes, it is complicated and this comes under the heading of a "bitching" column. But the truth is, things would be a little better if we had more choice. And it is certain government regulations from local to federal that makes this impossible. Remember in the very old days, like the 80's, where there were only a handful of television networks and the amount we have today is staggering? The cable industry is like that. Of course the handful of players now controlling the cable want to keep it that way, but I hope things change in the near future because I would love to watch them squirm!

It is comforting that more and more people are finding other options than their outrageous cable company. With new technology coming out and people unplugging cable, this kick in the pocketbook has to have an effect in the future. I really would not be upset watching a few cable companies take a dive as they pay the price for their legal extortion of their customers.

Do Americans Know History as Well as Star Wars?

March 11, 2013

It's tough to be President, no doubt about that. President Obama, who in the midst of budget problems, trying to improve relations with Congress, and dealing with a nut job in North Korea, compounded his problems by committing the ultimate *faux pas*: he got his Star Wars and Star Trek references mixed-up last week. As everyone has heard by now, he talked about a "Jedi mind-meld" when anyone knows it is a "Vulcan mind-meld."

Ok, I found the whole thing funny. And to give him credit, President Obama has continued to make fun of himself over the whole incident. And, as could be expected, there were tons of tweets put out on Twitter commenting on the remark as well as numerous media reports over all mediums.

This got me to thinking: what if President Obama or some member of Congress accidentally said in a talk that the fifth president of the United States was James Madison instead of James Monroe? I am sure it would have been greeted with 2 tweets and a correction issued by the Monroe Presidential Library. That would have been it. It would have been dealt with in proportion to its importance. Which is exactly as the Star Wars/Star Trek should have been treated.

We certainly live in a day where people know more about pop culture than the history or make-up of our own country. And that pop culture is given more credibility than what has gone into the 250 year making of our country. (And before I get called on my math, I am including the formative years before 1776). Hey, I am a huge fan of both Star Wars and Star Trek. I grew up with it. But it disturbs me that so many people know more about the plot lines of those movies and shows, or who Justin Bieber is dating, than where the state of Wyoming is in our country or the significance of the Alamo!

Speaking of Wyoming, a few years ago I was at a ranch in the state. I was having dinner and drinking with a group of folks who were there from Germany for a couple of weeks. I was taken aback by how much they knew and understood our country from a historical and political perspective. A month later I was there with an American group and threw out a lot of the same topics. The understanding and knowledge were down quite a bit from the Germans. And both groups were the same age range and fairly well educated – everyone had a degree in something.

This is the ignorance we have here in this country that I want people to think about. It is why "intelligent debate" is as rare as Donald Trump being humble. People don't know what they are talking about. There is the saying that "those who do not know history are doomed to repeat it." Granted, I may have been a freaky student who loved history, and still do. It just seemed logical to me that everything in the past led up to where the world is today. And I know of soooooo many young people, my kids included, who did not like history because it was boring. To me, that is the fault of a teacher, or more likely how we do not relate history to the present. Just listen to people. We are so self-centered, it seems that only the "here and now" matters, and not anything before. Follow interviews of people in government, movies, music, sports, and even church…the ignorance of what came before is widespread.

When we are talking or debating a point about our government, we have to refrain from knee-jerk reactions (for one thing, it tends to make people sound like jerks). It is so important to speak from a position of knowledge…and not knowledge bent and twisted. I do believe if this effort was made on the part of politicians and the media, as opposed to 10-second sound bites, we can start solving our big problems. Until then, neither the Federation nor Rebel Alliance can save us. (And if you do not get the last sentence go watch Star Trek and Star Wars!)

I am continuously shocked how little of American history people know. I wager that an immigrant who takes the test for U.S. citizenship knows more about our country than a recent high school graduate. Congrats to the immigrant, but shame on the rest of us. We can learn so much from where we have been. If nothing else, we may not have to live with certain mistakes if we see that they happened in our history...and we take the time to learn from them.

What's Going On in Our Schools?

March 12, 2013

Since I touched on education a bit yesterday I thought I would continue with the theme. I saw something in social media last week posted by a high school student that said:

Things I never learned in High School:
How to do taxes
How to vote
How to write a resume
Anything to do with banking
How to apply for loans for college
How to buy a car or house
But thank God I can tell you about the Pythagorean Theorem!

I have learned so much about the workings of schools by talking to my daughters who teach in high school and conversations with administrators. You could write a book on what school teachers and administrators have to deal with in terms of unmotivated students, meddling parents, emphasis on standardized testing, unmotivated teachers, great teachers who go above and beyond, etc. It is another example of something that has gotten so complex and confusing and expensive in the fabric of America. Here is where we need to take a deep breath and take a look at it.

Because with all of the money and programs and changes in curriculum we have put into schools, we seem to get a lot of high school graduates that aren't prepared for life. Let's look at a just a couple of things starting with the list above of things not learned in high school. I know this list does not cover all schools, because some have very practical "life" courses. But there is room everywhere to better prepare kids to enter the world with some common sense solutions to life. Heck, I know there are adults who need training in some basics of living. The world is more complicated day-by-day. We cannot afford to send our young people out there with one arm tied behind their back.

There is a big cry on how the United States is behind in the sciences and other knowledge as compared with other advanced countries. This is a problem and needs to continually be addressed. But a more important issue is how the biggest classes at community colleges and other schools are the remedial math and writing programs! These are high school *graduates* who do not have basic skills down enough to take advanced classes. I think that is a big indicator of a problem. It is hard to be an engineer if you cannot do math or be able to write a coherent paper about your work.

I see what my one daughter who is a high school chemistry teacher goes through in time, personal expense, and dedication to try and give her students a good learning experience. I like to think most teachers are this way. For those that are not, keeping them around because of archaic traditions of tenure is a mistake. A teacher should be measured by their effectiveness, not by how long they are around. And I will devote a column to it in the future, but standardized testing should not be the sole measure. Apparently we are getting better at kids passing tests but they still cannot read, write, or do math.

And the last bit is for the parents out there: you are part of this education process. There are two extreme sides here: the parents who dump their kids at school and expect the school to teach their child everything from history to morals, and those that are in the teacher's faces defending their kid constantly. My daughter shared an example with me:

Parent: Why aren't you passing my child?

Daughter: Why don't you tell your kid to show up for class?

Good parents know that more than ever it is a true partnership. I believe the majority of teachers and parents are in the middle of the extremes to get their child educated and poised to move ahead in life. But as with most things, we sometimes have to be proactive in a positive way. If your school board is wasting money on some new program because everyone else does it and it is ineffective, speak up! Look at the graduation stats of your schools and where kids go after graduation. If you have a child in school, really listen to the answer when you ask, "How was school today?"

No child learns the same way as another or has the same aptitudes. One size does not fit all in education. And many school districts, especially in the cities, have bloated budgets and are highly ineffective. If you live in areas where the education is sketchy, you have 2 choices – move away or try and make a difference. As with so many problems in our country, this is a fundamental issue where it is time to make a change one student, one parent, or one teacher at a time.

School politics are as local as you can get. Here is a place where a parent or group of parents can make a difference. As with all things here is where a real dialogue between all parties is needed. School officials know education (supposedly) but parents know their kid (supposedly). The point is that if everyone does not talk, the best interests of the child are going to be lost. There is more here than dumping more money into the education funnel. It would be nice that things work like in the old days – a person who graduates from high school can read, write, and do enough math to function in the real world.

Teacher of the Year

March 15, 2013

My daughter, Jessica, was named yesterday as the "Teacher of the Year" at her high school. She is in her fourth year of teaching chemistry. It came as a surprise to her and she was understandably excited. And I am a proud Dad, of course. It made me want to point out some things for our future.

And in case her siblings actually read this, I am proud of all of them as I was of Jess before she got this award. I know I am blessed with four kids who are now in their 20's who have all graduated college and out on their own and embarking on their careers. Their growing up was one where nothing was handed to them and they all worked hard to get to where they are.

Getting back to Jess, her work and dedication are what impressed whatever committee in the district awarded this honor. She is as active as a teacher as in everything she has ever been involved in. She does her chemistry classes, conducts an AP chem class, is advisor to the prom and I don't know what else. I have known plenty of teachers in my life and know how hard they work, but in our conversations I know how much time Jess puts into her classes from getting there early to staying up late at night grading papers and tests. And this is done while she had to work a weekend job to make ends meet.

The big point I want to make today is I believe that Jess and her brothers and sister are part of a generation that are not afraid of hard work and want to make a difference. I have seen a lot of comments by people on some of my articles and others where they are dismissive of these 20 to 30-somethings as expecting everything to be handed to them. Every age group has those with a sense of entitlement, but it is the minority. Young people today need encouragement to excel. Just as some people have blinders on with what political party they follow, age also creates its own blind spot. Whatever we do in life – business, government, charity work, etc. – we have to look at a person as an individual; not dump him or her in a convenient category. A person in their 20's has enthusiasm and is up on new techniques. Someone in their 60's may have wisdom and experience. Too often, one is dismissed as too young and the other as too old. What a waste.

A lot of the unemployment and government policies coming out today directly affect Jess and her peers. They have one of the largest percentages of unemployment. The country's financial state is going to put such a strain on them that in 20 years they will be referring to 2013 as the "good old days!"

I have several calls to action here. Continue to pound on your representatives at every level of government that they have the future of our country in their hands and have to look ahead more than to their next election. For those of us in the age range of the baby boomers, we need to encourage the younger generation in whatever we are involved in: work, politics, church, etc. For the younger generation, get out there and push. Do not be intimidated, but don't forget there is a lot to learn from the older folks' experiences. For the older people who think they know everything and put down the youngsters: get a life.

The coolest thing I hope Jessica takes from this award is the reminder that she is having a profound impact on lives of teenagers. She does not know who yet, and may not know for years, but she is going to be that one teacher that one or more students will say was the most important person in their life. We all need to remember that even we non-teachers can play the same role. You never know when you can positively impact someone. To me it is clear that our current crop of politicians could not run a bake sale without screwing it up. Let's pray that the future leaders do better.

So I am a proud Dad. Sue me. More importantly, this article did remind me that there is a lot of hope for our future. It is the present that gets depressing at times. But there are a lot of good, smart young people out there. As long as they are not intimidated by the slugs in charge now, we do have an optimistic future.

Can Republicans Come Back?

March 18, 2013

Let's start Monday with some controversy. The Republican Party is going through a lot of soul searching lately. Better yet, the reasonable members of the Republican Party are doing the searching. In the last couple of weeks there has been Rand Paul's filibuster, CPAC having their conservative meeting, and various Republican House and Senate members having dinner with President Obama. There is mixed messages in everything that has been happening and the jury is still out on how the Republican Party can appeal to mainstream America again. Somewhere in this mess of mixed signals is a plan the Republicans may be able to work with.

As with anything a Paul does, Rand's ramblings in the filibuster had some good points but were also very radical. CPAC had a mix of speakers who wanted to bring the party back to the middle and others that are living in some kind of fantasy land that just is not going to happen in America again. And it is with a prayer that Obama and Congress breaking bread together can lead to a framework of decisions. I am not looking for much here…just a start towards working together.

I think there are three things Republicans have to consider when trying to reform a party that represents a *viable* viewpoint for many Americans.

One is recognizing what the mainstream of America is. The American landscape is no longer that of the 70's, 80's or even 90's. Just look at the census data and the projections. We are becoming more diverse in cultures. Economically, less people are doing as well as in previous decades. Just take into account those two factors and the extremism of the Republican Party, and you realize that you are not going to win many national elections. Congressional districts may still allow Republicans to get elected locally in some areas, but if you look long-term (not that many people do), it is the Democratic areas of the country that are growing in population. The simple math is that if that keeps up, Republican states are going to lose Congressional districts while Democrats gain them.

The second item is that Republicans may want to try and brand themselves as *compassionate conservatives*...and actually mean it. I am all for fiscally responsible government...and we desperately need it. But the fact is the government has gotten into many social aspects of life: social security, Obamacare, Medicaid, etc. The fact of government is that once something is institutionalized, it becomes a way of life. A lot of people are hurting. Since nobody seems to have a handle on bringing back jobs where a person can actually support themselves, these safety nets are needed. You cannot forfeit the population on outdated principles that have to take into account real life.

And the last thing that needs to be done is that folks like Rush Limbaugh and Sean Hannity need to be put out to pasture. Hate is gasoline on the fire of ignorance. At one point they rationally advocated the conservative side of the line...which is fine and needed. But when every attempt to do something by the Democrats is treated with derision and outrage, then you become a cartoon of what you wanted to be. They are getting rich and are anything but the voice of reason. They cater to their audience, but have turned off that majority of Americans they had one time hoped to influence.

The Republican Party can work to attract more Americans than they do now. But leaders with common sense need to get a hold of the rudder of this ship before it hits the proverbial iceberg and sinks for good.

I stand behind everything I wrote here. Unfortunately, the far right of the Republican Party wants everything their way which is some utopian view of America that never actually existed. And that America sounds more like an exclusive club that I wouldn't want to be a member of. They need a reality check that balances the needs of individuals with the national concerns of the country — which if you take the time to look at it — are inexplicably intertwined.

Universal Lessons from the New Pope

March 20, 2013

First of all, I am a retired Catholic. I now look at myself as a devout Christian who has a lot of rough edges and is in a constant state of trying to learn how to live my life better. I am saying that because this is not an article going through the pros and cons of Catholicism. (Besides, that would be at least a three volume set of thick books.)

This is simply some observations on how the man who is now known as Pope Francis has conducted himself in the first few days of being elected Pope. There is a big lesson here for all of us. And that lesson is humility.

Pope Francis showed this quality right after his selection as Pope. When leaving the election conclave he skipped the papal limo, choosing instead to ride the bus with the cardinals. He donned simple white vestments rather than the more ceremonial, colorful outfits. And when it came time to check-out of his hotel, he went down the front desk and did it himself. (Man, there is a wonderful credit card commercial there.)

But the story that really brought a smile to my face was the one reported in the *Daily Mail* where the pontiff rang a Vatican receptionist directly, which is apparently a papal no-no. The disbelieving man thought the call was a prank, and said, "Oh, yes? And I'm Napoleon." Luckily, Francis has the patience of a saint, and he convinced the man he was the real deal. He wanted to be connected with Adolfo Nicolas, the superior general of his old Jesuit order, according to the *Mail*. Francis told the disbeliever, "I really am Pope Francis. Do not worry, Andreas, just connect me with Father General, I would like to thank him for the charming letter."

The receptionist realized his error, because who else talks like that? (And I would have loved to hear the conversation at the dinner table when the receptionist went home that night. I wonder if thoughts of hell went through his mind as he contemplated how he talked to the Pope!)

Whatever your opinions of the Catholic Church, here is a man who is in charge of an incredible number of people's spiritual life. He has a daunting task in front of him. But he seems to be determined to stay as one of the people, even to the point of jumping out of his car to shake hands with his followers, kiss a baby, and blessing a disabled man in the crowd.

As a Christian there is a huge lesson here. Throughout the New Testament, Jesus was one of the people. He ate and taught with all types of people including sinners, adulterers, the poor, the lame, enemies of the country, etc. He refused the offers to be put up on a political pedestal. He was humble in all of his dealings right down to sacrificing himself on the cross.

Do not mistake humble for being a pushover. Jesus certainly was not that. He showed that you can be strong without arrogance, and that you can influence others and not making it all about yourself. (Jesus always made it about God).

Pope Francis seems to be trying to walk in those footsteps. And that is something we should all try to emulate. It does not matter if you are President of the United States, a member of Congress, a business leader, a church pastor or the head of your home. What matters is that we all need to show humility in whatever we do. For one thing, I believe it enables us to make better decisions. People react positively to it. Whenever we put ourselves up on that pedestal or let others do it for us, it just makes our potential fall happen from a greater height.

"I rather see a sermon than hear one." That describes Pope Francis. He is such a breath of fresh air. Leaders from all walks of life should take him as a fitting example of how to act. So many things would improve dramatically in performance and perception. I shake thinking about the improvement in our country alone if our leaders acted with a degree of humility and out of human concern.

The Power of "Free"

March 21, 2013

Here in NJ and throughout the Northeast we have a store called Rita's Italian Ice. They open up about this time of the year through the fall and sell great tasting Italian Ice, custard, and stuff like that. This year, as is traditional on the first day of spring, they give out a free Italian Ice to all customers. Yesterday was anything but spring- like: cold, damp and windy. My weather app said that with the wind chill, it felt like 29 degrees outside. But as I was passing a Rita's there was a long line of people standing *outside* waiting for their free treat. I don't know if you can sell ice to Eskimos, but I am sure they will take it if you gave it away!

Which got me to thinking... what if we made a big deal out of things that are free and we pushed that word heavily in the advertising? Could you imagine the results:

FREE Voting Here!

Maybe we would actually get more people to the polls.

FREE Education!

No more high school drops outs.

FREE Courage!

You would have the cowardly lion followed by 435 Congressman and 100 Senators in line.

FREE to All Sinners

Churches will be packed!

FREE Cardiac Exercise

Hiking paths in parks would be overflowing

FREE Enjoyment

Libraries will be popular again.

FREE "Believe It or Not"

Everyone will be watching presidential debates.

FREE Obamacare

Ooops, sorry — that isn't happening.

FREE Viewing of the Bulls and Bears

Wall Street would be too crowded to move.

FREE Display of Greed

See above

FREE Magic Show

An explanation of the budget of the United States

FREE Accurate News Reporting

OK — this line would be pretty empty. The media really doesn't care about accuracy.

FREE Kardashians

Hopefully this will be at a barge that will be set adrift out to sea when all the Kardashians are on board.

FREE Tour of Your Taxes at Work

Hmmmm…this might be difficult to find.

FREE Hot Air

One way to get all the pundits in one place.

Feel free to send your own suggestions. (No pun intended) And here is hoping that you take advantage of the freedoms we have!

I do manage to get all my pet peeves out in one single column from time-to-time. The sad thing is that stuff like voting and going to church are free — and not enough people take advantage of it.

Obamacare: You Can Fool
Some of the People Some of the Time...

March 22, 2013

I get so frustrated when we talk about healthcare in America. We need some type of program. For being a "superpower" it is a sin that getting adequate healthcare is such an issue for so many. But I admit I don't have a simple solution for it...probably because it is not a simple problem.

But I certainly do not think Obamacare is going to be the answer. Like most government programs it is going to make a complicated and expensive problem even more complicated and expensive. If I had a dollar for every member of Congress who voted for this who did not really understand what they were voting for, I would have a lot of dollars! They voted for the 'idea' – without any bloody idea what would happen with its implementation (which seems the case with most legislation).

As we are getting close to the total enactment of this plan in 2014, the ramifications are becoming clear – and it is not a pretty site. When the tsunami of regulations hits, signs are pointing that instead of the healthcare burden easing, it will be increasing overall.

These are the findings of a recent report:

- Insurance costs will go up instead of holding even or going lower. Obamacare was supposed to lower costs for families. If you buy insurance through the still-to-be-set-up federal exchanges you have the added cost of a 3.5% surcharge on the insurance plans. Employers offering health plans pay a $63 fee for every person covered at the business. And the medical insurers pay the government $100 billion over the next 10 years for the program. And if you think insurance companies are going to do that out of the goodness of their hearts (which they do not have), I have some swampland you might be interested in. That cost will be passed on to their customers somehow. "Rate Shock" is predicted for skyrocketing premiums.

- The Congressional Budget Office predicts that 7 million people will likely lose their employer coverage thanks to Obamacare — nearly twice its previous estimate. That number could be as high as $20 million, the CBO says.

- People will lose their jobs. The Federal Reserve's book on economic activity noted that businesses "cited the unknown effects of the Affordable Care Act as reasons for planned layoffs and reluctance to hire more staff." Gallup polling shows a surge in part-time work in advance of Obamacare's employer mandate. It found that part-timers accounted for almost 21% of the labor force, up from 19% three years ago.

- The middle class is taxed even more. It looks like that much of the $800 billion in tax hikes imposed by Obamacare will end up hitting the middle class, including $45 billion in mandate penalties, $19 billion raised by limiting medical expense deductions, $24 billion through strict limits on flexible spending accounts, plus another $5 billion because Obamacare bans using FSAs to buy over-the-counter drugs.

- Another bureaucratic nightmare begins. The Health and Human Services Department released a draft insurance application form of 21 pages. Let's face it, this is going to give our IRS forms some competition for complexity.

- Make the shortage of doctors even worse. A study by the Association of American Medical Colleges found that the country will have 62,900 fewer doctors than its needs by 2015, thanks in large part to Obamacare. At the same time, a survey of 13,000 doctors by the Physicians Foundation found that almost 60% of doctors say Obamacare has made them less optimistic about the future of health care and they would retire today if they could.

- Big surprise here: cost more than promised. The Congressional Budget Office now says Obamacare's insurance subsidies will cost $233 billion more over the next decade than it thought last year. (I am surprised whenever the President or member of Congress talks about budget projections, their noses do not automatically start growing.)

- And the final irony: millions will still be uninsured. There is a good possibility that if the law causes premiums to spike so much, people will drop coverage despite the law's mandate.

So Obamacare is shaping up to be like those drug commercials on TV: 15 seconds telling us what the drug treats, and 45 seconds of the possible, fatal side-effects. It is no good when the cure is worse than the disease!

I am no prophet — I just review the news. But most of this article is accurate with the launching of Obamacare. Actually, the launch was about as bad as anything could be with the well-documented issues of a lousy website, people losing their health plans, etc. It baffles the brain how many things could go wrong…and they did! Here is a sterling example of how inefficient the United States government operates. We would be a scary country if we approached projects the way a business would.

Microsoft and Yahoo—Game of Shadows

March 26, 2013

I had a miserable time over the weekend with my computer. In one of the recent updates Microsoft made on my laptop, they automatically updated my Internet Explorer to version 10 from 9. The problem is this completely screwed up so many basic functions that I use. I could no longer attach files to my email to send people. When you write for people for a living, it is kind of important to be able to send them their work back. And the stress-level and frustration increased yesterday when I tried to upload this column to my web site. That system was not yet compatible to IE 10. I finally got around both situations by utilizing different browsers to accomplish different functions. Now I juggle multiple browsers trying to remember who does what.

This problem cost me a lot of time because I am ok with knowing my way around a computer, but I am no whiz. And I almost lost my laptop when my urge was to hurl it out the window, but I realized it was not the computer's fault!

All of this showed me two trends that are increasingly battering society: our dependence on technology companies who may not be all that concerned about the consumer, and the pitiful customer service in many large companies. And to illustrate this I give you Microsoft and Yahoo! (Please, no comments on how I should not be using either – I am used to them.)

First Microsoft and Internet Explorer. I am ok with upgrading Microsoft programs if they are going to help. I think IE 10 is made more for the new Windows 8 than anything else. Well, my computer has Windows 7 and I do not have the means, or inclination, to run out every time there is an upgrade in hardware or software. You know those commercials where everyone is in line for some new phone or device? I wouldn't be there. If it works fine, I am happy with my stuff. I'll get around to an upgrade later. I think what made me the angriest as I discovered what my problem was, is that I could not switch back to IE 9. If there is a way to do it, I could not find it. I tried a couple of help articles I found on the internet, but they didn't work. And of course, Microsoft doesn't cover it on their website and if there is a way to delete Internet Explorer off my computer, it is well hidden. Why? Because Microsoft controls the operating system!

I felt powerless. Still do. It is a funny feeling when you think you have some freedom and discretion with the products you own, but you find a technological Big Brother exerting control over your stuff. And try to actually contact Microsoft with a question or problem! You are thrown into an electronic version of Russian Roulette as you navigate through pages of procedures and gobbledygook to try and ask a question. God forbid if your question is not part of their pre-programed help package. So an easy way to make sure a consumer cannot delete a Microsoft program like IE is to not allow them to ask the question!

Yahoo was similar in their customer service approach. I initially wanted to contact them because of the attachment problem I was having with the email. Trying to contact them with a question and waiting for an answer is like watching grass grow. I did this once with another difficulty. By the time I got an answer back I forgot what I asked and I had to go back in my emails to find out what it was. And then I realized their canned answer did not address my problem anyway. Maybe the new CEO of Yahoo should concentrate on the company practicing a little customer service instead of worrying about if the employees should work at home or the office.

If I painted pictures instead of writing, I would show companies like Microsoft and Yahoo as these huge castles perched on top of a hill, surrounded by several moats and with guards lining every parapet, window, and doorway. The consumers would be the village people holding pitchforks and torches and not allowed within 5 miles of the place. But this is more of what everyday life is becoming: companies who are in competition to outdo each other for the sake of having the newest and coolest – and not necessarily having the best interests of the consumer at heart.

I still stick by everything I said here. I think we all believe how technol-

ogy will free us up in our lives. Funny how it seems to end up controlling us. I suppose there is a lesson there. But I am so busy checking my smartphone or texting, that I do not have to time to ponder it.

Wal-Mart: Greed and Damned Greed

March 27, 2013

The consulting team of Howard, Fine and Howard are ushered into the Wal-Mart Corporate offices. Company management requested them to help straighten out some issues they were having. The operating officer started the meeting:

"We are facing the beginning of a crisis. A news story hit the internet yesterday describing how a steady customer is taking her business to other stores now. She said that on a recent visit to a store in Delaware she failed to find more than a dozen basic items, including certain types of face cream, cold medicine, bandages, mouthwash, hangers, lamps and fabrics. As she put it, the cosmetics section 'looked like someone raided it'. We are getting reports of this all over. What can we do about it?"

Moe Howard looked up from the file he was reading, "Well, retail stores are our specialty. Why don't you order more merchandise?"

A senior store manager spoke up, "That's not the problem. We have plenty of stuff in the back rooms. The problem is getting it up on the shelves"

Consultant Larry Fine said, "This isn't rocket science, even for us. Hire more people for the store. If you do not have stuff for people to buy, you will lose sales and be in big trouble."

"Well, you have to look at our history," said the operating officer. "In the past five years, we added 455 Wal-Mart stores throughout the United States. This is a 13% increase. In that same 5 years we cut about 20,000 employees, or 1.4 %."

"You know, I never finished sixth grade math," said Curly Howard, "but that does not seem to make a lot of sense to me. How do you have so many more stores and cut the number of workers? What's up with that?"

"Labor is so expensive," said the store manager. "If we hire the number of people we need, then our profit margin will be smaller."

Moe said, "But if you have stocked shelves and good service, you will actually get more people into the store and make more money. That should keep your profit the same or growing."

"Geez," said the operating officer, "where did you ever get that idea!? Wal-Mart was number one last year in customer dis-satisfaction and we made scads of money."

"So why are we here?" asked Larry. This type of problem is right up our alley. It's simple and all you have to do is apply a little common sense."

"That's because our stockholders like to see us addressing a problem – even if we don't follow your advice. We have been running our stores for years and know what we are doing."

"Uh, yeah, sure," said Curly. "So why don't you just hire more people and pay them a decent wage like Costco, build up morale, and you will stop that revolving door of employees that you have. People will stop leaving because you have the stuff on the shelves they want and you can have customer service again."

The store manager looked quizzical.

"Customer Service," said Curly slowly stretching out the words. "Look it up on the internet. It is a great concept!"

"We obviously hired the wrong consultants," said the operation manager. "You aren't here to fix the stores. You are here to ensure that our stockholders continue to get their dividends and our profits and stocks rise. Who cares about the customers? Our loyalty is to our stockholders. After all, that is the American way of business!"

I think this sums up how many corporations are run more for stockholders than anything else. It is a shame. For a tad less profit, everyone can be satisfied and happy. Stores used to have this attitude that everything was for the customer. Due to some magical formula (customers would spend more money), this attitude led to more profits. Sometimes redesigning the process to be "smarter" is not really the most intelligent way to go.

Style over Substance Is Killing Us

March 28, 2013

This is a follow-up on two recent articles I wrote: the state of our Veterans and Obamacare. I saw some facts and figures on both that were mind-blowing. Here they are:

Veterans waiting on disability benefits:

2009 – list of 11,000 veterans waiting to be processed for benefits

December 2012 – list grew to 245,000

March 2013 – 900,000 on the list with an average wait of almost a year (in some areas it is more)

Obamacare: The Congressional Budget Office (CBO) is a nonpartisan federal agency within the legislative branch of the United States government that provides economic data to Congress. It has been around since the 70's. In its recent re-evaluation of Obamacare, which does not begin full blown action till 2014, it has ramped up its estimates of the cost and problems. Three key observations: Obamacare is going to be more expensive than the Obama administration thought, disrupt the marketplace more than they thought, and be tougher to implement than they thought.

- The CBO's new baseline estimate shows that Obamacare subsidies offered through the insurance exchanges — which are supposed to be up and running by next January — will total more than $1 trillion through 2022, up from $814 billion over those same years in its budget forecast made a year ago. That's an increase of nearly 29%. The CBO upped the 10-year subsidy cost by $32 billion since just last August.

- The CBO has long said it expects the new federal health law will prompt some companies to drop millions of employees from health plans because workers have new options to buy insurance on their own. In August, CBO put the number at four million over 10 years.

Now it's seven million.

- The CBO isn't buying the administration's repeated assurances that everything will be ready to go on time when it comes to the health insurance exchanges. The CBO thinks the marketplaces won't have many insurance choices, the Medicaid enrollment systems will not be ready for new people to enroll, and people will be less enthusiastic about signing up for new insurance options.

As a conservative- minded individual I get on the Republicans case for saying stupid things, being reactionary in some of their views, and putting up lousy candidates for President. But these two huge problems fall directly on the Democrats.

On the Veterans issue, just look at the time frame. This has all happened since President Obama has been in office. He's the CEO of the country. He has a department that sucks. A real CEO would be kicking ass and taking names and fixing the problem. And he cannot blame the Republican Congress. They have voted more money to the Department of Veterans Affairs while other agencies get cut. We have no problem giving the best training and equipment to these brave men and women – shouldn't we do the same in taking care of them? Once again, the only thing I believe Obama can do is win elections: he certainly cannot actually do anything!! To quote Jon Stewart on the Veteran's problem: "This is f#$@ing criminal!"

As for Obamacare, I think if I had a dollar for every Democratic Congressperson and Senator that didn't understand this law before putting it into effect; I could take a dozen people out for a really nice dinner. They voted for an ideal! These people who are elected to run our country hardly ever take the time to THINK. It is more important to carry the banner of the party and get on Sunday morning talk shows.

I am all for some type of health care program in America. It is probably more necessary than ever. But be honest with yourselves as politicians and with the people about how it will work and what the consequences and costs are going to be. We will never see a headline that says "Government Program Costs Less than Original Estimates," but stop trying to rationalize your out-of-control programs.

Spring is always time for renewal and optimism. I see nothing in our government to give me any hope but a continual descent into winter.

One thing I learned as I reread this article is that the Congressional Budget Office (CBO) is pretty darn correct in their observation. They were dead on about Obamacare. I know that more often than not they are fairly accurate in their estimates, and are continually ignored by all branches of government. Maybe we should listen to an impartial observer more often. The numbers by Democrats or Republicans tend to be more fiction than fact. As for the problems our Veterans face — It is is f#$@ing criminal!

"What Is Truth?"

March 29, 2013

Today is Good Friday. This is the day Christians of every sect commemorate the dying of Jesus Christ on the cross. Why did he die? The simplest theological explanation is that He died for all of our sins. He went to that cross wearing the sins of everyone in the past and future. It was the ultimate showing of Love as God had his Son sacrificed by the hands of humans. With this final step of death, humans could have a close intimate relationship with God. Which comes in very handy since God doesn't do things like take away our human nature. We still sin…a lot. But it is no longer a wall between us and the Lord.

And don't forget that Good Friday isn't the endgame. Three days later, Jesus rose from the dead and lives on today. It is through him that we have a future to look forward to when we die and make the transformation from this world to the everlasting one.

I know my limitations. I know what I believe, I understand some of the Bible, but I am no scholar. It comes down to faith to a certain degree. But there are two short messages I want to share here.

In the gospel of John (18:38), Pontius Pilate, the governor of Judea for the Roman Empire, interrogates Jesus before he sends him to his death. Jesus tells Pilate that men come to him for the truth. Pilate blurts out, "What is Truth," and promptly turns on his heel and walks away. We have here, I believe, the first recorded example of a politician asking an important question …and not bothering to wait around for an answer!

But it is also a question we all need to ask ourselves, and take the time to find an answer. I will use Christians here as an example, but if you are of a different faith, you may be able to apply this to your circumstances. I think we get so caught up in the hustle and bustle of life, we forget that our spiritual beliefs are supposed to be our guide.

Too often we let circumstances and other people wear us down. We may spout out the main points of our spiritual beliefs, but we don't necessarily remember to live them. This is hard stuff to do. The Bible is full of people in the Old and New Testament who fell by the wayside till God picks them up. There is always hope. After all, we have to do it through him; this is not something we do on our own.

Which leads me to my second point. The whole reason Jesus Christ came here to die for our sins traces back to Adam and Eve in the earliest part of the Bible. In Genesis 3:5, they are tempted to eat the fruit of the tree of knowledge by being promised that "you will be like God." It is that quest of arrogance that fuels a lot of people. The atheists and doubters believe that the bible is just a bunch of stories; that God doesn't exist; and man can only rely on himself. How is that working out for the world?

And I am not talking about the fight over religious doctrine that has led to more wars than you can count. I believe that is a case of man taking what God taught and putting their own spin on it and perverting it. To me this is a great example of how we can screw up a good thing – we start to insert our own arrogance into something that is supposed to be for all men and the real lesson is lost.

Let's look at the theory of evolution. What never seems to be stressed enough is that it is a theory still. There is more documentation on the life of Jesus Christ than hard evidence that we descended from apes. (Ok, maybe a study of Congress would strengthen the theory.) It really bothers some people that there may be somebody smarter out there who actually has all the answers; which means they have to step down off of their self-imposed pedestal.

If you are a Christian take the time this weekend to reread the biblical passages on the passion, death and resurrection of Jesus Christ. If you are not Christian, give it a try yourself. You may be moved…at the least you may understand the basic beliefs of Christianity. You don't even need a Bible. There are plenty of internet sites devoted to the Bible. And at the very least, really think about your own spiritual beliefs. It is only going to be through the weaning of our arrogance that we have a chance to do what is right in life for ourselves and for others.

Writing passages like this one help me to get my thoughts and beliefs in order. Sometimes the spiritual side of our life…whatever we believe…

can get so abstract that we forget about the basics. I enjoy writing about Christianity. If I cannot give glory to God in my writing, than I am doing something wrong.

Let Kids Be Kids

April 1, 2013

According to the Centers of Disease Control, a shocking 11 percent of all school-age children have received an official diagnosis of Attention Deficit Hyperactive Disorder (ADHD), including a full 20 percent of high-school aged boys. Of course the drug companies like this type of news as they salivate over the amount of drugs they will be selling with all of these new cases.

I am extremely troubled by this in several ways. The first is I wonder about the diagnosis. I know some parents with kids who have this diagnosis. Their kids fidget, can't stay focused on one thing and are always running from one thing to another. In my layman's observation they are...kids! Children have enough excess energy where a group of them could power a city block. You want a work out? Go herd a bunch of 7-year-olds around for an hour. You will be looking for a chair and a liquid beverage to take the edge off. And there is a reason kids have a lot of toys: their brains have not developed to the point of extended concentration. That takes time on the part of parents and teachers.

Just a disclaimer here: I do not doubt that there are kids who suffer from ADHD and need help. But I am afraid that the numbers are out of synch. You know one thing that happens when a child is labeled this way. Well, they definitely have a label they may have to live with the rest of their school lives. Geez, that really gives them confidence. But that label also serves as an easy way out for the parents and teachers: well, Johnny has problems because he has ADHD. Maybe we coddle our kids a little too much sometimes where a little tough love may be more appropriate. Or maybe a little effort. Instead of sticking kids in front of the TV or video games, sit down and read a book to children. Help them through the difficult homework problems. Encourage them to do chores around the house that take a little concentration or time, like cleaning up their toys or room, instead of the parent or cleaning woman doing it.

And as for the diagnosis, I remember way back when my oldest son was in kindergarten or first grade. The teacher and some specialist observed him and came up with the idea that he was hard of hearing and should go for different tests. You know what we found out? HE WAS SHY! He could hear fine. He is an adult now and it seems impossible he was shy at one point, but that is the truth. Why is everyone so eager to shove kids in some narrow cubbyhole and keep them there?

As far as 20% of high school boys being labeled this way, is it any wonder? With the constant text messaging and onslaught of media and technology it is a wonder anyone over the age of 15 can concentrate on anything for more than 10 minutes. I know some self-described brilliant adults with advanced degrees from great schools who cannot keep facts straight in a 5 minute conversation. Their excuse is that they are big thinkers. The reality is they are incapable of focus and then wonder why their career or business came tumbling down. When I write for others, I counsel them on keeping it short and sweet because the average person's attention span is miniscule.

What makes me the maddest is how the pharmacy companies feast on reports like this. Remember most drugs control symptoms…they do nothing to cure you. That means a person theoretically has to be on a particular drug forever. And since they have been convinced they cannot concentrate, they aren't going to pay attention to the laundry list of side effects. And I am afraid there are many parents who don't care either. They want to feel they are helping their child.

You really want to help your kid? Then don't be afraid to spend time with your child and get other opinions. Don't start them at the age of 6 to think that a pill is going to solve every problem. This is what our society is getting conditioned to. (Besides, by the time your child becomes an adult the healthcare system in our country will implode – then what is he going to do?) There are often alternative ways of diet and exercise to help many issues. Let a kid go play and run around in the fresh air and sunshine. It is amazing how more receptive a child who burns off excess energy is to sit down and read a book or color for 30 minutes. And for a young child, that is a nice little step toward focusing better.

We are an immediate gratification world. That is not how life really works though. The time is now if an effort is made to stem this tide before it gets more out of control.

Too many parents take the easy way out with their kids. Use drugs to calm them, blame their teachers, etc. – whatever it takes to take the parental responsibility off of themselves. It is a shame because a lot of kids are getting launched into the world with the wrong attitude and misguided support system. We would all be a little better off if we accept responsibility for what we are supposed to do, and then try our best to do it. What an interesting world we would have if we did that! And our children would have a better outlook in their approach to life.

Washington Does Go Back to the Future

April 2, 2013

"We find our population suffering from old inequalities...In spite of our efforts...we have not weeded out the overprivileged and we have not effectively lifted up the underprivileged...

We have, however, a clear mandate from the people, that Americans must forswear...the acquisition of wealth which, through excessive profits, creates undue private power over private affairs and, to our misfortune, over public affairs as well..."

This sounds like a speech by President Obama, doesn't it? If nothing else, it could be targeted at the wizards of Wall Street. You could also picture this directed against the overwhelming influence big-money lobbyists have on our government.

Actually, it comes from Franklin Roosevelt's State of the Union speech given on January 4, 1935. It was his preamble to launching the second New Deal. The country was still fighting its way out of the depression and government was still looking for answers.

I saw this in a book I am reading on Eleanor Roosevelt and it hit me hard that things have not changed much in 78 years! Thank God, we have more safety nets in place to help people so shanty towns aren't being built in Central Park, but the truth is we are not doing a great job progressing as a country. There's enough homeless people around and many hanging on by the sheerest threads to know we aren't out of the woods.

I have stated I am a die-hard capitalist, but I also am not happy at the massive gap between the have and the have-nots. If you look at our country's history, it was not until after WWII that America's coveted middle class thoroughly bloomed. The world was devastated and the USA has the resources, capital and people to have the greatest industrialized nation in the world. And there were plenty of markets to sell to since the rebuilding countries had nothing of their own yet, and bought our products.

But somewhere around the 1990's, the world caught up with us. There was credible world-wide competition for almost all products and the world started evening out, more or less. Which by the way, is exactly what happens in a capitalism model. More competition, cheaper prices, etc. – companies, in this case nations, go through a cycle of ebb and flow.

But what strikes me the most about FDR's speech is that because our government has not adjusted to the reality that is going on today, they cannot make up their minds of what direction to go in. Many people in the government fall into the category of being on the side of the rich and powerful. If they pulled themselves out of a modest livelihood to where they are now – well, they tend to forget what it was like in the trenches. And the influence of the lobbyists and their money is downright scary. When the rich and powerful control everything, those without either are trying to climb an icy slope and keep sliding back.

Politicians love to stuff their war chests with money. Money gives them the advantage in elections. It may mean they have to vote a certain way that is more helpful to the money-givers than for the people who put them in office, but that is how our government works.

This walk down memory lane is to remind people that we are a democracy. And we can all vote. And we can all write and call our representatives no matter if they are local, state or federal. Hey, I periodically send some of these columns I write. At least sometimes I know they are being read. Whether it has any influence or not – who knows – but at least I feel I am being heard. Politicians have a love of money and power, but they do have something that overrides that love – fear. Because if they are held accountable by the ones who put them in office, they know the gravy train may end. I don't think we use this singular power as much as we should. It takes effort if we want to see any positive changes.

If you are an American citizen or legally here, never be afraid to let your opinion be known. We do not need an American revolution with guns and cannons again, but we could use one where people get a little more active instead of bitching about it.

This is why knowing history is so important. It helps to prevent past pitfalls. We do that as a country at times, but we do an awful lot of repeating the same problems and supposed solutions over and over again. The financial gap is growing at an alarming rate in the U.S and nothing seems to be improving…if nothing else, it is getting worse. Capitalism can still work to the benefit of all, but the greed concept has to be curtailed on the corporate level.

50 is the New Limbo

April 3, 2013

"The silver-haired head is a crown of glory, If it is found in the way of righteousness." (Proverbs 16:31)

In a previous article I wrote about the struggles of college graduates in finding jobs that actually paid them enough to live on and take care of their college loans. Statistically, this is the most unemployed and underemployed section of our economy. But today I want to talk about the other end of the spectrum...those over 50 and looking for work.

Turning 50 today is different from what it was even thirty years ago. People who are in this middle age bracket are healthier and more active than ever before. It is not far-fetched to state that people in this age range are doing as much...or more...than they did in their 30's. In my case I am much more knowledgeable on the value of healthy eating, exercise, and keeping the mind sharp and stimulated. I certainly don't feel like I am in my 50's. OK, I am damn disappointed when I look in the mirror, but such is life.

There are a lot of people this age who have a lot to offer any number of companies or organizations. And you would think they would be sucked up by companies because there are plenty out there who are out of work and eager to use their gifts in a constructive way. But once again, the short-sightedness of bottom line management in business leaves many good people out in the cold.

When our economy went south several years ago, many companies cut their labor force in order to save on expenses. Lots of times the older workers were let go because they made more money than anyone else. Companies lost a great deal of experience in their operations and many businesses lost ground trying to make up for that loss. And this put a lot of good people in the unemployment lines.

When it comes to hiring, many companies are frankly too stupid to look past their set criteria in hiring. Even though it is age discrimination, I wonder how many HR people pass on really good resumes because they can figure that the person is over a certain age. Their decision is based on the idea that younger is cheaper and is more up on technology.

Bull. I know plenty of people who have adapted and are just fine in all manners of computer, software utilization, communication and social media use. The overwhelming amount of companies are more concerned with protecting their bottom line. Don't they realize that having people with real experience in business and a proven work ethic is going to make them more money? And I have worked with a lot of young people out of college over the years who are hungry to learn from someone who has been around. I think most college grads are smart enough to know that they still have a lot to learn.

As Proverbs points out in the Bible, age is usually something to be revered. Not because the person managed to get old, but because of the wisdom that accumulates with time. You cannot put a price tag on that. Yes, you are going to have people in jobs who feel a sense of entitlement and really aren't productive. That is where HR departments have to actually work and get to know the people in the company instead of relying on computer programs and set-in-stone metrics. It is time to put the humanity back in "Human" Relations.

Coming out of church on Easter I heard 2 guys talking about the trouble they are having finding work. They were both in this limbo age range. I do not know their qualifications at all but they were talking about if they could just get an interview, they would have a chance. It is time for corporate America and the small and medium businesses to strive for a balance in hiring. "Penny-wise is pound foolish" – meaning that if you save a few cents now, it is going to cost you dollars later. There were new stories yesterday about how Wal-Mart is taking a beating from customers because so many stores are poorly stocked. Why – because they opened scads of new stores while cutting their work force. Is this what they teach in MBA classes these days?

If you are in your "later years" and looking for work, keep at it. Someone will appreciate your talents and pick you up. If you are a company, think outside the box. Because those who stay in the box tend to suffocate!

It is a crime that employment in America has come down to these shortsighted visions of employment. Work and being able to work is a foundation of our country that is constantly being chipped away at. And as long as companies concentrate on wringing every penny by adopting "best practices" instead of thinking for themselves, we are going to continue not hiring people who can do a job, or not pay them adequately for the work they do. Then companies wonder why people do not have money to buy the products they make. Duh!

Scary Being Attacked by a Reality Show

April 8, 2013

It was a wonderful weekend. My oldest son got married and I have a wonderful, new daughter-in-law. They put on a fun wedding and I pray for nothing but the best for them.

Their wedding was at a place called the Water Gap Country Club in the Pocono area of Pennsylvania. Originally the plan was to stay there. My son warned all of us that "Hotel Impossible" was going to be filming there. Apparently the hotel/country club had a very recent change in ownership and was starting to renovate the place. And there was a good reason they needed to give the place an overhaul. The rooms were very outdated and rundown. I can stay in almost anywhere and have camped in some odd places, but I get put off by dead bugs all around the room. Making the decision to go somewhere else came quickly and I knew I had to alert my mother who was also on the way up that they might want to look for someplace else. I know my Mom and knew this place wasn't going to fly. The people at the hotel were fine about it. After all, there was a reason they had "Hotel Impossible" there. (And they did a very nice job with the wedding the next day.)

And this is where it got interesting. One of the crew from this reality show wanted to interview me about why we were leaving. I cannot say I am shy because I do theatre and video and movie work when I get a chance, but I was not comfortable with this. I declined but still had to sign a waiver giving them permission to film me walking to the car and leaving. Ok, not a great drama moment in my mind, but fine. Heading back to the car, my Mom did pull-up since I didn't get the word to her in time. Going over and talking through the car window about where to find a place to stay, I heard some noise and looked up. Descending on us like a swarm of locusts were about eight people with microphones, cameras, clipboards and who knows what. It was ridiculous. I did mention in no uncertain terms to back off. Some producer-looking type started to say something and I cut him off and asked them to go away.

Someone came over to apologize a little later and I said it would be nice if they had some respect for the wedding. I know the kids weren't happy with this turn of events and didn't want them interfering. They did stay in the background for the event and I was thankful for that.

It was so weird being on the receiving end of a reality show. Personally, the only reality show I enjoy watching on TV is sports. For the most part I believe reality shows are lazy and cheap television. Producers do not have to worry about scripts, actors, and sets plus all the money they cost. But others like them and they get ratings. If watching a lawn growing got ratings, we would have the grass channel!

I don't know if a reality show can be classified as the "media," but their aggressiveness is certainly a lot like what you see on TV news. It is rather frightening if you aren't used to it. I guess it brought home to me how much privacy is non-existent in our day and age. There is always that saying that everything is in "the public's right to know." Unless you are in public office or do work in the public interest, or do something that affects others, the public does not have the right to know! People can go out of their way putting their daily lives on Facebook or whatever the social media du jour is, but that is their problem.

I will be much more forgiving of people who say something stupid when descended on by reporters in the future. It does take practice and experience not to be overwhelmed by a tidal wave of cameras in your face. But even if you are not in the position to have to put up with something like this, don't be afraid to protect your privacy. It is a right we have in this country. But it is getting harder to keep than money in your savings account!Ó

I cringed watching "Hotel Impossible" when my episode was on. I did have my close-up telling the reality crew to back off, and they erroneously said I checked back into the hotel, but that just proves there is not a lot of reality in "reality" TV. This was not an experience to be welcomed, but it is great to have nice memories of my son's wedding on television. The show did a great job with that footage.

We Could Use a Margaret Thatcher

April 9, 2013

I am no expert on British politics. I just know watching the House of Commons having a debate is a lot of fun. But I do know that Margaret Thatcher brought England out of its own doldrums kicking and screaming when she became Prime Minister after the 1979 General Election. She was the longest serving Prime Minister of the 20th century and her reign ended in 1990 when her own conservative party challenged her leadership.

By saying the Unites States can use a Thatcher in today's government, I mean someone with her leadership qualities. She had a vision for her country and marched toward those goals by wading through opposition from all sides – and often from within her own party. She had courage and an inner strength we do not see too often in a politician. She lived the Davy Crockett model of "Make sure you are right, and then go ahead."

Sure, her single-mindedness ended up being her downfall, but she had a hell of a run before it got to that point. (Her Community Charge - popularly referred to as "poll tax" - was widely unpopular and her views on the European Community were not shared by others in her Cabinet and led to her resignation.) But this woman who came from the everyday ranks of citizens (her Dad was a shopkeeper) demonstrated the strength of leadership that is in such short supply today.

And this is the courage that is so absent from our current Washington government…and has been for quite a while. There have been flashes of leadership in our nation's capital from both parties and through several administrations, but that is all they were – a flash. It seems like the most politicians are able to do today is be a flare – a bright light that quickly goes dim. The Presidency is as much symbolic as true power. As the President Lincoln of Steven Spielberg's movie says, "I am the President of the United States of America, clothed in immense power!" I'm sorry, I don't see much of that feeling radiating from President Obama nor was it there in President Bush except for the initial period after 9/11.

The Senate used to be the halls of political heavyweights and progressive thinkers. And I am not talking about the 1800's with Henry Clay, Daniel Webster, and John Calhoun. It was not that long ago we had senators with the names of Kennedy and Dole, who knew how to get things done. Now we have a Senate whose most courageous action seems to be inaction.

As for the House of Representatives there is an image that leaps to mind. Unfortunately that image is a kindergarten classroom running amok at recess. They are still learning the fundamentals of sharing and communicating. And I am not sure how much longer we can wait for maturity and graduation from them.

Nature abhors a vacuum. I guess we as voters tolerate it. The extreme members of the right and left would support Donald Duck if that was their candidate, but the rest of the country would love someone who would emerge as a leader who can connect with most people. And that someone needs to have some political skill of getting the opposition to some middle ground. Just look at this week. Technically unemployment ticked down a point, but more people than ever since the days of Jimmy Carter have just given up looking for work. 90% of Americans are ok with some modification to gun laws but the NRA bullied enough politicians with their money so that isn't going to happen. There is a huge disconnect here.

Maybe a Margaret Thatcher will arise one of these days in America. There are a handful of governors who demonstrate leadership skills every day in running their states. Only time will tell if they want to jump into the shark infested waters of the national stage. It is time to stop letting events run America, it should be people. It has always been men of strong character that shaped the early years of our country. Where are the men...and now the women...who have the guts to say "Follow me!" It is way past time to "make sure you are right, and then go ahead."

Lack of leadership in our country is the biggest theme that ran through a year's worth of writing. We just do not have it in this country on the national stage. We have pretenders, but no one with the guts and intelligence to lead from the front. I do not think it is a stretch to say many of our current problems are from the wishy-washiness in Washington. I really look forward to someone to look up to again.

Everybody Works Today

April 10, 2013

The headline is from the movie *Dave*. That's the film where Kevin Kline is the director of a small employment agency and also happens to be a dead ringer for the President. Great movie, but one of his beliefs in running the agency is that everybody who wants a job should have one. This should be the philosophy in America. And I believe it is the feelings of most Americans. Unfortunately it seems to be the second or third thought of those who can do something about it.

First let's look at corporate America. You know - those businesses that have been enjoying such a staggering growth in the stock market. Job creation isn't in their game plan. They are usually at the forefront of cutting jobs so that they can increase the bottom line. If creating more jobs is needed to increase profitability, then it is a good by-product. If they are actually created in the USA rather than overseas, it is even better. I have to wonder what many of these companies do when sales are down in our country because people can no longer afford their products or services because people are unemployed or severely underemployed. Do they blame the government?

So let's look at the government. It does not exist to create jobs. (*Even though they do that a great deal, and not very well. It can be argued that a successful company can afford to carry a few extra employees, but a government cannot. And the federal and many state governments are hopelessly bloated.*) But a government does lay out policies for taxes, regulations, business incentives, etc. On the state level, some are very good at this and makes their states attractive for businesses to relocate to and bring more jobs to the residents. As for the federal government, this is just something else they cannot get their act together on.

It is so discouraging to look at the unemployment figures. And confusing. In sports, statistics give you a very good idea of the performance of an individual player or an entire team. Our country's unemployment figures are a mess of contradictions. Last week we were told unemployment was down a point and there were more jobs available for people. By the same token, fewer jobs were filled by a significant margin than forecasted and more people are completely out of the workforce at any time since 1979! Confusing, isn't it? But percentages can certainly be manipulated when you lower the number of folks actively looking for a job. And this does not even take into account people who did find work, but at a significantly lower wage than they were previously getting.

Conclusion: we need less empty talk from the President, Congress, and the corporate kingpins and more effort to do something. A working nation is the foundation to being a successful country. And if the foundation continues to crumble at this rate, it becomes harder and harder to shore it back up. Lawmakers and corporations are pros at doing things in their own self-interest. If they can look past immediate gratification and look at a couple months or years down the road, maybe they will see how important this is to deal with NOW!

Let me put a face on this. I mentioned in Monday's column that my son got married over the weekend. I saw some guys there who I remember being 10 years old and my son's childhood friends. One's name is Matt who is now a young man who got married last year and looking to start a family. This is a great guy who has two degrees already and is working as a manager for a Starbucks and also does landscaping to make ends meet. And his degrees were impressive; he wasn't a Theatre Arts major. But it is so hard for him to find a job in his field. It certainly isn't an issue of work ethic; he demonstrates that every day. The jobs just are not there!

It's not a joke. Again, let your government reps know they are falling on their faces. It seems everyone in government is happy to complain about getting nothing done when they are the ones who are supposed to move the country forward. I really worry about our future. Sooner or later a house of cards come tumbling down!

This problem is not getting any better. I have come to the conclusion that since neither side of the aisle has a plan for more jobs that the government is completely lost in what to do. The problem with that is the government then sounds like they do not care because they avoid the subject. Maybe if the President and Congress all said, "We don't know what to do," they will be able to sit down and have a real discussion and possibly start coming up with real ideas. Avoiding the topic does not solve anything and lots of people are in difficulty.

Guns Determine Real Courage

April 12, 2013

This isn't a discussion about the on-going gun debate. There isn't enough room here to spell out all of the fact and fiction. Rather it is a commentary on the motivation of our elected representatives.

As a democracy, we like to think our vote counts and our congressmen and senators do exactly that for us – they reflect the will of the people. But one thing the current gun debate once again showcases is the power of such organizations as the National Rifle Association. Now the NRA is in the forefront here because guns are their thing, but there are dozens of lobbying concerns that exert their influence and money…especially money…at politicians to impose their will on them. The truth is that sometimes the lobbying side of Washington is the fourth branch of government and has more influence that the other three that are spelled out in the Constitution.

The NRA has a rating system they use on Senators and House of Representative members. It is the grade they give each politician on how they vote on gun-related matters. Just the announcement that the NRA is going to give a grade on a certain vote seems to be enough for a member of Congress to lose their backbone. It seems in some cases, it doesn't matter what a rep's constituents want. Apparently the NRA knows more than the people and their support is more important. Take NRA and substitute their name with the pharmaceutical lobby or the banking lobby and you see why we are such a mess.

I talked earlier in the week of the leadership Margaret Thatcher exercised in England during her reign. She was called the "Iron Lady." I cannot think of one Senator, Congressperson, or President currently in office, where "Iron" would be used anywhere in their title. "Jello" or "wishy-washy" or "available for the right price" maybe, but not any word that illustrates strong leadership.

If any type of gun legislation comes to a vote, I would be very curious to know if a legislature's vote reflects the area he represents. If an area overwhelmingly wants better background checks and some modification of gun laws, and their rep votes against it, then you know where that politician stands. That should be the report card that counts.

Money is what makes Washington turn. And that is a shame. This is certainly not recent. I have a feeling that the whiskey lobby was trying to influence Congress back in 1793 when they were coming up with the first interstate transportation laws. Though an honest politician is sometimes a contradiction in terms, I don't think we would want to hear someone say, "the NRA gives my campaign a lot of money so we got to keep them happy – that's why I voted against this bill." But that is the sad truth about how the USA operates. We have the highest of ideals, and very gray areas of implementation.

The solution – keep being an active participant in our democracy. If you are in government, don't be afraid to show leadership and back-bone, no matter what level you serve. If in the media, start a new trend – report the news accurately…don't bend it to your personal bias and actually try to look at both sides of an issue. For the rest of us, never be afraid to let your opinions be known to the ones that represent you. Even if you did not vote for the guy or gal currently in office, they are still your representative. Be heard and vote…that is our right and that is still our strength.

You know the saying of how money is the root of all evil? In the case of politics, it is. One of the big problems with Washington today is when the Supreme Court in one of its rulings deregulated the campaign contribution process. Now more money than ever flows into the coffers of the candidates and it seems to have made those moneylenders more important in the eyes of the politicians than the people they are supposed to represent.

Native American Insights

April 15, 2013

As a Christian I do try to attend church on Sundays. Yesterday I found myself in a Methodist Church and happened to hit 'Native American Ministries Sunday'. I was treated to a sermon and talk from a member of the Ute Indian Tribe. She had been involved in ministry for many years and the talk was enlightening on two points.

The first point had to do with my further education on how Native Americans were treated both in the early days of our nation, and also currently. One thing I discovered is how these people have a great distrust of almost any Christian church because the church and government often walked hand-in-hand with getting the Native American population to move off the land, or to physically wipe them out of an area by killing them. Yes, fellow church-goers: hypocrisy is not a recent occurrence. There is not much our country can be proud of in the handling of this population by our ancestors. I really would love to hear some moron rationalize the terrible treatment that was done to them over several centuries.

And Native Americans still have a tough time today. Government administration of Native American affairs often is inadequate. Like the problems in the Veterans Administration, a department set up to help people seems to be constantly bogged down with inept management and poor resources. I think the best use of the government's money would be to send in independent management consultants to each and every government agency and then the departments would be required to follow the recommendations. Life on and off the reservation may become more positive for the Native American population.

I also received more insight to why Native Americans aren't happy with team names like the Redskins (Washington), Chiefs (Kansas City), Indians (Cleveland), etc. People say they admire the heroism and romanticism evoked by the classic Native American image, but many view the use of mascots as offensive, demeaning, or racist. The controversy has resulted in many institutions changing the names and images associated with their sports teams. But Native American images and nicknames nevertheless remain fairly common in American sports, and may be seen in use by teams at all levels from elementary school to professional. (And by the way - I just learned the office dealing with Native Americans in the US government is called the Bureaus of *Indian Affairs*. Shouldn't we start by changing that name?)

The second thing I liked about the sermon was learning the Native American attitude toward age: they embrace it. They honor their elders and look at them as a great source of wisdom and experience. I recently wrote how the trend in the workplace is to distain the older worker. I smiled as she talked about revering the elderly – it is something the rest of America should take a lesson from whether it is in business, government, family, academics, or other walks of life. There is a valuable place for everyone in society: the young, old or in-between. We have to stop making knee-jerk assumptions about someone just because of their age. If people take a few extra minutes to really look at *the person*, they may not be so dismissive of pushing aside someone who has true ability to contribute to the job, organization, church, or whatever.

There are many lessons to learn when looking at the past of our country. But it seems like most Americans have an ignorance and aversion to our own history. The plight of Native Americans is as sad a chapter in our history as was slavery. It doesn't cost much to make an effort to demonstrate some sensitivity and understanding. The United States was founded on great principles. There is no reason we cannot continue trying to reach for those principles regardless of what was done in the past.

Here is another case where so many of us do not know our history. I am also a little embarrassed that I do not write more about Native American issues. Living in New Jersey is an excuse I guess because they are not a familiar group of people that are around like I see when I travel out west. But it still needs to be addressed and something Americans should rally around. Sometimes it strikes me just how many issues we have throughout our great country, and how most of us are pretty ignorant about them.

Rise Up!

April 16, 2013

It has been very hard watching so much on the news about the explosions in Boston yesterday. I was writing with ESPN on in the background when I started to hear about what was going on. The footage of the explosions and people running and then video of the hurt and bloodied was hard-hitting. One thing about it being the Boston Marathon meant plenty of cameras to record the happenings.

It is quite a paradox of feelings that happen when we are exposed to violence like this. It is one thing when it happens in Baghdad or Jerusalem. We see things like that and it is almost like watching a movie. There is a certain detachment from the event. But when something explodes in one of our cities at a long-running and world famous occasion, it feels like a kick in the stomach. With all that is going on in our country, some of which I write about here, it often seems like we are coming apart at the seams. It is frightening and stressful as more and more people struggle to get from one day to the next. But then this happens and it puts life in perspective. Yes, we do have problems, but usually we feel safe. It is events like 9/11 or Sandy Hook and now the Boston Marathon explosions that jolt us from that perception into reality. Whether this turns out to be terrorists or a nut job, we have real fear thrown into life.

And then at the same time there is immediately a sense of the country pulling together. Our hearts and prayers go out to everyone in Boston. An eight year old boy and two others have died. Over 100 were injured and some badly. An iconic day in the city, Patriots Day, will never happen again without some reference being made about the one in 2013. In a tragedy like this, there is a temporary hold on our two parties being at each other's throats. The news media is reporting the news. Yes, there is a lot of speculation going on among the talking heads and the politicians that get face time, but it is no different than the millions of conversations going on around the country. We are all rooting for the different law enforcement agencies to get to the bottom of this and solve the crime. If whoever did this is found, we would probably like to see him dragged through the streets of Boston, but our justice system will do its thing. President Obama gave a short speech last night that was calming and presidential. America always seems to do better in a crisis. It is the day-to-day we have to work on.

This sense of unity won't last, it never does. But it is a glimpse to how we feel as a country, and what we can do as a country. It would be nice to be able to bottle it and bring it out of the medicine cabinet when we all need a tonic...but without the destruction that brings it about.

The suggestion for today is pray for the victims and families that were affected by the explosions. Pray that the law finds who did it. And be thankful that this does not happen on a regular basis in the United States. We live in a safe country compared to much of the world. Not everything can be prevented. But if this is one of the periodic wake-up calls life brings us, reflect on what we do have here and rejoice in your fellow Americans.

There is a great sense of coming together when things like this happen. And it was a wonder to see law enforcement in action as they got to the bottom of this attack quickly and efficiently. Let's hope events like this are kept at a minimum, but it is important to never, never forget.

We Are America

April 17, 2013

In light of the events in Boston on Monday, here is a reminder of what makes up America.

America is the brave men and women whether they were professionals or not, who put thoughts of their own welfare aside to carry, comfort, and help their fellow Americans when explosions are going off around them. In the midst of the horror that was videoed on Monday, you saw firsthand the efforts people made to help. America is the marathon runners who finished a 26 mile run and ran another 2 miles to give blood.

America is the law enforcement people who are determined to find out what happened. She is the first aid and medical professionals who found themselves in the middle of a M*A*S*H ward. Our country is the first responders who demonstrate that they will go headlong into danger to help others. It doesn't matter if disaster happens in Boston, New York, or whatever town you name.

America *IS NOT* the coward or cowards who made and set off these bombs.

America is all of those people who went out on Facebook, Twitter, and other outlets expressing their thoughts, outrage and prayers for the people in Boston. In a country that tends to downplay God as the years go on, it's illuminating how many of us pray.

America is the professionals who report the news. It is astonishing how good all of the news outlets are when they get out of the business of offering their opinions and actually let us know what is going on. America is the openness of officials to let us know how things are being handled. They cannot always give details on the investigation side of things, but they reassure us by operating out in the open.

America *IS NOT* the morons who in the midst of such a tragedy start mouthing off how such an event is a conspiracy of some section of the government. I also hope we are not the people who actually listen to this BS.

America is the politicians who put aside their party differences when the chips are down. You can see this in the actions of Boston's mayor and Massachusetts governor and other legislative folks. This was Governor Christie in NJ when Sandy hit. It is their determination to look at and reassure all of their people.

America is the National Guard and other military branches that rush in when asked to whether it is a domestic terrorism incident like this or to some volatile part of the world. It is also the families that support their loved ones in their military careers.

America *IS NOT* people who take guns and go in and shoot innocent little children or a movie theatre full of people.

America is people who believe in our democratic process and are not shy about their voices being heard. This is also the country that allows this freedom of speech and press. When channeled correctly, it can be a powerful force to guide our nation's policies. America is also those politicians who actually listen to what people need, and ignore the minority who just might be louder than the majority.

America is a nation who believes that the people have the power to bring about change. We may have to endure ridiculously long election processes and assorted BS, but many go to the polls anyway. The ideals of the USA are still something people in other countries would love to have.

America *IS NOT* lobbyists and other groups who pour money and influence to get the government to see their point of view...and to hell with the general population. America is also not those jellyfish politicians who roll over on demand for these people.

America is the country that licks its wounds after something like Boston, dusts itself off and goes after the cowards of the world who dare to get in its way. Where righteous anger is concerned, America is not pretty and woe to those who screw with us.

Nothing else to say on this!

NRA -1, Common Sense — 0

April 18, 2013

I write for a living because numbers hurt my brain. But it doesn't make any sense to me how a Senate can vote against a bill requiring background checks for people purchasing guns when (and I will go with a low number here) 80% of Americans supported the measure…including many gun owners.

Oh, right – the lobbying arm of the NRA reared its ugly head. Did they reenact the scene from the Godfather where they told Senators, "I have an offer you cannot refuse?" It seems like the heavy promise of campaign money or the NRA's propaganda machine going against a Senator voting for the bill was more than enough to have people not listen to public opinion. And when you strip down how our government is supposed to work, aren't these representatives supposed to respond to public opinion? Or are these Senators so full of themselves that they feel that we are little children and they know better?

Nah – it has to do with money, greed, and fear.

If these Senators are so fast to "defend" the Second Amendment – something written more than 200 years ago – shouldn't they also be ready to embrace our entire concept of government? Which is also something that was set down more than 200 years ago?

I am angry, not about the law being struck down (I have my doubts how effective it would have been) but at the blatant and transparent power behind the throne here. I have been a member of the NRA as a shooting instructor and all of their material on gun training, safety, and shooting instruction are great. But where does the NRA get the majority of its money? From dues of members…or from gun and ammunition manufacturers whose best interests are served by an unrestricted gun culture? If you ever read any crime novels, one of the recurring concepts in solving a crime is "follow the money." And to me this has been a crime against our whole concept of government. And it is not just the NRA. There are lobbies like pharmaceutical, insurance, banking, etc. that can make a politician wilt faster than a corn stalk in a drought.

All the Senate has shown to the country and the rest of the world is that it can be bought. Yup, that is the American way – everything does have its price. I would love to see the individual poll numbers from all the states where at least one of their senators voted against the bill. If that state had 51% of their people against the background check law, then their Senator did their job. But it doesn't seem like this was the case.

Sometimes a government has to do something for the nation in purely symbolic terms. Passing this legislation would have done that. People are really sick of the shooting events we have had in the past decade. People are frustrated with a government that seems detached from reality. I hope somebody sends those Senators pictures of every child and teacher who died at Sandy Hook. I am ok if they are haunted by that the rest of their lives. It would be an interesting psychological experiment to see if they really have a conscience or if money can trump it every time.

Nothing is more frightening than looking at a gun barrel pointing at you. One second is all that separates you from being ushered into whatever awaits us on the other side. I am sure this is how at least some Senators felt when the NRA was bullying them. This is where their insides turned to jello and their already weak backbone collapsed. Be proud, America: this is our leadership and the people shaping our country for years to come. And we wonder why we are in such a state of confusion!

Money is truly the root of a dysfunctional government. Besides the lobbyists, the unregulated campaign finance laws have made every election a free-for-all. The vast sums of money can shape any message – whether there is any fact behind it or not. This has been a part of politics since the first small villages elected a leader. But now the influence behind the throne is on steroids with nothing to put the brakes on it. The NRA and other influencers are going to win as long as they have a big enough checkbook. What is disappointing is how many Americans follow the checkbook like a bunch of lemmings.

Gotta Love Our Law Enforcement

April 19, 2013

It was very exciting to wake up this morning to the news of the police activity in Watertown, MA near Boston where one of the suspects from the Boston Marathon bombers was killed and the other is on the run. We have our share of problems in America, but when it comes to finding someone who committed a crime, the USA is second to none.

Perhaps the other suspect will be found by the time you read this, but I marvel that within 5 days of the horrific events on Monday, the police and FBI were able to find 2 people as the possible bombers out of all the video and photos they received. Showing their photos was enough to set these two on a rampage last night which unfortunately let to the shooting of an MIT campus police officer. Right now, many towns in the surrounding area are on lockdown as a mess of police and National Guard are looking for the other guy.

It is too soon to tell if the explosions on Monday were organized by some outside group or if these two acted on their own. But now the FBI has information to start figuring out what links these guys had to terrorism, if any. For anyone to attack the United States like this is akin to a suicide mission...sooner or later they are going to be found. Just ask Osama bin Laden...well, you can't ask him, but that's the point.

It's a shame that sometimes we get to see the law's fine work after the fact of a tragedy like this. The truth is that the counter-terrorism groups in America do a good job preventing things like Boston. Some things reach the news but I believe many do not. Unfortunately in this day and age, it is practically impossible to stop all incidents of terrorism. It is the climate of the world. For whatever misguided beliefs...or just pure hate... people operate under, this is the world we are now stuck with. We may be a little safer in America than many other countries, but obviously not by much.

Where these guys got their explosives, expertise, and guns from will be very interesting. And another good thing in our country is the press will let us know this information as soon as they are told. I think it is important that we get more of an understanding how these evil people think and operate. We have already had incidents where an everyday citizen saw something odd and reported it which led to a bomb being found before it was set off. Americans chip in when it comes to stuff like that. The more people are aware of what to look for, the harder it will be for terrorists to operate in such an environment.

Hopefully, this drama will continue to unravel today and come to a conclusion. Hurray for the hard work and dedication of every law enforcement department that led to these suspects being run to ground so quickly. No, America is not as safe as it used to be, but we are not defenseless either. Be vigilant!

There is a lot wrong with how our elected leaders attempt to lead in our country. But the professionals in the government are great. These are the police, FBI, rescue workers, etc. who perform above and beyond their job. I feel the same way about the military: there are professionals in charge there. I guess this means our leaders are purely professional politicians. They may be good at politics but they are worthless at doing the actual leading. I just hope we are in a "down cycle" and men and women will appear on the national stage again who aren't afraid of putting the country on their back and say "Follow me!"

Our Education Deserves a D-

April 25, 2013

"U.S. students are falling behind their international rivals. Young people aren't adept at new technology. America's economy will suffer if schools don't step up their game."

This was the summary of "A Nation at Risk," the report issued 30 years ago by President Ronald Reagan's Education Department. It was quite an eye-opener of our country's education system. It spelled out where the United States was coming up short in education and what steps could be taken to avert a crisis.

And after 30 years we still have a country where 1 in 4 Americans fail to earn a high school degree on time, and the U.S. lags behind other countries in the percentage of young people who complete college. The report brought about changes in content to curriculum and accountability to schools, but the fact is we spend as much money on education as we did in '83 and the results haven't changed all that much.

The Program for International Student Assessment measurement found the United States ranked 31st in math literacy among 15-year-old students and below the international average. The same 2009 tests found the United States ranked 23rd in science among the same students.

Between 1980 and 2008, 13-year-old students posted only a 2-point gain in reading scores and 17-year-old students saw just a 1-point gain during that time. The tests were scored on a scale of 0 to 500, meaning the change was statistically insignificant.

The fact is that 30 years later, our education system leaves a lot to be desired. Once again, our country automatically thinks that throwing money at a problem will bring about a solution. When are people at the local, state, and national levels of government going to realize that it is not a question of how *much* you spend but *how* you spend it? If you went into each and every school district in America, I will wager that the majority of the districts have a bloated administrative staff that were hired to fix the problem, and that their salaries do not result in a comparative change in the district's success. This is particularly true of the big city schools with the biggest problems.

And how about where the rubber meets the road: the teachers. I know for a fact the amount of time, stress, and personal expense many teachers put into their profession. I have learned firsthand the amount of abuse a teacher has to handle from the administration, parents, and students. Many are frustrated by the fact that they have to spend so much time teaching with standardized tests in mind, rather than teaching for knowledge. Plus many schools are going to start rating teachers on their students' results on these tests. Will the teachers be marked on a curve? Will it be taken into account if they have a class full of unmotivated students with no parental support or a school that has trouble providing the necessary learning materials to be effective?

Here is a problem that the average citizen can have a say in since so many school issues arc dealt with on a local level. School budgets are a big part of where property taxes go. So don't be afraid of speaking up for how your money is spent.

Two things I would constantly be harping on for your local schools: One is the make-up of the administrative state of your schools and school districts and just how effective they are being. I often think that all government departments should go through an independent efficiency study. Schools are no different. You don't know how well or bad something is doing unless you evaluate it. And I don't mean the grades of the kids. That may be just the symptom of a much deeper problem.

Second, is helping the parents realize just how important they are to the process. There is the extreme of having the hovering parents on one side (ready to fight to the death for a better grade for their kid whether they deserve it or not) to those who want the schools to do what they can't be bothered with: the raising of their children. The majority are somewhere in the middle and need the encouragement to be active in the schooling process. For the most part, parents are clueless when they have kids. We all learn as we go, and understanding our role with our children in school is no different.

We are doing such a disservice to our children with so many of the decisions of the government and the direction we are going in. If we want to look toward the next generation to start fixing what we broke, let's give them the tools to do it. We cannot be like Peppermint Patti in the *Peanuts* comics and be satisfied with a D-.

Education is a constant problem in America. In some places it is because of a lack of resources, parental involvement, or a history of bad administrations. It is probably one of the most complex problems facing the country. While I understand using standardized tests to get a feel for how a school is doing, the results shouldn't be used to hold a school or teacher hostage. Statistics and numbers tell a story, but there are quite a few human elements involved in education. The federal and state governments need to back off coming up with these educational mandates when every area, town, and school district is different.

Obamacare: Congress Will Never Lead by Example

April 29, 2013

Back in 2009 when Obamacare was going through its final steps of becoming law, Sen. Chuck Grassley (R., Iowa) stuck an amendment into the package requiring that members of Congress and their staff enroll in Obamacare's health insurance exchanges. The concept was that if Congress was going to impose Obamacare upon the country, it should have to experience what it is imposing firsthand. But now, word comes that Congress is quietly seeking to rescind that provision of the law, because members fear that staffers who face higher insurance costs will leave the Hill.

One subtle point needs to be made: Large employers in the private sector are not required to put their employees onto the Obamacare exchanges. Given that Congress is a large employer, this isn't, in the purest technical sense, about subjecting Congress to the same laws it imposes on other large employers. But it is about subjecting Congress to the laws it imposes on those who will have to buy insurance on the exchanges: individuals who don't get coverage through their employers, and small businesses.

There is a lot of correct conversation about how America is turning into a country of two extremes: rich and poor with the middle class slowly deteriorating. But this is also a symptom in Washington. The rich are the politicians elected to office and the poor are the people they are supposed to represent. The highway beltway that encircles Washington could be the Great Wall of China that repels any sense of the real world from penetrating the halls of government. When the Senate and the House of Representatives get around to actually passing a law, it seems like little thought is given to the high cost, implementation, and practical applications of the law. And the President is in on this mess too as made evident by the healthcare law that unwittingly bears his name.

These people who we elect should walk in the shoes of the average person now and then. They need to sit down in front of the spreadsheet for a small business and look at how all of the taxes and regulations make it difficult to make a living. Give them a $100 and have them go to a supermarket and buy a week's worth of groceries for a family of four. Walk through an unemployment or a local social services office and find out how many people are happy to be there rather than being able to go out and having a job where they can make a living. Let the politicians actually go through the process of trying to find a job and realize the ridiculous amount of hoops a job candidate has to jump through to either finally be told "no – we cannot hire you" or they get the job where it is still a struggle to survive.

And this is the America of 2013! Government will pass laws that affect all of us, but don't want to get their hands dirty by having it applied to them. Obamacare is reported to have the real potential of being more expensive for people getting health insurance, for companies, for the government and still it will not give every American medical coverage. Like so many laws concocted by the United States, it is a 10 year Pandora's Box. Like the Box, bad things come pouring out. Because much of what the Congress and President does, a law has to be in force for a while before we see the true overwhelming costs of it that puts our country further and further behind. And if I remember the fable of Pandora's Box correctly, after all the evil comes out of the box and affects the world, there is one last offering of the box to the world: *hope*. And that is the one thing that is still in short supply.

Since I wrote this Obamacare has already gone through more changes than Joan Rivers with plastic surgery. If nothing else, the program has validated this article. Our government just does not think anything through. Here we had the Democrats, led by the President, talking about the benefits of Obamacare when they had no idea what was going to happen. Most famous was President Obama famously saying, "If you like your health plan, you can keep it!" That turned out to be the biggest lie of all.

Guess Congress Knows More Than the Army

April 30, 2013

Here's a recent conversation between a Senator and Army General:

General: Hi, Senator. Look, can you do me a favor? Stop approving money for upgrading the Abrams tank. We have enough right now.

Senator: Nonsense. Nothing is too good for our fighting men and women. We are just going to keep rolling them out of the factory for you guys.

General: But, Senator, you upgraded 2/3 of our fleet. Really, we're good. We could use the money on other things: food, supplies, bullets.

Senator: Don't worry, son, there is plenty of the money in your budget for all of that.

General: Uh, Senator, do you read the newspapers? Thanks to your "sequester" bill, we have to figure out where to trim $42 billion off our budget by September. Call me silly here, but at $7.5 million to refit one tank that we don't need right now, and multiply it by about 700…well, I think that would be a good place to start.

Senator: General, I'm surprised at you. Do you know how many people in my state are involved in tank manufacturing? Do you want to see them out of work?

General: That is really not my concern, Senator. But why can't you have the factories make something else for us? We have a pretty big wish list of toys that we do need.

Senator: It doesn't work like that. Why have them change when they are already equipped to do tanks?!

General: Let me try this again. WE DO NOT NEED THEM! We have new tanks that are going to be produced in 2017. These tanks you are upgrading are 3 years old. Kim Kardashian doesn't even upgrade her boyfriend that quickly. They work fine.

Senator: General, General…our support of the military is always a priority.

General: Yeah, then why are we looking at a reduced budget of $487 billion over the next 10 years? Huh…can you explain that? And that's on top of the sequester cuts I already mentioned. By the way, what's up with that sequester BS? Can't you guys make a decision on anything?

Senator: I won't bore you with politics, General. But that deal had to be made to keep the country going. Nobody thought it would ever go into effect.

General: But it did. You know, if we made decisions like Congress we would be speaking German and Japanese in our schools now.

Senator: General, I find that highly offensive. What kind of fools do you think we are up here?

General: You would know that better than me, sir.

Senator: I am afraid this conversation is going nowhere, General. I am sorry you wasted your time. But the bottom line is that we know what is best for our country. If we are going to spend money on tanks, then you will be grateful that you are getting them. Good day.

The General looks at the phone in disbelief. He dials another number.

"George? Bob here…Yeah, the family is fine…yours? Good. Good. Listen I just got off the phone with one of our brain-dead Senators. They are going to keep spending money on the Abrams…I know, I know, I kept telling him that. Listen, I have an idea. It may be a bit radical, but hear me out. You know those unmanned exploding drones you guys are always playing with? I know you can put coordinates in them to hit anything or have them zero in on a heat source, but I have a question. Do they have a "stupid" setting?...No,huh. Can you program it that way?...I guess you're right. It would be overkill – no pun intended. And we would need too many. Maybe we can get Congress to buy us more of them. Now, that would be poetic justice!"

Politics is in all governments. Actually it can be found in any group that has more than two people there: a business, church, charity, etc.

But it boggles the mind when you see how much money is wasted when the politics is the priority, and not the governing part. The money we waste in the United States could fund several small countries, but we just let it keep on going. Logic and common sense are none of the watchwords governing our leaders. And on a side note, this one was a lot of fun to write!

Obama: Style Over Substance Is Getting Old

May 1, 2013

"Paper Tiger" is a literal English translation of the Chinese phrase zhǐlǎohǔ, meaning something that seems as threatening as a tiger, but does not withstand challenge.

After yesterday's press conference, I reckon it is time to officially put President Obama in this category. Here we are only three months into his second term with over three and a half years left and already there is a sense of gloom around his Presidency. Obama did laugh off a reporter's question about whether the defeat of a bipartisan bill to enhance background checks of would-be gun buyers and other legislative struggles meant he lacked the political "juice" to advance his second-term agenda.

"If you put it that way," the president said with a chuckle, "maybe I should just pack up and go home. Golly."

The problem with this question officially being asked to the man himself, is that it could very well become a self-fulfilling prophecy. In this day of 24/7 news coverage, the amount of time from something merely being an idea or a rumor to becoming fact is about 17 minutes. And a fact of life from business, sports, war, and politics is that one of the hardest things in life to change is momentum. Success breeds success, but disaster also breeds disaster. A very skilled and wise person may be able to turn something around, but we have over four years of this and there are absolutely no indications that anything is going to turn around.

Besides being something less than upbeat at his press conference, an example of President Obama's inability to get things done is reflected in his wanting to get the detention facility at Guantanamo Bay, Cuba closed. One of the most high-profile promises from his history-making 2008 campaign was to shut this place down. It is back in the news because 100 prisoners are on a hunger strike there. Now, 5 years have passed since he vowed to close the joint down within his first 100 days of being President. President Obama is making Americans yell out the saying, "I rather see a sermon than hear one!"

As Americans we need to have confidence in our leadership. Yesterday, Obama also voiced his frustration with Congress and blamed them for a lot of our ills. And Congress does suck. But like it or not, pal, part of your job is to figure out how to get things done. Somebody needs to step forward from either party to begin acting as the Great Conciliator and get people to focus on moving the country forward. And, President Obama, you are automatically in the best position to do this. As Abe Lincoln said in Steven Spielberg's movie about him, "I am the President of the United States and clothed in vast power!" Melodramatic or not, it is the truth.

I think we would all love a President where we would be willing to follow him to hell and back. I don't think too many people would follow Obama to Disneyland. He has a gift for oratory, but that seems to be where his gifts stop. I don't have a lot to say for the people in this country who "hate" him. Hate is not good nor is it constructive. I think most people hate him because he won, and their party didn't. This sore loser mentality is hurting our country big time. President Obama seems like a genuinely nice guy. I would enjoy sitting down and talking with him. But if we played a game of "Clue," I think I would win because he still doesn't seem to have one in how to be an effective President.

This really hurts me to say this: I guess we can hope for better in 2016. The sadness is: what the hell do we do till then?

I still have not come up with an answer for the last question. The only good thing is that the politicians are showing a little sign of working together. But I think a lot of this comes from the exhaustion of constantly fighting and hearing that their constituents are getting fed up with it. However, the President must be the least effective President since Jimmy Carter in getting his office and Congress to work together. Yes, we have separation of branches, but this one seems as wide as the Grand Canyon.

Johnny Can't Read...Or Write!

May 3, 2013

I write for a living. I usually do corporate work and help folks who are writing novels or books. I get many inquiries from students in college to do their reports and papers for them. I decline these requests since I really believe that if they don't do their own work, they aren't getting anything out of college. I will on occasion, edit a paper for someone.

What I have noticed is a declining ability in so many young people to be able to communicate. It is evident in not only papers that I receive, but also in their e-mails to me. I am not sure if it is laziness, lack of ability, or only possessing the ability to text on the phone that brings this about, but it is disturbingly prevalent.

We rightly make a big deal out of American students lagging behind other countries in science and math. We dump all kinds of money into programs, more bureaucracy to work on the problem, and targeting students to do well in standardized tests, and what happens? We still lag behind!

It is frightening when the classes with the most college students in it are the remedial English and math classes. These are full of high school graduates who are supposed to know all of this stuff. So what did our schools prepare them for? To be able to pass a bunch of standardized tests to justify the existence of the high school and then send them out into the world woefully unarmed to move forward?

Not everyone has the aptitude and desire for college. But they should at least leave high school with sufficient skills to thrive in a job or some other type of training. Maybe I am biased because of the work I do, but you should be able to write a simple sentence that can be lumped together with others to form a single paragraph and thought. I read some stuff from college students and have to just say "Huh?" Unfortunately, there is no dictionary to translate gibberish.

What I find hilarious is when reports are filled with phrases or abbreviations that are suitable for texting, but not a psychology report. I understand why young people need help in editing papers. I just hope they actually know what they are writing about even if they cannot articulate it.

It seems we have a real crisis in education. There are all kinds of excuses like poor teachers, ineffective administrations, or every student has ADD. While there may sometimes be truth in reasons like this, I don't believe it covers all of the ills. There are a lot of good teachers out there who are very frustrated in what they have to work with in terms of administrations and unmotivated students. There is nothing wrong with keeping a student's feet to the fire to get him or her to achieve in school, but it takes teachers, administration, and especially parents to make it happen. Besides, it's good training for the crap you are in for as an adult.

If we are going to throw our money at the problem, then let's do it constructively. There is obviously a great many problems in our country's educational system. We really need to remember that we want these kids to be able to function out in the world, and be able to do simple things like communicate and make a budget for themselves. Until they start giving prizes out in literature for works done in 140 characters or less, we have a long way to go.

As you may have guessed I think education is important. The world is more complex than ever and we are sending our kids out into it with nothing more than a smartphone. That's mainly because we can't get them to let go of it. They figure if there isn't an app for something, it's not important. And the ones who do go on to college aren't exactly prepared for it. The same is true for the kids who know they won't do well in college and go for technical training of some type. But as long as a school has their kids do well in standardized tests...forget about them being able to think...they are happy.

Nothing to Fear, But Fear....

May 6, 2013

I saw some of the excerpts from the NRA national convention on the news this morning. It showcased how fear or perceived fear is still the lowest common denominator in getting a political point across in our country. Yes, I am picking on the NRA here, but they manage to have a cast of characters that make anything they do look like a Saturday Night Live skit. The truth is that what they do is the same thing every cause remotely connected to politics does whether they are Republican or Democrat. It seems like rather than give a coherent thought on why a group is against something, it is much easier to bash the other side and attempt to scare the hell out of anyone thinking of supporting it. (The Liberals pushing Granny over the cliff in reaction to Republicans wanting to exercise some budget discipline leaps to mind.)

Now the NRA was speaking to their people and is going to cater to the audience. Nothing wrong with that - however, if they possessed any brains, they would realize their messages are going to be televised and people who do not look fondly at them are going to react. When a great majority of Americans support background checks for buying a gun and it gets shot down in the Senate, and this mismatch of logic is put on the shoulders of the NRA, then why would a group want to alienate even more people? If the NRA has a public relations firm, their mission obviously isn't to win over more people to their thinking.

And I say this as someone who is fine with the Second Amendment and have been part of the NRA. But like the extremists in the NRA who believe in having their own personal bunker stocked with supplies and guns, the NRA seems to be taking a bunker mentality. Encourage the troops and circle the wagons. It is a formula that could hurt them more in the long run. For once an organization becomes more insular and incestuous, its power fades and could eventually spiral into oblivion. If you do not have outreach and tweak your message to bring in new blood, you will eventually wither and die. (Hmmm, am I talking about the NRA or Republican Party?)

And for the morons who write me whenever I dare talk about gun control, I am not talking about gun control. I don't believe that having background checks leads to the abolition of guns. Look, the biggest problem with guns is all of the illegal ones that are out there. But if a background check keeps a gun out of the hands of even one person who shouldn't have one due to a violent past or mental illness, then it is a good thing. If the NRA tried just a little to lean this way, the perception of them would skyrocket. But once again it is more important to stick to their guns (pun intended), than using a little common sense in their approach.

In his speech, NRA chief executive and vice president Wayne LaPierre linked the gun-control debate to the aftermath of the Boston bombings, arguing that as police searched for an armed suspect in a place where guns are heavily regulated, residents were sheltered in place with no means to defend themselves: "How many Bostonians wished they had a gun two weeks ago?" LaPierre asked the crowd. It was the first time the NRA connected the Boston bombing with the gun control debate.

La Pierre advocates the old national defense policy of MAD: mutually assured destruction. The idea of this concept was that if the USA and Russia had enough nuclear missiles to obliterate each other, then a war would never start. And it worked. But there is enough history to show that not everyone has enough brains to keep an itchy trigger finger from shooting. And most gun owners I know feel the same way. The NRA can be a force of reason if it wanted to. It has the money and the clout. But they choose to constantly shoot themselves in the foot (another pun intended). But maybe that is why Wayne LaPierre is against the background checks: he couldn't pass the mental health requirement.

I support the Second Amendment and think the NRA has gone around the bend. That may make me contradictory, but I personally think it makes me someone who sees through their BS. When push comes to shove, the first thing they want to do is scare all the gun owners. The sad thing is that they usually succeed. And then they wonder why gun owners are a misunderstood lot.

All for Woman's Rights, But What about a Parent's?

May 7, 2013

While in Mexico last week, President Obama said on Thursday he was comfortable with his administration's decision to allow over-the-counter purchases of a morning-after pill for anyone 15 and older. Obama, speaking at a news conference while in Mexico, said the FDA's decision was based on "solid scientific evidence." What's still unclear is whether the administration will prevail on its appeal of a court order that would lift all age limits on purchasers of the pill.

That decision to appeal set off a storm of criticism from reproductive rights groups, who denounced it as politically motivated and a step backward for women's health. "We are profoundly disappointed. This appeal takes away the promise of all women having timely access to emergency contraception," Susannah Baruch, Interim President & CEO of the Reproductive Health Technologies Project, said in a statement late Wednesday.

In appealing the ruling Wednesday, the administration recommitted itself to a position Obama took during his re-election campaign that younger teens shouldn't have unabated access to emergency contraceptives, despite the insistence by physicians groups and much of his Democratic base that the pill should be readily available.

I have several concerns with this entire issue.

I do understand the need for this type of product being made available. And it should be made available for any girl under 18 – but with parental permission. Noticed I used the word "girl" here, not woman. It seems like girls physically grow up quicker than ever before. (And some scientific studies attribute this to all the artificial hormones put into the milk and food that young people ingest.) And while President Obama is using other "solid scientific evidence" to make his decision, is he also looking at the maturity level of the girls who have to deal with this situation? Physically, young people are miles ahead of where they were years ago. The same is true of their sexual activity and knowledge on the subject. But emotionally and intellectually, they are just kids. And it seems like emotional growth is regressing at the same time physical growth is progressing.

And guess what folks? That's where parents need to fulfill a role. First of all, according to all the other laws, a parent is responsible for their child until he or she is 18 years old. I don't think it should be left up to the courts to decide when it is convenient to circumvent that concept. If a parent can be sued for something their kid did up to that age, then they need be a total part of their life – even in the case of sexual activity. There is a great need for family court in this country to help very difficult situations, but the court needs to stay out of the family in day-to-day life.

Ok, it sucks for a girl if she went too far with a guy and now is scared to death. Yes, being able to buy a pill at the drug store like a pack of M&M's makes part of the problem go away. And she avoids having to tell her parents. But then she also misses out on being told about responsibility, the dangers of disease, other options available, etc. It is also a wake-up call to the parent that maybe they better start paying more attention to their daughter. If a parent has their act together even a little, it is a good time to show the girl just how much she is loved and how the parent or parents are there for her.

There are an awful lot of good kids out there who are going to screw-up. We all do in one way or another. And the family unit is not as strong as it should be. But continually undermining the responsibilities between parent and child should not be in the hands of our courts. Knowing or interpreting the law is not the same as having wisdom. There is a lot of trauma and tension when the subject of sex comes up in a household. But it is an opportunity to get everyone to focus on the ideal of love, while battling over the mechanics of sex. And it is a necessary growing experience – for both the child and the parent.

When you look at one legal decision, you can miss the fact that the government is constantly becoming intrusive in every facet of our lives. When you look at a bunch of decisions or a collection of laws, it becomes even more evident. Where does it say that the government can override a parent while their child is still underage? This does not come under the heading of parental abuse like when the authorities have to step in. Even with the writing I do, I miss the fact that we aren't too far away from "Big Brother" being everywhere...if we aren't there already.

The College Con Job

May 8, 2013

In a far-reaching interview on Yahoo's *Daily Ticker,* former Secretary of Education William Bennett, author of *Is College Worth It?* said, "We have about 21 million people in higher education, and about half the people who start four year colleges don't finish," Bennett tells The Daily Ticker. "Those who do finish, who graduated in 2011 - half were either unemployed or radically underemployed and in debt."

Not exactly the stuff we were told while growing up on why we should go to college. Furthermore, the average student loan balance for a 25-year-old is $20,326, according to the Federal Reserve of New York. Student debt is the second largest source of U.S. household debt, after only mortgages. And, Mr. Bennett also pointed out that out of the 3500 colleges and universities in the country, only 150 institutions provided a student a positive return on investment. This is where the cost of tuition is well-worth what a person can look forward to in his or her career. That's 4.3% of our colleges if you are keeping score!

The U.S. is home to some of the greatest colleges and universities in the world. But with the student debt load at more than $1 trillion and youth unemployment elevated, what is happening in higher education is a crime. It seems like the mission of most colleges is not unlike big corporations: bring in as much money into the institution as possible but don't necessarily have it trickle down to the employees...or in this case, the students and the employees.

An example of this is how more and more colleges rely on adjunct professors and teachers to instruct a course. These are part-time folks who have no benefits, no tenure track at the college, and no professional security whatsoever. They often do this because they love the subject that they are knowledgeable in and enjoy teaching. If they are doing this to supplement their income, most can make more working part-time at Home Depot. And while many of these people are extremely good, the fact is that a student, his parents, or his future mountain of school loans is paying top dollar to the college for this type of system. Think about it: if tuition is $30,000 a year and a student has 10 courses in that year and all are taught by adjuncts who are maybe making $2000 a class, that is $20,000 in expense to the college. We will go low here and say that the average size class is 20 students. Well, that school is raking in 20x10x30,000 = $6,000,000. Yes, this is a ballpark figure and there will be overlap of students in some of the classes, but you get the picture. If we were dealing with organized crime here, it would be called extortion. In America, it is called Academia!

When archeologists examine our civilization 1000 years from now they are going to come to the opinion we imploded from the weight of greed. Colleges are leading the way. Because if they have a slight drop in enrollment (usually because tuition is too expensive), the first thing they do is raise tuition which has the domino effect of students going there needing even more loans to pay the school. Like so much of our government, the concept of becoming efficient and cutting back on costs is not the first thought that comes to their mind.

What can be done about it? A little more sense on the part of parents and what a high school teaches kids about colleges will go a long way. As a parent we generally want our kids to go to college and want them to go to the place they like the best. But if a parent allows them to go all the way across the country to some school to get an art degree at $70,000/year plus all the other expenses, is the parent doing their job? Where is the teaching of being realistic, budget-minded, and fiscally conservative coming from? When the kid graduates (hopefully) in four years in a crater of debt the size of the Grand Canyon, and then finds out it is difficult to live on your own and payback his four years of fun with a file clerk job, then what? Because this is what happens to the great majority of kids out there! And high schools have to do more than breathe a sigh of relief that they manage to get another kid graduated and out the door. Kids who have college aspirations should have a mandatory class on all the ramifications of going to college, how to make a wise decision on where to go, and what to expect when they get there. Since the high schools are sending too many on to higher education who cannot adequately read, write, or do math, they can at least do this.

Sometimes we need a collective face slap to get our heads back into the game. Whatever influence you have on a kid as a parent, relative, friend, or teacher, take the time to paint them a real picture of what they are in for. It is never too early to do some critical thinking. Then maybe when these kids grow up, we will actually have a generation who can fix what ails us.

I do not know who is more delusional when it comes to the college decision — kids or parents. I cringe when I hear of the college path some kids take. Going for a theatre degree is not going to translate into a good paying job for many, but parents are just as happy to see their kids go in that direction. Maybe the parents are just glad they are out of the house and in "college" and maybe they do not want them to grow up yet. That's why I think more than a "college night" is necessary in high school for kids to figure out one of their most important life decisions.

Bad Bosses Are the Plague Not Listed in the Bible

May 10, 2013

Sometimes I marvel how the United States is the most successful capital-istic country on earth. We have so many people in charge of businesses and organizations who couldn't run a lemonade stand. Through my working years I have had one fantastic supervisor, several mediocre bosses, and two who were absolutely terrible. It boggles my mind that when a person is at the top of the food chain in a company, they do not try to learn how to do their job better. Whether someone is the top dog or one of the management team, having a position of authority does not automatically endow a person with wisdom.

And the economic evidence of where this leads is evident. Psycholo-gist and workplace intervention expert, Michelle McQuaid, conducted a study of one-thousand people. The study showed bad bosses can cost the economy $360 billion annually in lost productivity. McQuaid says three out of every four people report the most stressful part of their day is dealing with their boss.

There are many factors that contribute to a bad boss. We'll focus on two today – the first of which is when an individual is promoted to a leadership position for the first time. What often happens in a company is that somebody does great in their job whether it is in corporate sales, doing marketing, conducting research, selling on the department store floor, etc. That person is then thrust into the position of supervising others doing the job he or she used to do. If a person has never had any leadership opportunities in any capacity, they are going to flounder. What ends up happening is that they are going to try and be a boss like one of their supervisors…who may be equally inept at the job because they also do not have a clue. It is like someone who becomes a parent for the first time and repeats all of the mistakes that his parents did. It is the only example they ever had.

Another problem occurs when a person makes himself the boss. This often happens when a person has their own business. They think that since it is their business and idea, they have the perfect right to be king and do whatever they want. I was recently in this situation where the head guy would not listen to any advice and stubbornly did what he thought was right. This arrogance led to disaster where the owner lost a lot of money and the enterprise never got off the grown. What is that saying, "Pride goeth before the fall?"

There is such a difference between being a leader and a boss. This is the distinction that people have to make an effort at learning. Being in charge means possessing a combination of skills in organization, communication, psychology, goal orientation, and particular knowledge of whatever the business is. Leaders motivate and guide people to being successful. Bosses tend to crack the whip and do not understand the concept of "grace under pressure." And these differences do not just show up in work. They can manifest themselves in churches, volunteer organizations, sports leagues or teams, etc. A few people have an innate talent for leadership. The good news is that everyone else can learn the necessary skills. This is where companies and people make a mistake. By not investing a little in some training for a person, a business has nobody to blame but themselves if a new manager fails. The same is true for a person who owns their own business. Read or take the initiative to learn how to be a great supervisor. It matters so much to the success of the business, the happiness of employees, and the bottom line.

One other thing to those that go through such training: Leave your ego at the door. I have taught such courses and you can tell the people who believe they have all the answers. They put down such training because they have no use for all the "touchy-feely" stuff. It is the saying: "What happens when you train an idiot? You have a trained idiot!" Like it or not being a leader is 90% people skills. Without those abilities the person is going to fail which in turn can hurt the company or organization and bring it to its knees. Anyone in the position of being in charge has to ask the question: "Do I want to be a leader or a boss?" And remember, BOSS spelled backwards is a double SOB!

Going by the comments I received on this article, I hit a nerve. There are tons of bad supervisors out there. The truth is that it does not have to be that way. But for all of the training material and courses out there on how to be a good leader, it all starts with a person realizing he or she needs some help. Ego does get in the way here. I personally admire those that work on being better at their job, especially if they are a supervisor. The know-it-alls just bring out the disdain.

Obama's Intelligence Service

May 15, 2013

President Obama walks into the Oval Office dressed in his golf clothes and heads over to his desk. Sitting down, he picks up the copies of the *New York Times* and *Washington Post*. Starting with the *Times*, he looks over the headlines. Suddenly he sits up straight and shouts out for his Chief of Staff, Denis McDonough. Denis comes running in. "Yes, Sir. What's up?"

"Denis, what's this headline about the IRS targeting those Tea Party nut jobs? Shouldn't they be spending time on squeezing every last dime out of the middle class?"

McDonough starts to turn a little red, "I just heard about that the other day, Mr. President. They are targeting any organization with "Patriot" or "Constitution" in their names. It seems like the guys in the tax office were going out of their way to give those organizations a hard time to get their nonprofit status. But don't worry, our groups are approved right away."

"Well, that's all well and good, but isn't the public going to get mad at me? You know I'm the President. What was that saying Harry Truman had? 'The Penny Ends Here.' 'A Clean Desk Is the Sign of a Sick Mind.' What was that thing?"

"Uh, 'The Buck Stops Here,' Mr. President."

"Yeah, that's it. I am going to hear a lot about this. People actually expect me to know what's going on here. Why wasn't I informed?"

"Weelllll, it seemed like a bunch of overzealous employees who were just trying to help."

"I have to check on this, but I'm pretty sure the IRS is supposed to be a nonpolitical agency. They should be holding people's feet to the fire, no matter what side they support. Oh, well, I guess we should ask someone there what's going on. Get my Treasury Secretary…what's his name…on it."

"Jacob Lew, Sir."

"That's it." President Obama picks up the *Post* and looks at the headline. "Geez, Denis, what the hell is this headline? The Justice Department took records from the Associated Press? Isn't that going against the Seventh Amendment or something?"

"The First Amendment, Sir. Yeah, I've been meaning to tell you that one. It was a National Security issue. We were tracking down a leak. We didn't think you needed to be bothered with details."

"I appreciate that, Denis. We have to be careful with leaks. It would be impossible to pass all of my legislation if we had leaks. Did the Attorney General head that one up?"

"No, he took himself off of it. He didn't want it to seem like an administration witch hunt."

"Glad he was looking out for me. I will need a full report on this. I'm sure those pesky newspeople will ask me about this. Get me the file on it so I can read after my golf game."

"It will be on your desk, Mr. President. It will be in the file marked "Administration Witch Hunt."

The President threw the papers on the desk. "I have to quit reading the papers. All they tell me is what is going on around here. You know what they say, 'Ignorance is Bliss'."

"Yes, they do, Mr. President. Uh, sir, shouldn't you keep a little more on top of things? You say you want to get back to governing. Even MSNBC is coming down hard on you for all of these issues. We have that Benghazi thing hanging over us this week too."

"Yeah, I know. That's why I need to go relax on the golf course. Besides, I'm the President of the United States , clothed in remarkable power… or whatever Lincoln said in that movie. I keep on top of things. I never miss a fundraising event. Why should I bother with details? That's what I have my staff for. And it's a good thing I have Jay Carney as the Press Secretary. I wouldn't want to face the press today. Is he getting ready for the daily press conference?"

"Yeah, I think I saw Jack Daniels and Valium on his desk when I went by his office. Don't you want to know what he's going to say today?"

"Nah, I'll read about it the papers tomorrow."

President Obama must lead all of his predecessors in saying, "I didn't know about that." Talk about someone needing a leadership course, it's him! I do not expect anyone, including the President, knowing everything that is going on in something as complex as the federal government, but you should be familiar with the high points. Moreover, when something does go wrong, like the stories mentioned here, do you notice how nobody is ever reprimanded or fired?

Snatching Defeat From Victory

May 16, 2013

The current issues confronting President Obama with Banghazi, the IRS, and the Justice Department slapping around the 1st Amendment by taking phone records of reporters is nothing to crow over if you are not a big President Obama fan. And the reasons for this are that these events just highlight the deficiencies of all the leadership in Washington…of BOTH parties.

First the Democrats and President Obama. I've said it before and here it is again: if this was the end of his second term, the biggest thing historians could say about Obama is that he was good at winning elections and premature Nobel Peace Prizes (God, that is still the biggest joke). Anyway he is the chief executive of the United States. The definition for "executive" in terms of government is "the branch of government that has sole authority and responsibility for the daily administration of the state bureaucracy." I really hope we don't find out that President Obama had any knowledge of any of these events before they happened. If he did, then he should be shown the door! (Oh my, except then we have *President Biden.*) If there is some phantom memo that indicates he knew about these events and did nothing to acknowledge them or stop them, it would send the country reeling.

Regardless, he has done a pretty crappy job of being this country's chief executive. The three government offices in this week's scandals: State Department, IRS, and Justice Department are ones he is responsible for as CEO. You can get away with fluffing off problems by claiming ignorance or blaming the last person in the position if you are new, but the credibility of that argument dies when you are into your fifth year as the boss. I am not sure if Mitt Romney would have been the answer, but Mitt did have extensive experience as a chief executive. I believe that he, or someone like him, who understands the art and power of leadership and delegating is what our overly complex country could use right now. President Obama has shown he is all style and no substance. And he is not doing well at "on-the-job-training."

Now for the Republicans, especially John Boehner and Mitch McConnell, the republican leaders of the House and Senate. Get out! Every time I see them on television, I cringe. Here they have been lobbed several softballs to blast out of the park and all they ever seem to do is hit a pop fly to the pitcher. I don't know what it is. They are obviously skilled politicians to get where they are, but as national leaders, they suck. I watched both on the news this morning speaking out against these events and they could use the expertise of an acting or speech coach. I think the average American can predict what these two lukewarm bodies are going to say before it comes out of their mouth. Maybe not the exact words, but you know it is going to be trite, predictable, and said with arrogant glee: "Hah, hah...you screwed up, White House, and we are going to let you know it...again...and again...and again..."

I keep waiting for a Republican that is a strong leader who can obviously think for him or herself and not be afraid to connect with Americans... and waiting...and waiting... Why do we keep going back to Ronald Reagan? That's like us Mets' fans reminiscing about the last time the team won the World Series. (Damn, that WAS the last time the Mets were champions – 1986). Ok, now I feel like a double loser today. But the point is that there is no viable alternative in leadership for an American to find. And I am perplexed by the Republican Party's inability to start looking at the big picture. If the Republican Party won the Powerball Lottery, they would probably lose the ticket!

Only Washington DC can be so dysfunctional that it can screw up a law of nature. It is said that nature abhors a vacuum. If that is the case, why are we still waiting for real leadership to come swooshing in to take the place of the empty suits in our government?

I wonder how historians will look at this time for America. Will they call it the "Dysfunctional Years?" Time will tell. I have to say my admiration of Speaker Boehner went up a bit when he blasted the far right for preventing anything getting done. It is nice to see our leaders get mad every now and then. At least you know they aren't oblivious to what the rest of America sees.

House of Mouse Not Immune to the Arrogant

May 17, 2013

There was a story in the NY Post on Tuesday that talked about how a handful of upper-crust Manhattan moms have a pricey, secret way to get their kids to the front of the lines at Disney World. The moms pay $130 an hour to hire a disabled, "black-market" guide, who uses her position—sitting in a motorized scooter—to help entitled families gain special access to rides.

A disabled person at Disney and most theme parks get to go to the front of the line with their family. So in this scheme, the mercenary disabled person can take his or her new found "family" past an endless line of people to have almost immediate access to all the Disney attractions.

As one mother bragged, "My daughter waited one minute to get on 'It's a Small World' — the other kids had to wait 2 1/2 hours. You can't go to Disney without a tour concierge...This is how the 1 percent does Disney."

According to the park's official policy, guests using a wheelchair or motorized scooter, plus up to five members of their party, can use auxiliary entrances "intended to offer guests in wheelchairs or with trained service animals a more convenient entrance to the attraction" and are "not intended to bypass waiting lines."

What this does is hurt people with disabilities who legitimately can't stand in line. As more people do it, the more resentful other park guests will become. I can just imagine how a disabled person will feel when people in line start giving grief because they question if the person is really disabled. It ends up hurting people who really need the services.

I have no problem with people making or having money. But money doesn't make you better than others. This fallacy of people having this "holier than thou" attitude because they have a few bucks is one of the biggest things wrong in our country today. Arrogance because of money, position, or supposed superiority of some type only leads to resentment. As America becomes more and more a nation of "haves" and "have nots," there is great potential where the arrogant will be shoved off their pedestals at some point. It is much better to be nice to everyone as a person rises, because he may meet the same folks on the way down.

And what about the kids that are getting to the front of the line via trickery? They are learning that as long as you have money it is ok to use it to break or bend the rules because that is what money is for. I hope the mothers that use this despicable practice have their kids make their life a living hell in another 10 years when they feel like everything in life should be handed to them. Can you say "entitlement?"

Speaking of living hell, I can think of an appropriate punishment for the Moms who aren't afraid of spreading their money around to beat the system. I think they should be duct taped into the seat of a small boat. And that little boat is part of the "It's a Small World" attraction at Disney. And those Moms have to go through the ride again…and again…and again…and again…"

I actually like "It's a Small World," but can you imagine listening to that song for hours on end? Disney did some things to curtail this practice, but just the fact people did this is sickening. There is a small group of people who are bringing up their children with the "money is everything" mentality. What happens if the bottom falls out and they are with nothing? Civilizations are marked with the haves being taken to task by the have-nots when there is a revolution. I am not saying that is where the United States is heading, but the resentment factor is inching up.

Prayer Is Never Out of Fashion

May 21, 2013

The awful news that came out of Oklahoma yesterday with the devastation and deaths from the tornados that descended near Oklahoma City has to make all but the most hard-hearted feel grief for those people. As of this writing, 51 people were already confirmed dead with more expected to follow. Something you hear newscasters say when a disaster like this happens, or folks express in social media, is: "Our prayers go out to all of those affected."

That is all well and good. I have found myself stopping for a minute and saying a little prayer when I hear those comments. As much as I would love to be aware of God in everything I do, it doesn't happen. And I can mentally kick myself when I actually have to be reminded to pray when such a tragedy happens.

I guess I could be cynical over this but I am happy that so many people, whether in the public eye or part of everyday life, can freely offer and ask for prayers. It strikes me that so many people that avoid talk of God or think science can solve everything, revert to the basic need to reach out to Him when things get really bad. One of the greatest theological questions constantly posed is that if there is a God, why does he let bad things like these tornados happen where people are killed?

I am not seminary trained or anything, and I certainly don't speak for God, but I have to think that life is filled with tough events to remind us that there is a God and we better have faith in Him, because faith in whatever *man* does is going to lead to a dead end. And prayer works. I have seen it in my own life and I know others that have seen it in theirs. That doesn't mean I got everything I ever asked for. I wasn't the winner of Saturday night's Powerball, but I have come to believe that it simply wasn't meant to be. Many times I have found that by not getting what I want, life for me really worked out best in the long run.

After all, the whole concept of God is a being who knows all, can do all, and it is only arrogance or ignorance that can make a person believe they know more than God. I have believed that there is a script for our life, but we don't get a chance to read ahead. For God didn't make a bunch of puppets to jump when he says jump, he made people who he wanted to freely accept Him and love Him as He does us.

So don't be afraid to pray when we are reminded or asked to. Yes, people have died in Oklahoma, but there are many people left behind who have to cope with the death of loved ones, or the absolute destruction of their homes. There are many who are going to be mentally, physically, and spiritually injured from living through this catastrophe. These are the ones who need our prayers. They are the ones who are going to need the Lord's help.

I have never been the type who could openly evangelize to people about God. I am getting better at it, but it is not easy. This, however, may be the time to explain to others why you pray and who you are praying to. I have seen in too many people, especially young people, the inability to want to know God or even grasp who He is. Often this happens because of no exposure to any spiritual teaching, or a really bad experience in the past. Share with others your beliefs and why you pray. You never know what and when something is said that will create a spark inside another. God does listen…we just have to remember to keep talking to him.

I am happy with the way this came out because I do not express myself well when speaking about God, but I write about it ok. The other thing that struck me is how many times in the short months that I wrote these columns did we have a need to call out to God? Sandy Hook shootings, Boston Marathon explosions, these tornadoes, and many other horrific events happened. It is a rough world we live in and if that doesn't scream out how we need God in our lives, I don't know what will get us there.

Things Don't Change

May 22, 2013

I just finished Jon Meacham's excellent book: *"Thomas Jefferson, The Art of Power."* In this book he gives us a portrait of our third President and his 60 years in public service. This was a man who at a young age hung out with the royal governor of Virginia and who died on the 50th anniversary of the signing of the Declaration of Independence, the document he initially authored. His public and professional life is fascinating, but it is that political life that got me to thinking of how this country has grown in over 225 years…yet the way government business is conducted has not changed a lot.

I found it fascinating that the early founders of the country deplored having political parties in the United States, yet they sprang up almost from its inception. The Federalists and the Republicans started the entire scenario that has grown to the extreme factions we see in Washington today. (*Republican* here is not the same thing as today's party and are sometimes called *Democratic-Republicans.*) Trying to boil it down to a sentence, the Federalists believed in a strong government and wanted to strengthen the ties back to dear Old England, and the Republicans leaned towards state rights and keeping the government as democratic as possible. One of the real fears of Jefferson and those Republicans is that the Federalists really wanted to bring a monarchial type of government back to the USA. I was struck on how fragile our early country was and that just because we had the Constitution did not mean we were a slam-dunk to become the country we grew into.

Looking at the Jefferson presidential years from 1801-1808, I was struck by three things that could have come out of the news 200 years later. One is the "them vs. us mentality" of the political parties. The extremes of both groups were apparent. We all know about the Civil

War, but the first talk of a group of states about breaking away from the country were some of the northern states in the early 1800's, who were predominantly Federalist. They wanted to start their own country. The animosity between the two groups was such that they could have debated in Congress whether the sky was blue or not.

Second, is the vehemence of the media. I make jokes of how Fox News and MSNBC should be paid political arms of the Republican and Democratic parties respectfully. Back then, there were newspapers that made no attempt to hide their allegiance. And, like now, no scandal or rumor was too little or devoid of real facts not to publish. There is no reason to think that someone who strongly supported a particular party would go out of their way to look at the other side of a story or to look for an unbiased version of an event. To them, the newspapers that supported their side were the Bible.

Third, is the fact that the one thing that can bring political factions together is war. When either the British or the French rattled their sabers at the young country, the politicians came together and tended to put differences aside. Unfortunately, it took 9/11 to get a glimpse of this happening in our present day.

The differences? I would have to say leadership. It was stronger on both sides of the historic aisles, but we will look at Jefferson here. He was absolutely hated by many in the other party. But you know what he used to do? He constantly entertained politicians of both parties at dinners and other interactions. While people may have still disagreed with him, they at least had a chance to get to know the man, and he got a better understanding of them. A main nemesis of Jefferson was Alexander Hamilton, the leader of the Federalists for a long time. But in one of his letters, Jefferson talked about how it was the man's policies he couldn't stand, not the man himself. Indeed, in retirement Jefferson kept a bust of Hamilton in a prominent position at Monticello. Hamilton indicated similar feelings toward Jefferson. It seemed like people made an effort to separate the person from the issues. Unlike now in Washington, it seemed as if leaders like Jefferson had a clearer head for what was needed to get the country moving forward. Party was certainly a big consideration, but strengthening the country was more important.

I would like to think our supposed leadership would take a lesson from our history, but I would bet that many in Washington have no clue of what came before them.

I would love to do a history survey of Congress and see the knowledge level of its members. I would not be surprised that a majority do not know basic facts of the early days of the United States. But what I really miss today are those people throughout our history who were up to the task at hand, whether it was war or economic difficulties. That I have not seen in our leadership in a long time.

Know-Nothing Party Returns?

May 23, 2013

For you non-history buffs out there, the Know-Nothing party was an American political movement that operated on a national basis during the mid-1850s. It promised to purify American politics by limiting or ending the influence of Irish Catholics and other immigrants. Mainly active from 1854 to 1856, it strove to curb immigration and naturalization, but met with little success. Membership was limited to Protestant males. The origin of the "Know Nothing" term was in the semi-secret organization of the party. When a member was asked about its activities, he was supposed to reply, "I know nothing."

While the "Know-Nothings" faded away quickly, as all bigoted movements should, another version of this party seems to have popped up all over Washington lately. Not in terms of being racially or culturally biased, but in the way leaders in the government are so ready to say, "I don't know." We have three messes in Washington all vying for number one in the hit parade. There is "who did what" in the State Department and CIA in the manipulating of data concerning the attack on the American embassy in Benghazi. We have the Justice Department secretly checking out phone records from the Associated Press. And to round it out, we have the esteemed IRS using their power to blunt the formation of certain political groups in America. Not scandals, but if you throw in how we have veterans waiting forever for benefits from the Veterans Administration and everyone looking like a deer caught in the headlights as they try to explain how Obamacare will be implemented, there is a total lack of confidence in anything going right in Washington DC.

And recently, all we hear from high-level politicians or top-of-the-line bureaucrats is that they never seem to know what is going on. Starting with our President and going to his staff and down to people who work in the IRS, this is the rallying cry: "I don't know." In Congress' hearings with the IRS, it seems like nobody knows who gave the order to give conservative groups a hard time. If I had a dollar every time an IRS official said, "I don't know," during the hearings the other day, I could pay my tax bill. And we get the same reactions to the other issues of the day. It is like the shell game where you try to figure out where the ball is under three rapidly manipulated shells. Under the hands of a skilled scrambler, it is almost impossible to locate the correct one.

Maybe Indiana Jones could discover the Ark of the Covenant, but he would have a hard time finding truth in Washington. It is like a child that you catch with an empty box of cookies, and when asked who ate the cookies, he blurts out, "I don't know!" Ignorance may be bliss, but it is doing nothing to promote confidence in our leaders.

Perception is very important for any organization. That is true of the United States government. And I hate to break this to you Mr. Obama, but like a large corporation, it DOES start at the top. The chief executive sets the tone, steers the policy, and is responsible for the actions of the lieutenants under him or her. Go to a stock holder meeting of a company and see how long a CEO is kept in place when they plead ignorance to a major problem. If an underling went off on their own to make a decision that severely hurt the credibility of the company, a true leader will kick ass till he got to the bottom of the problem.

I have this horrible feeling the White House will say all the right things about these problems and fervently hope they will just fade away. It won't matter that the credibility of important government agencies like the IRS, State Department, Justice Department, Veterans Administration, etc. is shot to hell. The country doesn't need this and more importantly, we don't deserve it. The "Know-Nothings" had a short time in politics back in the 1800's. It's time that the current "Know-Nothings" are treated the same way.

Looking back, I guess I was right. The White House does let other news stories move to the forefront and the old scandals do fade away. Part of the problem is news organizations seem to always be looking for the next big story but do not have the old perseverance to get to the bottom of an old one. Could you imagine if Woodward and Bernstein decided they were bored with Watergate and went on looking for something new?

The "Sting" of U.S. Colleges

May 28, 2013

'Tis the season for graduation. Young adults are graduating college and old teenagers are leaving high school. Having the chance to talk to some of these young people marking these milestones in their life, it is interesting to hear some of their comments. Of course they are happy to be done with this stage of their life, but there is a great deal of apprehension for the future. Actually, the parents tend to feel the same way. In these uncertain times there is a lack of confidence in what the future holds. If a high school graduate is heading to college, he or she wonders what it will be like, did they choose the right place, and what kind of career are they going to work toward. College graduates wonder if they are going to find a job sufficient to start paying back all of their loans in 6 months when they become due. And parents wonder when their kids will actually leave the house!

At the center of all of this are our nation's colleges and universities. The title of this piece refers to the Robert Redford/Paul Newman movie about a bunch of con men that go after the big score. And that is what a lot of our colleges' main mission is: to get as much money out of students and parents as they possibly can. And they all talk about how their school will make a difference in a person's life. Oh, it will make a difference. The question is whether it will be good or bad.

There was a great article last week by Bernice Napach talking about some of the myths in American colleges. The first one made an impression on me. It was how U.S. schools are the best in the world. According to Jeff Selingo, editor at large of *The Chronicle of Higher Education*, and author of *College Unbound: The Future of Higher Education and What It Means for Students*, the U.S. now ranks fourteenth in the world in higher education. This is a kick in the pants. Part of our national pride as Americans is feeling we have the best of everything. Much of what made America great is exemplified by the colleges: they rested on their laurels too long and are happy to prolong the illusion without actually doing the work to maintain the reality.

This is evident in further studies showing that a college with over-priced tuition may not be all that much better than a state college that is cheaper to go to. In fact, many state supported institutions are fine places of higher learning. But some people are so enthralled by name recognition and prestige that it overwhelms and clouds their judgment. I have heard some parents talk so much about getting their kids in a big name university that they aren't looking to see if there is any substance to the education behind the name. I believe many parents and kids look at colleges the same way they buy a car. If it looks good and sounds good, they'll buy it. Not many people really research the car they are going to buy, and I see the same thing going into choosing a college. Except there is no lemon law to fall back on if the college ends up being a bad fit for the student.

I see this whole name thing promoted by the business world. I have seen people turn their nose up at people if they did not come from a name college. Maybe I am too much of a realist but there is more that makes up someone than the school they come from. Don't get me wrong, there are some great schools out there and it is something I weigh if hiring an individual, but it is not the end all in figuring out if a person is a good fit for your business. The irony of this is that the individual I am thinking of graduated from MIT (a really good school) with an MBA, but was an utter moron when trying to run his business. He kind of proved the fact that just because you went to a good school, it doesn't mean much if you cannot produce.

It may be too late for this year's crop of graduates, but I urge parents and high school students to think with your heads and pocketbooks, and not your hearts. First of all, not every kid is cut out for college. I said before in a column that in this day and age, everyone needs some type of special schooling after high school, but not necessarily college. But if you go the college route, every kid is different and you have to look at a school to see if it is a good fit for the student. There is no sin in going to a two-year community college first and then finishing up the last two years at a four-year school. It is a hell of a lot cheaper, and the diploma does not distinguish where the first two years of courses came from.

This is where a parent needs to be a parent. 18 year old kids are chomping at the bit to get out of the house and on their own. Of course, it does not quite mean the same when the parents have co-signed loans that could easily buy a second home. A parent may have to say "no" when their kid wants to go to the $80,000 a year college nestled in the beautiful Vermont mountains. But if a parent is going to spend a lot of money so their kid can get a degree in theatre arts or philosophy, don't bitch when they are 30 years old and still live at home.

The college myth does have to be shot down. To me it is like buying designer clothes. They may be much more stylish than something you would buy at Kohl's, but they both serve the same function. Many times the Kohl's clothes will wear better than the designer duds. Parents and kids need to educate themselves on what they are looking for in a decent school and not be seduced by smoke and mirrors.

NCAA — Not Capable of Anything, Anytime

May 31, 2013

The National College Athletic Association is supposed to administer the vast array of sports that college men and women participate in. This includes the two huge moneymakers — men's football and basketball. They are supposed to crack down on all the violations that would make one team not have an advantage over another.

So I would like to add my congratulations to the NCAA for penalizing a student-athlete from a West Coast Conference school for the unspeakable crime of washing her car with the university's water and hose.

A WCC school self-reported an extra benefits violation to the NCAA when university officials caught one of their women's golfers washing her car on campus, according to the source. The NCAA ruled a secondary violation had occurred because the water and hose were not available to regular students and requested the golfer pay back $20, which was deemed to be the value of the water and use of the hose.

In the meantime, we have football and basketball programs at many big-time colleges resembling minor leagues for their pro counterparts. We have enormous amounts of money being paid to coaches to be ego-driven rulers of their little kingdoms. We have universities reaping big cash payouts from getting into bowl games with football or the March Madness tournament for basketball.

Yes, college athletes get scholarships if they are very good to attend the school. And many do not squander that opportunity. But they are also hamstrung with little, stupid rules that can screw up their life if they are not careful. This happens while we constantly see coaches not being very responsible whose only loyalty is where the next big paycheck is.

Cheating has gone on in college sports forever. At the beginning of the 20th century, colleges were routinely bringing in ringers to play football. One reason the NCAA came into being was to prevent cheating and abuses.

What we end up having in 2013, though is another institution which has lost its way due to power and money. Sometimes this seems to be the America we have "evolved" into. Power and money have corrupted so many things we used to look up to, or felt confident they are doing their job. And we have come to accept that situation of as the "new normal."

I love sports, but the NCAA has been majoring in the minors for decades. They zero in on some kid while missing the corruption going on around them. I have written a couple of articles in the past few weeks on the condition of our colleges in how they administer themselves where the welfare of the student is a minor concern. Now here is a governing body of the entire culture doing the same type of thing. The status quo is not acceptable anymore. It would be nice if somebody could be held accountable for their actions for a change.

It is way past time to gut and revamp the NCAA. It is unbelievable the money that goes through this organization and how inept they consistently are at dealing with the big problems in college sports. Sports are good for colleges but sometimes they are the tail that wags the dog. Talk about misplaced values. And we wonder why there are issues in our higher education system.

Audit the Untouchables

June 5, 2013

The IRS is under such a microscope lately — and for good reason. First we are told how they were targeting and impeding conservative groups from organizing. Definitely not part of their job description and we may never get a good answer on how far up the ladder that order went. Then we find out how much money they spend on conventions and rather stupid staff "motivators" — videoed skits and such. Most Americans kinda like this since we all have a built-in resentment toward the IRS. It seems like this is payback time.

And Americans should be outraged. When institutional abuse happens in a government agency, it not only feels personal, but it is our tax money financing the exploitation. The irony is greatest with something like the IRS because they collect our tax money. However, we really have to look past the IRS and at the government as a whole. Aside from the scandal issue, I would bet a large amount of money that if you look at every government department agency and department in Washington DC, you would discover that the waste of money is going on at epidemic proportions.

The "Untouchables" according to the movie, was a band of federal agents who battled Al Capone and organized crimes in the 1930's. They got that name because the members of the group were supposed to be immune to bribes and pressure from carrying out their mission — they were untouchable.

In our government there seems to be an institutional mentality that they are immune from any fiscal rules that would govern any other entity in the country: like a business, charity…even a church. The money will always be there and there is a lack of responsibility for spending our tax dollars. Yes, these government institutions have a budget, but there is no sense of urgency that they actually have to follow them.

It is time for our government "untouchables" not to be so untouchable anymore. I think a good outlaying of funds would be for the government to hire a bunch of business efficiency experts to go into every office in Washington and find out how they operate. Then produce a report without all of the government lingo and show all Americans and our representatives in government how things are run and where the wasted money is. This would make everyone in Washington quake from lobbyists to middle management in government and all the way to the top. Why? Because it would be so bloody embarrassing just how badly our country is run and all the wasted money!

In our system of government, the people we elect are supposed to be the stewards of our money. If Congress and the President were a board of directors for a business or members of a church council, they all would have been fired long ago, and a new team brought in. And forget party affiliation here. This has been going on for way too long and has transcended all administrations and whoever had the power in Congress at the time.

I really believe Washington looks at money like they are playing Monopoly. It isn't real and there is plenty of it around and to hell with how much something costs. What's a million here and a million there when your budget is in the trillions? These are figures that nobody can relate to as being real. Government offices know this so they spend without a great deal of oversight looking at them. They take advantage of business in Washington going on as usual. It is only when something blows up in their faces like the scandal within the IRS that other abuses come to light.

If we have any hope of strengthening our government, we need to insist on fiscal responsibility. The national budget will keep going up as inevitably as more reality shows coming to TV, so let's at least look at how we really spend our tax dollars now. It can only lead to good. Because even in Monopoly, if you make too many stupid decisions and get the wrong roll of the dice, you go bankrupt.

I would vote for someone who ran for President who wanted to audit all the agencies in the government. I really believe it would be an eye-opener of a report and could lead to some sanity returning to Washington. Nobody in D.C. would like this idea and many would be quaking in their boots. I really believe the waste is appalling. I always believed if you are trying to improve something, you have to first make sure your foundation is solid. This reality check would do wonders in being a little more efficient as a government and a country.

White House — Game of Secrets

June 6, 2013

Now we find out that the Federal government had another "secret" memo ordering a wholesale report on people's phone calls. Under the Foreign Intelligence Surveillance Court (FISC) order, Verizon Business Services must provide the NSA "on an ongoing daily basis" with information from calls between the U.S. and overseas – but also with calls entirely inside the United States. Calls made entirely overseas were not affected. It was unclear whether phones in other Verizon divisions -- its regular cell phone operations, for instance -- were similarly targeted.

The White House initially declined comment, but a senior administration official defended the activities described without confirming the specific report: "On its face, the order reprinted in the article does not allow the Government to listen in on anyone's telephone calls," the official, who requested anonymity, said by email. "The information acquired does not include the content of any communications or the name of any subscriber."

Ok – they are the National Security Agency. It isn't going to take them long to put names to phone numbers (it's not like they have to call directory services) and they certainly have the technology to listen in if they want. And it is not like they are targeting actual suspected terrorist. They are looking at all records. I am not even sure how they sift through everything but the point is that nothing is safe and sacred in this country anymore – like privacy.

This may have been going on since the Bush Administration under the Patriot Act. The irony here is that President Obama campaigned on being the anti-Bush: protection of civil rights, open government, blah, blah, blah. And it turns out his administration is Bush on steroids: unlimited phone records, targeting reporters' information sources, and a proliferation of drone attacks. Maybe the White House did not know about the

IRS targeting conservative groups, but the atmosphere created by the administration certainly fostered such abuse.

So where does it end? Government is becoming intrusive in people's lives while losing its concept of what it is supposed to do. You know, we are slowly drifting to that horrid police state usually reserved for lessons about Communist Russia and Nazi Germany. If you read history, things usually start slow and grow under "national interest." I am not saying things will progress to that point in America, but it is getting tiring of all of these "secret" activities of the government. Makes you wonder what else is going on that we do not know about.

You know who I feel a little sorry for today: the Liberals and Democrats. Maybe I do not agree with them most of the time, but they are a big part of our country's make-up. And it is tough to be betrayed. They may publicly support President Obama, but everything coming to light in the last month or two must make them feel sick to their stomach. Everything they got on their high horse about when Bush was President is haunting them in their own leader.

Our country has been a product of compromise since 1776. Finding out about things like this ramps up the rhetoric between the parties and makes it tougher to get anything done in the country. And our Chief Executive still manages to dodge responsibility like it is radioactive. It will be interesting what we hear out of the White House today on this subject and all of their other current misfortunes. Sometimes I think the White House press conferences should start their opening statement with, "Once Upon a Time…"

I think it was President Reagan who was called "The Teflon President." Everything said about him by the news media or the opposition just seemed to slide off. I am afraid Reagan has lost that title to President Obama. It would be interesting to see his campaign promises from 2008 and hold that up against everything he has done since. As for the NSA, the scope of their activities continually sees the light of day. I get that they are a spy agency. Most Americans have nothing to worry about since they aren't doing anything wrong. But don't you feel like taking a shower when you become aware just how little privacy we have because of our own government.

Whither the Middle Class?

June 10, 2013

Here are some statistics that should give people pause:

- Only half of American households are middle-income...down from sixty-one percent in the 1970s.
- Median middle-class income decreased five percent in the last decade.
- Rising college costs have put more pressure on middle class families. Students will graduate this year with an average of $35,000 in total loan debt.
- The income inequality gap is growing. The wealthiest one percent of the U-S population is now 288 times richer than the average middle class American family.

It is no coincidence that the emergence and the growth of the middle-class after World War II dovetailed with America's growth into a superpower. It seemed like the American Dream was alive and well because with a little bit of hard work, anyone could secure themselves a decent life. Jobs were plentiful, paychecks kept pace with the cost of living, and there was a sense of confidence that life in America could only get better.

Now, fast-forward to the months leading up to the election in November last year. We heard a lot of talk from both candidates and both parties on how important the middle class was and how steps had to be taken to strengthen it and make it strong again. Here is a list of accomplishments doing that very thing:

Ok, that space wasn't a typo. Nothing has been done. People are still looking for work or have to juggle several jobs just to make ends meet.

What people earn in their jobs was outpaced years ago by the cost of living. Benefits are becoming a thing of the past. We are about to enter a new world of healthcare in America and it seems like nobody has any accurate prediction of where that is going to lead - but the government's track record is not good at it being a success. American companies are earning big bucks, but they aren't creating jobs in America.

Pretty soon we are going to be out of time for talk. While the news media worries about whether Republicans or Democrats are winning, the people are losing. Do you ever wonder what our country is going to look like in 10 years? 30 years ago, we were starting to rise up from the political upheaval and bad economy of the 1970's. 20 years ago the country was maybe reaching its zenith in terms of financial security and confidence in the country. 10 years ago we were making our way out of the confusion and horror of 9/11. At the rate we have been going for the past ten years, we are definitely on a slippery slope downward.

Sometimes when things are dark, you manage to see a light in the darkness. You can find a group of people or at least one individual that can give hope. If this was a movie, a hero would emerge from the mist to put the country on his or her back and lead us forward.

I can't help it, but when I look into the darkness, all I see is more darkness. Let's stop settling for what we have been electing. Don't be afraid to call your representatives onto the carpet. Don't blindly follow party. Back people who understand what America really needs and who actually care about people. I think we have had enough of the Obamas, and Boehners, and Pelosis of the world. But words aren't enough. It takes action and our greatest action is our ability to vote and speak directly to those who are in government. That is a right nobody has taken away from us yet. To quote a famous movie line, "I'm mad as hell and I can't take it anymore!" Many of us feel that way. Let's do something about it.

Seems like the middle class is given a lot of lip service every four years. Then after the Presidential elections are over, the subject becomes dormant for the politicians. The problem is that it is not dormant. As the stats show, the middle class is slowly slipping away. And it isn't like members of it are moving up to the wealthy title. They are slipping down into the poor/poverty area. Safety net programs have become lifeboats for people and instead of working on policies to strengthen jobs, our government would rather scuttle the lifeboats. Someday, the people are going to get sick of it all and vote everyone into retirement. Either that or we are going to have violence in this country that has not been seen in some time!

Bank Robbery by the Banks

June 13, 2013

I read with great interest yesterday the article by Jessica Silver-Greenberg for the *New York Times*. In it she details how banks allow tainted money to flow through branches, how they fail to safeguard against suspicious merchants, and for originating transactions on behalf of businesses that they know make unauthorized withdrawals from customer accounts.

A great many of these transactions originate with senior citizens who are targeted with certain scams that persuades them to give the merchant their bank account information. That account is then charged for some "service" and a withdrawal from that account is made. If the owner of the account says the charges were unauthorized, they can request the bank to take action. Which is what the bank gladly does…for a fee.

Even if a bank sees that certain merchants are a problem at an alarming rate, they do not take action. Why? Because the more questionable the merchant, the more fees a bank stands to collect. Every time victims flag an unauthorized charge and demand money back, banks collect fees to process the return. Those fees are far larger, according to banking documents, than the ones charged for processing the original transactions.

In prosecuting the fraudulent marketers, court records show that banks kept handling the transactions, even though they knew what was going on. The reason: one payment processor executive suggested an answer: the business was a gold mine. "Turning them off and sending them somewhere else is not an option," a bank executive said.

This is our banking system. Not all banks do this (at least I hope not) but it is another example of where greed and lack of morals is taking our country. I belong to a neighborhood-type of bank that does not have a lot of fees for checking accounts like a lot of banks have, but whenever I have had to stop payment on a check I wrote, or requested a bank check for something, I am shocked at how expensive it is for 2 minutes of work. If I go inside for something and see the chart showing the rate of return for purchasing a CD, the rate of return is the reverse of the national debt – it is an amount too small for me to comprehend.

Throw in overdraft fees, debit card fees, penalties for your account going below certain amounts, etc., and you have legal extortion. It is okay to charge fees to cover the cost of certain transactions or events, but when did the light go on in some executive's head where they realized that here was a new extreme revenue stream? And what is worse, are these cases I listed above where the banks allow questionable activities to go on so that they can reap the benefits.

Our economic structure is such that we need banks. But like so many parts of our life such as the government and companies, the emphasis is not on the customers or constituents anymore. It is on what those in charge of these institutions get out of it. The more I have been writing about stuff like this, the more I realize it is an epidemic. Yes, there are exceptions, but the bottom-line is the power, profit margin, or what the stockholders receive. It has gone way past the idea of making a profit. Banks and other companies used to have a philosophy of making money through service to the customer. Now when they get to a certain size, or are perceived as indispensable, it becomes ok to legally pillage and dictate terms.

The banking lobby is one of the largest on both the state and federal level. That is probably a big reason laws are passed to protect what they do. It is quite a paradox: they scream about government interference when laws are passed to protect the consumer, but are the first ones with their hand out when their greed takes them to the edge of ruin as in the last financial crisis. If you are sick of your bank, shop around and look at other options: credit unions or a more local bank (if they still exist in your area). God forbid if the banks get in trouble as they did several years ago, but if they do, we need to exert pressure on them to do the right thing for their customers if they need to be bailed out again.

The banking profession used to be a solid profession in any community. That can still be true on a local level but overall they are looked at like you would any other parasite. It is ridiculous how they nickel and dime the average customer with all of their fees. Actually, what they do charge is not close to nickels and dimes. It is going to happen again how some banks are on the brink of ruin with how they conduct business. I think it is time to forget that "too big to fail" cry. If financial institutions find themselves in the same place as they did in 2008, it is time to let them crash.

Don't Forget Dad

June 14, 2013

Father's Day is an odd day of recognition. It always seemed to me that after the hoopla of Mother's Day, somebody was sitting around and said, "Oh, yeah, what about the Dads?" Thus Father's Day was born – almost like a throwaway day. You go into a Hallmark store and it's always a slogan like "Don't forget Grads and Dads." Fathers are lumped in with millions of high school and college graduates.

No doubt that Mom should be honored and her entire day made special. After all, they had to go through the pain of childbirth and are always the "go to" parent for about 95% of the kids out there. (Let's face it: if men gave birth, every kid would be a single child!). Plus Moms have to put up with Dads. That qualifies many women for sainthood.

But it is not easy being a Dad. And we all tend to screw it up. Kids don't come with a manual, marriage is an interesting concept, and thousands of years of instinct lead to severe stress. What do I mean by that last part? Men were the ones that were responsible for supporting the family. For years that meant working from dawn to dark at business, or farming, or going out and hunting for the day's food supply. I think that instinct is still built into many men. But the world has gone topsy-turvy. I am not saying it is bad, just different. Now many women are the main breadwinners in the house, fathers are expected to spend more time with their kids in all endeavors (not a bad thing at all) and generally rules for family life are being made up as we go along. There is a reason many men have a confused look on their face – they really are. Throw in the stress of most jobs these days, what everything costs, and wanting to do the best for the family and you have a formula for insanity.

So keep Dad in mind this Sunday. Most fathers are going to say, "It's just another day. Don't worry about doing anything special." They don't really mean it! Everybody likes to have a little fuss made over them now and then. And for someone who has been a good Dad, he is not someone you should take for granted. None of us are going to be here forever and that is true of your Father.

In closing I want to leave you with the words from the brilliant sage of humanity, Grouch Marx. This is a song he often sang about Father's Day:

Today, father, is Father's Day
And we're giving you a tie
It's not much we know
It's just our way of showing you
We think you are a regular guy

You say that it was nice of us to bother
But it really was a pleasure to fuss
For according to our mother
You're our father
And that's good enough for us
Yes, that's good enough for us

You know, I just can't top Groucho, so I won't try. Remember Dad!

Government as Religion — Part 1 of 5

June 24, 2013

This week I am writing a series of articles talking about religion and how it is not enough of a priority in our lives. For my definition, I use religion as a personal belief in God, and trying to live the way we should. And it is something that should be at the forefront of a person's life, and not on the back burner. I am Christian but have respect for another's belief, so I am not going to dwell on any one particular denomination or sect. The point is that too many things in this world have gotten in the way of God…and it shows!

The United States government for way too long has operated with the belief that they are the "end all" of hope for people's lives. Nothing is more important and what they say goes. Over the decades we have "evolved" to this point. This kind of proves that evolution doesn't necessarily mean a progression towards something better.

President Obama proclaims to be a Christian and I will not dispute that. But he does what so many people do and not embrace his beliefs when trying to act for the "betterment of all." I look at some comments he made while in Northern Island last week. Talking about the situation that had plagued that country for years he said, "If towns remain divided – if Catholics have their schools and buildings, and Protestants have theirs – if we can't see ourselves in one another, if fear or resentment are allowed to harden, that encourages division. It discourages cooperation."

If these schools don't teach tolerance of others and respect for another's belief, then, yes, there is a problem. I think the majority of institutions today teach against intolerance. But there is a bigger message here that has been running through our government for a while now: that we all have to conform with one another in order to move forward. All of the major decisions coming down from the Supreme Court this week deal with issues of supposed "equality": gay marriage, affirmative action, and voting rights. We have to follow whatever these laws end up being, but it shows a mixed message. Some laws do bring about a necessary affirmation to what is morally correct, while others go the other way.

This is because the Unites States now operates on the principles of what is correct due to consensus, as opposed to what is right and wrong. In other words, we are now a country of rationalization. There is no moral compass. Separation of church and state got perverted to mean God is not a factor in any decision made by the government. It was supposed to mean that there would be no official religion mandated by the U.S. government; not turning the country's back to God. An old Meat Loaf song title leaps to mind to sum up our country: *"Where Everything Is Permitted."*

To me, what President Obama said about Catholic and Protestant schools in Ireland reflects his belief how government should work: eliminate differences and let the ones in power steer everyone to conformity. Personal beliefs and moral decisions cannot be left to the people; the government can decide what is good for all. That is why it keeps getting bigger and more complex and more intrusive in our lives. And it is like a snowball getting bigger as it rolls downhill squashing everything in its path. And what the government snowball is doing is taking out individual beliefs and initiative. You know – those things our country were founded on.

The final irony is that trying to bring the country to conformity is dividing it more than ever along so many fronts. The push to conformity is destroying the country's ability to constructively compromise. This seems to be the root reason of nothing much getting done.

We have sung for years "God Bless America." Sometimes our actions seem to have him saying, "Hey, you think you know everything then you fix it. I'll give you my blessing again when you wake up."

I truly believe God has blessed America. Look at our resources and our history. But God could very well stop those blessings at the rate we have been going. I really do believe that the arrogance of many of our leaders is such that they truly believe they know what is best for all. There is only one being who has that right...and he doesn't live in the White House.

Money as Religion — Part 2 of 5

June 25, 2013

If there has ever been an idol placed above God, it is money. It is bad enough when people pound their chest and figure it is because of their own ingenuity and ruthlessness that they are rich. But what is really bad and happening in this country more than ever, is people getting wealthy and not giving a damn for anyone else.

Before people start throwing stones at me (very Biblical) please listen to a few points. One - I believe in capitalism. Two – when I worked in the nonprofit field, I saw many wealthy people give of their time and money to help various causes. Many people with money do a lot for others. And three – those people that are really greedy, I hope they are annually audited by the IRS.

Where money bothers me is how so many individuals or boards with the responsibility of running companies, allows that gold ring of more profit govern their every move. If you carefully read the news stories of people who are unemployed or making a fraction of what they used to, you would think you are reading news stories from the turn of the century. That's the turn of the 20th century I am talking about, not 13 years ago!

There used to be labor wars a century ago. A lot more of the work force was manual labor and people really had to fight to get a living wage. Companies like coal mining and the steel mills cried out that cutting down to the eight hour work day would be the death of them! They needed to make money to grow and pay their stockholders. The money and the power held all of the cards – at least for a while. Slowly, they gave way to pressure and unions and there had to be some sort of compromise made. Working conditions eventually shifted and progressed to something tolerable.

It seems like a lot of that same negative atmosphere is back again, though in different ways. For one thing, the pool of jobs in America has shrunk considerably. Going by the unemployment rate the past six years, there aren't enough jobs in our country. Companies' profits are great, stocks go up, and the corporations do grow – just not in our country. With the zeal for profits at a no-hold barred pace, American corporations expand in other countries. Kinda funny when you think about it: American companies used to exploit the American worker, now they do it to workers in other countries.

American companies have now used the tight job market to their advantage. With an abundance of workers, companies can scale back on what it pays workers in wages and benefits (if they give any). Raises for many employees across all industries have seen little progress. Some people are actually making less than they did in the same job five years ago because everything has gone up, except their salaries. But we just got done seeing the stock market breaking all kinds of records again. If you take the country as a whole, a very small minority was celebrating that fact.

Most of us sweat out paying the bills and pray our jobs don't end or we will be in trouble. I have lived through that. It ranks up there as one of the more stressful situations you can find yourself in. It also makes you roll your eyes at all the BS in the government and the media about how to solve the problem. Excuse me boys and girls, but after a good five or six years, the only thing we have is talk. The numbers back this up. People have given up looking for work and many aren't making a living wage.

When I was a kid and we talked of a prosperous America, it was more of an overall ideal. Yes, there was poverty and struggle, but less people were on that side of the slope. And those that were down, had more opportunity to pull themselves up. As long as the emphasis is always on the dollar sign as the pinnacle of business, without some balance in worrying about the worker, then we will be in trouble for a long time. That may sound a bit melodramatic, but history bears it out. And as a wise man once said, "Those who cannot remember the past are condemned to repeat it."

And since our financial gurus, the high priests of greed, tend to screw up the economy because they will do the same things that caused it to tank the last time, things aren't going to improve. And the more that cycle keeps repeating, those folks now in trouble will only see their ranks grow.

One of the things that make me mad where the economy is concerned is how the government and pundits look at certain economic indicators the same way they did 30 years ago. Well, they don't work that way anymore. The one that always gets me is the stock market. In the past when it went up, it meant companies were growing and that translated into more good jobs in America. Now it means the company is growing but they are opening up new manufacturing plants in Mexico where they are paying the workers $6.00 an hour...and those workers are thrilled.

Education as Religion — Part 3 of 5

June 26, 2013

Being able to learn and expand our mind is a gift. Many creatures, especially mammals, can learn as they grow but nothing can do it at such a rapid rate as man. There are geniuses among us who know and understand certain things at a pace most of us cannot comprehend. So why do so many of these individuals start to develop an arrogance and superiority to such an extent that they believe they are better than anyone out there? Many even take the final step of rationalizing there is no God because they are of such superior intellect that they cannot comprehend a being better than they are. This effect is even filtered down to those who may be of average intellect but because of their advanced schooling believe they are better than everyone else. You know…lawyers!

For many people, if you went to college and where you went to school are the most important things in the world. Many people put more credibility into science than God because science is full of supposedly proven facts that are a lot more tangible to relate to. Actually, two of the biggest scientific explanations that atheists and doubters lean on are not factual at all – they are theories. The theory of evolution has so little factual evidence behind it that it is laughable. And this is what we teach in schools. What Darwin provided and others have added to is a logical progression of how life developed to the point it is today. Logical maybe, but fossil evidence is shoved into the puzzle that has been created because scientists are trying to prove a fact that has been manufactured. And it is arrogance that promotes the power of this theory because those scientists have a lot of explaining to do if they cannot prove it is true.

Then we have the Big Bang Theory. I enjoy the TV show but as a theory of how the universe came into creation, it is almost as funny as the show. Again, with what man now knows, there is a scientific logic to the theory but that doesn't mean it happened that way. And there is no way to prove it. All the money that is spent on super-colliders and finding the "God" particle...time would be better spent if people just looked for God. He is easier to locate.

Education used to be the route to enlightening and expanding the mind. But in recent years, it seems like minds are being closed. If man didn't develop the idea and teach it, then it isn't worth learning about. High schools barely prepare a kid for adulthood and colleges are becoming a technical school for a chosen career path. Education should prepare an individual to "think." It should enable a person to find an answer to something not known and to be able to communicate it properly. One reason I do ok in my work as a writer is because there are an awful lot of people who cannot do either – and many have been through college or higher.

I have seen employers put so much importance on where a person went to school and lose sight of the individual. I remember working for one person who thought so much of somebody when they had an "expert" label on them, that he would immediately switch gears from what the company was doing if that "expert" suggested doing something different. That business folded.

Education is important but it is not the ultimate shaping of a man or woman. If there are no morals or ethics with that education then what do you have? (I already used a lawyer joke so I will skip it here.) I titled my columns here "Common Sense" because I found this missing in many educated people I have run into recently. And when education convinces a person that they are so good and can rationalize there is no being better than them, then education has done a disservice.

When you look around our world, it isn't God that brings about the evil that leads man to treat their fellow man the way they do. The purpose of these articles this week is to show what has taken man away from God. Sometimes it seems that we have become too smart for our own good. God has given us the capability to learn and grow and to continue to come up with things that would have seemed like science fiction only 30 years ago. But since he did not want to create puppets, he also gave us free will. So the next time someone leans on science to talk about evolution or the beginning of creation keep in mind one thing: would you rather trust man or God? Let's face it – man has a lousy track record.

I find the common element in people who do not believe in God to be arrogance. They truly think they are all that and a bag of chips. This definitely runs true in some people's attitude to where they or someone else went to college. Princeton University is near me and it is a fine school. I think anyone who graduates from there has a good brain and a good work ethic. But that person is not "better" than another human being, just smarter. There is a difference. You could graduate from Princeton or MIT and still be an idiot who cannot apply your knowledge in a practical way.

Sports as Religion — Part 4 of 5

June 27, 2013

I love sports. I've played them on an organized basis or as a member of a pick-up group. I enjoy watching ESPN and keeping track of my favorite teams. While I am not one to sit down and just watch a game of some kind, it is often on as background music while I write or do things around the house. Sports has always been the true reality TV, and not contrived like most of the "reality" trash that is on television. I do not go to many live sporting events because of the ridiculous cost and sometimes obnoxious fans you have to put up with. But overall, it is a pleasant diversion from the normal hassles of life.

But somewhere in the past 10-15 years that all changed. Maybe it is the abundance of media coverage that ESPN started, but sports have truly become the religion for many people and what their whole life revolves around. Talk about a misplacing of priorities.

Actually I first experienced this back in the 80's when I moved to Syracuse, NY. Having grown up in NJ and gone to Rutgers University, I was raised in an area that had a glut of professional teams in every sport between Philadelphia and New York. Moving to Syracuse was the first time I lived in a true "college" town. I worked for a nonprofit organization and I remember calling a volunteer one night my first week there in January. Well, I called while the Syracuse Orangeman basketball team was playing a game that was being televised. I had my head handed to me for having the ignorance to dare call him while the game was going on! A great deal of the city revolved around the basketball and football team.

When I eventually returned to NJ to live, I started to listen to WFAN, the sports talk radio station in New York City. I listened to these poor souls who lived and died with their teams. I mean, it really ruined their week if the Giants lost a football game or the Yankees went on a losing streak. It seemed that their team was the most important thing in their life – possibly even above any family they had. As a New York Met fan, if I was like that, I would have been put on life support a long time ago. I cannot really relate to people who feel this way. I may get disappointed if my team lost, but I am over it in about 15 minutes. When you get right down to it, even with the millionaire players, the financial value of the teams, and all the hoopla that revolves around sports – it is only a game.

I think it shows how people need to believe in something bigger than they are. It illustrates the desire for people to connect with others over something in common. Sports become an easy place to find these needs that are part of us. By worshipping in the cathedrals of stadiums and arenas, a man or woman is not subject to hard questions and an examination of their life. They can have fun, drink, eat, and cheer while their team is out there on the grass or the floor or the ice performing. This can be enjoyable and I have nothing against it. I like doing it. But there is a problem when it becomes your total focus of life.

While you can look to the media, internet, and social media as a reason sports mushroomed to its place in our lives, there is a more fundamental grass roots issue where I see sports becoming an alternative for religion. This is in the grassroots problem of youth sports being scheduled on a Sunday. And I do not mean Sunday afternoon, but on Sunday mornings in direct competition to church services. While people do not attend church like they used to, putting up artificial barriers to families even thinking about going to church doesn't help. I often see children's baseball and soccer games going on by 10:00 AM Sunday mornings. This may not happen all over the country, but it does show a lack of respect that churches receive in this day and age. As a society, our priorities leave much to be desired.

I congratulate sports figures like Tim Tebow and Kurt Warner and many who aren't afraid to show their faith while they were playing their particular sport. And ironically, there is a lot of praying going on in sports. "Please, God, let him make this field goal." "Lord, help me get a hit." "God, don't let him catch it." You get the idea.

I can't help wonder what the world would be like if all of that passion and loyalty was directed to God. What if people tried to do what is right for others with the same intensity that they root for their favorite team? If people wore their devotion to God the same way they wear their favorite team jersey or sweatshirt, we could possibly live in one awesome world!

I grew up in New Jersey in an area where many people were fans of New York or Philadelphia teams. It was fun if you liked someone different than your friends. There was a lot of good-natured teasing. But when I returned 20 years later there was a marked change in a person's attitude with their teams. The teasing was not good-natured anymore – it could be downright mean and vulgar. There are a lot better things in life... like God...where that passion could be put to better use.

Religion as Religion — Part 5 of 5

June 28, 2013

Taking the Wikipedia definition, religion is an organized collection of beliefs, cultural systems, and world views that relate humanity to the supernatural, and to spirituality. Many religions have narratives, symbols, and sacred histories that are intended to create meaning to life or traditionally to explain the origin of life or the Universe. From their beliefs about the cosmos and human nature, they tend to derive morality, ethics, religious laws or a preferred lifestyle.

Through the course of this week, I have illustrated how people look at government, money, education, and sports as their religion. There is no supernatural entity in any of them but they definitely lead to a certain set of ethics, histories, and lifestyles that people use to guide their lives.

A religion based on God in its truest form helps people to focus and learn more about their beliefs while keeping God in the forefront of their lives. In my opinion, this is the only way to live one's life. It is a set of relatively simple beliefs that does take faith on one's part to believe in and follow. Faith takes effort. Believing in God is not always easy, and that is why so many find it simpler to adhere to something that is man-made: like government, money, education, sports and whatever catches somebody's attention. The bottom line is that where man is involved, something is not going to be perfect.

Unfortunately, this also becomes a problem with "organized" religion and churches. They are run by people. They are all going to fall short of being perfect, and some can do more harm than good. I have been in situations where I have seen first-hand the hypocrisy, arrogance, and questionable teachings of a church. And this is from the pastor! It can also be prevalent in the members of the church. For me, the hypocrisy and arrogance are the worse to see. I am a Christian and if you read the Bible, two words that do not describe Jesus are hypocritical and arrogant. So there is a large disconnect there between what a person believes and how they act.

Again, I always keep in mind that people are far from perfect. I have done my share of things that I am not happy with and that were sinful. Sometimes in a church body the perception of forgiveness goes by the wayside. It can be enough for a regular supporter of a church in attendance, time, and money to want to wash their hands of the whole thing. Imagine a newcomer coming into a church and finding the reality much different from the peace and spirituality they seek.

Sometimes the running of a church or religion becomes more important than the worshipping and learning of God. Churches need as much of a reality check now and then as we all do on what we are doing and what is really important. My favorite sign I ever saw that was on the outside billboard of a church was "Only Sinners Welcomed Here." That, ladies and gentleman, is what we have to realize when we look in the mirror each day. That is why God needs to be at the forefront of our lives, not on the back burner or substituted with something else.

Many polls - including those from Gallup - indicate that 92% of Americans believe in God. Not all attend church. Yet around 80% of these folks self-identify with a particular religion. Additionally, many polls indicate that American society is in moral decline and more emphasis on religious moral values is needed.

Not to be a melodramatic person here, but the moral values of America is on the Sodom and Gomorrah path of everything being allowed. America does it because we have to respect the beliefs of others. I can respect somebody's beliefs, but that does not automatically make them right. The paradox is that if you have a moral code that is shaped by your spiritual and religious views, your beliefs are being called old-fashioned and narrow-minded. It is what the state says that is the over-riding principle, not God! There is a reason we have a song called "God Bless America." He has for over 200 years. We have freedoms and a system of government unprecedented in history. But history also shows that God has taken his blessings away from people when they stop listening to Him. And that is the slippery slope we are descending at a rapid pace.

Amen!

Lessons of 1776
American Heritage Week: Part 1 of 4

July 1, 2013

This is a week we sometimes take way too much for granted. Thursday is the 237th anniversary of the signing of the Declaration of Independence. We also mark the 150th anniversary of the Battle of Gettysburg during the Civil War which occurred from July 1 - 3, 1863. For those of you who treat any mention of history with a yawn, I am not writing a history class here. It is more a case of reminding ourselves of our heritage, just as we look back at our family tree to see where we have come from. And sometimes looking back helps us to see where we need to change where we are going.

It is difficult to put ourselves back where our country was 237 years ago. There was no instant communication, no jumping in the car to travel 60 miles in an hour, and no bathrooms. There was a king, an colony occupied by his soldiers, and no freedom of governing by the people in the "colonies." A lot of that seems so foreign to us now. But back then it was a way of life to feel allegiance and loyalty to the king. Of course the laws were designed in his favor and anyone speaking out against the king was considered a traitor and arrested...and usually hanged...for treason.

This is the backdrop where our Founding Fathers cobbled together an alliance of 13 colonies and fought back against the mightiest king and nation in existence at that time. There had often been revolts against royalty for thousands of years, but they usually didn't last long. It is hard to imagine what those men of 1776 took on: breaking away from the mother country and forming a brand new nation. It was a unique effort of blending together many ideas, beliefs, and loyalties into one vision. There was a lot of difference of opinion back then. They had no blueprint to go on of what other countries successfully did in the same situation. They were paving the way for a totally new type of government where the voice of the people would be heard.

Some things have not changed in 237 years. The voice of the people back then was like now: the Tower of Babel! There were a lot of differences of opinions on how to move the colonies forward. Some men did not totally want to break ties with England. Others couldn't understand how the colonies could declare themselves free and independent with the practice of slavery going on. Some men were driven for pure ideological reasons and others pursued a change for the sake of making money. It is not unlike today's Congress: different viewpoints and different motivations.

What is different back then compared to today's government can be summarized in one word: "Leadership." Fortunately, back then the men whose viewpoints shaped our nation were the stronger leaders or we may be singing "God Save the Queen" during the seventh-inning stretch at baseball games. These leaders argued, persuaded, and compromised into moving the group forward to freedom. Not all of their solutions were correct, but overall it led to a new nation. The confidence and passion of men like John Adams, Thomas Jefferson, Ben Franklin, etc. got 13 distinct colonies to come together and work together for the common good.

On the battlefield, George Washington was the picture of leadership. The Revolutionary War lasted for six long years from the Battle of Concord and Lexington in April, 1775 till the British surrender at Yorktown in October, 1781. If you look back at the battles of the Revolution, Washington did not have a good winning percentage. The rebel army was constantly the underdog and was out-manned, out-gunned, and faced experienced leadership when it went up against the mightiest army of the day in the British. If Washington was a football coach he would have been fired halfway through the season. But Washington stood firm and worked with what he had. He never decisively lost a battle and managed to at least have many end in a stalemate. There were miracle escapes like when he got the army out of Manhattan as they were about to be routed, and upset victories like at Trenton on Christmas Day. And when everything was on the line and the British had miscalculated their retreat, he beat them at Yorktown with help from the French. But it was his presence and leadership that kept a ragtag bunch together as they morphed into an army instead of being scattered to the winds.

That essence of leadership is what is missing today. Part of leadership is having a belief in one's self and the determination to bring others into heading for your goals. Leadership is being in front of the crowd with others following. Leadership is not hanging back and seeing what everyone wants and then going with the flow. But we don't seem to have true leadership much anymore, at least on the national level. President Obama certainly doesn't have it, nor does the House of Representative or the Senate. The so-called leaders of the Republican and Democratic parties can't even lead their respective members. When there is no leadership, you have chaos and nothing gets done – and that is an accurate description of Washington DC today. How ironic that the nation named for one of our greatest leaders is absolutely rudderless.

The other quality of leadership is bravery. As they were debating independence, Benjamin Franklin said to the group, "We must hang together, gentlemen...else, we shall most assuredly hang separately." Talk about being committed to a decision. That courage by our leaders seems to be a thing of the past. Let's hope someone can start being a leader again to guide us out of the swamp our government seems to be stuck in!

When you look at the men and events that gave birth to our nation, you cannot help feel pride, patriotism, and wonder. It really is a miracle of history that the United States was formed and thrived. History really does teach us a lot and it is a shame many Americans are oblivious to it. It would make one heck of a mini-series for the History Channel to do someday. If people aren't going to read about their history, at least we can give them a chance to watch it!

Gettysburg: 3 Days of Hell
American Heritage Week: Part 2 of 4

July 2, 2013

It was 150 years ago between July 1-3 that the Confederate Army made its first and only push into the northern section of the country. What started out as an accidental engagement turned into a three day battle that proved to be one of the bloodiest of the Civil War and extremely pivotal. General Robert E. Lee pushed the Confederate Army but the Northern lines held and he had to retreat back toward the South. It would be almost two more years of ferocious fighting before the Civil War concluded, but Gettysburg was the beginning of the end.

The Civil War was one of America's worse wars, because the only people that died and were maimed were Americans. It was also the point in our history that cemented the country together. From the time the country's Constitution was adopted, there were many overtures from states, or portions of states, wanting to break away from the country for whatever reason. From the South's point of view, the Civil War was a fight for state's rights. Ever since the country was a bunch of colonies, people tended to identify themselves with their home state. Lincoln took his oath of office seriously about defending the Constitution and looked at the southern rebellion as something that was not allowed.

After the dust of the Civil War settled down, the identity of people as Americans became stronger than someone's allegiance to their state. Unfortunately, it took other wars to strengthen this concept, but America really did become the United States.

I am not sure if it is having the benefit of time when you look back at history, but it seems like the passions that drove our country and our leaders were strong and a little more definitive than today. The South was just as passionate of its cause as Lincoln and the North were to keep the country together. Good leadership shines in moments of crisis.

By every statistic, the Civil War should have been over quicker than it was because the North had the advantage of men and weapons. But the South had outstanding generals and leaders who were smart and could rally their men and made some tremendous stands in battle. The first batch of Union generals was a wishy-washy bunch that would have been congressmen and senators today. Lincoln kept the country together and he finally got a general who single-mindedly focused on victory when he appointed Grant to lead the army.

We are not facing a civil war today, but we are in times that seem perpetually muddled and confused where the running of our country is concerned. The president and Congress manage to pass budget measures at the last possible minute to keep the finance side of the country going, but are incapable of any long-range planning. The sniping back-and-forth between parties is beyond getting old. And we have a President who is quicker to pass the blame on to others than a child who blames his sibling for breaking the cookie jar that he actually knocked over.

Thank God we don't need to take up arms against each other, but we are definitely in a crisis. Whether you liked or hated Bill Clinton or George Bush, give them their due – they led. A leader isn't going to always make the right decision, but if they can galvanize people to do what they want, they are a leader. I pray that as we get into the next round of elections, and, yes, even the Presidential election of 2016, people start looking at the people running and start to demand that a leader emerges. Yes, politicians are going to be molded by their party, but they cannot let that be their single guiding principle. And neither should voters blindly follow their affiliation – that has not been working out too well.

Gettysburg had many lessons of leadership – good and bad. I will go out on a limb here that when historians look back at this time in our history 150 years from now, they are going to be searching all over trying to find a decisive leader. The question is: how did this vacuum of leadership of the men and women who were in today's government affect the USA in the future? I fear the answer would not be a good one!

The government of the United States has always met the challenge when faced with war and other tough odds. For some reason it is the day-to-day administration that we flounder in today. Maybe if the Congress and President looked at their jobs as battling for the good of America (which is exactly their job) they would work together better as if in a war. Because I think you need a "war mentality" to continue moving forward and allowing each citizen a real chance at the American dream.

Celebrate America Proudly
American Heritage Week: Part 3 of 4

July 3, 2013

Tomorrow is the 237th birthday of the United States. It commemorates the official signing of the Declaration of Independence. This was the official manifestation of an upstart country-in-waiting thumbing its nose at the greatest empire in the world at that time. If things had gone wrong our "Founding Fathers" would have been strung from the gallows as traitors. As it was, many people during the Revolution gave their life to bring about a new country that in its structure provided every citizen a say in its running. (OK – technically it took a long time before African-Americans and women could vote, but at least the concept was there.)

The United States was truly the little engine that could. Like the tiny steam engine that beat the odds to lumber up a mountain, the United States showed the same determination in its early days. Our first 20 years as a country constantly had states wanting to back out of the union and even gave us a dedicated group of government leaders who would have been very happy to be a part of Merry Old England again. Then we had a good 40 years where first we had to first throw the British out again (War of 1812) and then deal with the verbal battle over slavery which ended with the country physically torn apart by the Civil War. As we reached 100 years old we started feeling our oats a little bit as a strong country and started to deal with international problems. Near the turn of the 20th century we had the brief Spanish-American War and almost 20 years after that the country was in the middle of WWI.

That war was just a prelude to the big game. World War II ushered America into the forefront of being a true world superpower. After the war was won, America embarked on a growth spurt in business and manufacturing that was not seen again until present day China. America set the standard for so many concepts and ideals that the rest of the world wanted to imitate us. In a two-man race against Communism, America tried to be the beacon and example of what freedom meant, and won the fight.

And it has been quite the hodgepodge that made up this America that has plowed ahead for 237 years. As Bill Murray's character John Winger said at one point in the movie *Stripes*: *"We're Americans, with a capital 'A,' huh? You know what that means? Do ya? That means that our forefathers were kicked out of every decent country in the world."* America became a place where the beaten and down-trodden moved to for a chance. (And there were always movements to clamp down on immigration throughout the life of our country, so that is nothing new either.) But if ever a country showed how to bring together the rich and poor, both genders, and many heritages to mold into a winning team, it's America.

Yup, we have a lot of issues going on and a feeling of stagnation in the governing of our nation, but let's forget about them for one day. July 4th is a day to celebrate the long road America took to get to where we are. We have an awesome flag and you will see a lot of them proudly displayed tomorrow. Look at it and thank God that you live here. Remember that the red stripes in the flag are symbols of the blood that has been spilled to defend our country. There has been a lot of it and some is still being poured out in places like Afghanistan. Much has been done by many men and women who have given their all in government or military service to help bring about a country that gives us the opportunity to pursue "life, liberty and the pursuit of happiness."

Happy Birthday, America!

Continental Congress Reunion
American Heritage Week Part 4 of 4

July 8, 2013

There was an unusual barbecue over the past holiday weekend. Thomas Jefferson, Ben Franklin, and John Adams got together for hot dogs and beer and to compare notes of what their grand experiment in democracy had been doing for the past 237 years. They settled in to some chairs and started comparing notes.

Ben Franklin: I have to tell you that I am absolutely amazed. This country stretches from one ocean to another. Who would have thought America would get this big? Back in 1776, we were just hoping to see 1777!

John Adams: You are right, Franklin, and who would have thought they still follow so much of the ideals put down in the Declaration of Independence and actually go by the Constitution? Well, more or less where the Constitution is concerned.

Thomas Jefferson: They finally did away with slavery. But at what a cost in blood!

Adams: We predicted that in 1776, Tom. That's why we tabled that whole slavery question back then.

Franklin: You know, gentlemen, the country has greatly perverted some of our ideas. When we came up with the whole separation of church and state, we did not want the government to run a church or a church to run the government. We never meant for the country to take God out of the equation.

Jefferson: What I marvel at is how in debt the country is. One thing American government does not take seriously is managing the finances of the country. That was built into the Constitution. Who would ever think that they would treat money as something infinite so that they can ignore it?

Adams: I think it is horrible how nothing seems to be getting done in the country. These Republicans and Democrats seem to have trouble on agreeing what day of the week it is.

Jefferson: John, I seemed to remember writing you in 1813: "Men have differed in opinion and been divided into parties by these opinions from the first origin of societies, and in all governments where they have been permitted freely to think and to speak."

Franklin: Really, Tom, quoting yourself!

Adams: Quiet, Franklin, you are quoting yourself all the time. Jefferson, I remember that letter. And we had some form of parties ever since George's first go-around as President. But we got through it and kept operating as a country. These people just seem to spend their time putting each other down.

Franklin: I think I once said, "How few there are who have the courage to own their own faults, or resolution enough to mend them!"

Adams: See, I told you that you do that self-quoting stuff. We know you are a sage, Franklin.

Jefferson: Maybe the difference is we had good leaders. When you think back to the men who put together the Declaration and the Constitution, there were a lot of good men in those rooms. I think today's expression is that we had a room full of All-Stars.

Franklin: So what is the difference now?

Jefferson: It seems like these men, and now women, don't have their own moral compass. They do whatever will get them elected the next time around.

Adams: You know what surprises me is how much power the Supreme Court wields. I don't know if any of us foresaw how that part of government would operate in the country. In the last couple weeks there have been decisions by the court that apparently turned life upside down for some people.

Franklin: One thing hasn't changed – the newspapers and all of those other media things they have these days can be pretty vicious. But I guess that is what you get with free speech.

Adams: And people can still own guns. But what are these assault weapons I hear about?

Jefferson: Gentleman, one thing for sure is that the years have taken our principles and expanded them to a degree we never would have guessed.

Franklin: But the question is if it is for the betterment of the country, or for its detriment?

Jefferson: You are the philosopher, Dr. Franklin. It is a little bit of each I would think.

Adams: From how I look at things, it will be interesting where the country is in 13 years from now when the United States is 250 years old. They seem to be on the edge of going one way or the other right now. They can either go forward or backwards.

Franklin: I know what you are saying, John. And for the life of me, I cannot predict where she is going.

Adams: Modesty, Franklin?

Franklin: You know me better than that, John. Not enough data to go on. Everything I have read or listened to seems very confused about where the country needs to go.

Jefferson: I am happy we had a clear idea of what we wanted 237 years ago. Otherwise we would be having tea and scones right now, instead of hot dogs and beer.

I enjoy writing like this. It's fun. And as I reflect on it, this was a good way to end American Heritage Week. You see, the title is not original. Back in 1978 I worked at Yards Creek Scout Reservation. As we were about to start a week full of rain for the scouts and their leaders, American Heritage week was born. The staff came up with different skits at meals that brought our history to life. Some were downright hysterical, and it got a bunch of people through a very wet week. To that staff of my youth I dedicate this American Heritage week.

Obamacare: Mission Impossible

July 10, 2013

Health and Human Services Secretary Kathleen Sebelius walked into her office early in the morning. Putting her coffee down on her desk, she spied a flash drive next to her laptop. It was taped on a piece of White House stationary with "Play Me" written next to it. She rolled her eyes, sat down, and inserted the drive into her computer. There was a quiet whirl, and her machine began playing the following:

Hello, Ms. Sebelius. This is your President speaking. As you know we are about to launch the Affordable Care Act. A great deal of the implementation responsibility falls on your shoulders. October is not that far away when the bulk of the program is launched. Here is what needs to be done:

We need this program to come rolling out the chute seamlessly. It is up to you to make sure that happens. Every piece of this law has to start on time. However, we will make exceptions of anything that is going to royally screw that up. So for now, feel free to put on hold that part of the law where employers of…hang on…I know I have that figure here somewhere. Oh forget it – you know how many employers a company has to have when they are absolutely mandated to provide health coverage. Anyway, that mandate is not set in stone. So let's delay for a year or so. We'll revisit it later. Come to think of it, we won't worry about it until after the mid-term elections next year.

And you know where we were going to have all kinds of computer networks hooked up to immediately verify someone's income if they come to a government insurance exchange for health insurance? That's not going to happen either. Apparently that is more tangled up than the plot on *Game of Thrones*.

Speaking of those insurance exchanges, that's looking a little iffy too. I know I said that our goal was to have sort of an Amazon "one-stop shopping experience" when people came into the exchange. You know, so a person could fill out a form and purchase insurance in one sitting. They might not all be ready to fly on time. Hmmm, maybe we should have gotten Amazon to run the damn thing. Whatever…you may have to take some bullets for the administration if they are not all up and running by then.

Oh, and the budget we set up for this thing…that may have to be revised. You see, since we can't verify how much people make, we are going to operate on the "honor" system. We have said that in the law's first year, we would accept the testimony of applicants when they apply for health insurance. That means that if someone tells the government that they make $10,000, we simply believe them. So we'll be shelling out a heck of a lot more money for subsidies since we aren't completely ready yet.

And since we dialed back requiring employers to comply with the law; we are going to lose billions in penalties. So you are going to have to fudge the numbers a bit. I asked the accountants here to run some numbers, but they ran screaming down the street to the bar and we haven't been able to get them back. So do what you can on that.

There you have it, Ms. Sebelius. This is your mission, if you decide to accept it. As usual, if you or any of your team is caught lying or screwing up, this office will disavowal any responsibility whatsoever with what you are doing. Good luck. This recording will self-destruct in five seconds.

There was a series of clicks and then Sebelius heard, "Damn it. I can't get this thing to shut off. Where is the techie guy? Doesn't anything work in this place?"

I didn't do bad predicting the future in some of my columns. When you look at the bullets Secretary Sebelius did take when Obamacare came rolling off the assembly line like an Edsel, I hit it right on. Even with all of the talk and changes happening at this point in time — 3 months before implementation — I didn't expect it to be quite the fiasco that it was. I am constantly amazed at how poorly President Obama rolled out his signature program.

Sometimes No Is No

July 15, 2013

If you have ever been a parent, you have probably had a child question you about one of your decisions. If you are not in the mood to debate your child, you most likely resorted to the answer parents have used since Adam and Eve: "Because I am the parent, and I said so!"

There are sometimes decisions made in America as a result of the systems that we have set up that have the same bearing. One of these is our justice system. I will be the first to say that using the word "justice" is an oxymoron at times, but it is the best we got. Win, lose, or draw – the decision made by a group of the accused's peers is the final verdict. Like it or not, it is just tough if we are not in agreement with that verdict. Arguments about the conduct of the lawyers on either side of the case are like debating an umpire's call in a ballgame: you may disagree about it, but that's life.

And that is what we have with the "not guilty" decision handed down in the 2012 shooting death of unarmed Florida teenager Trayvon Martin by George Zimmerman. This should now be done and over with, and both sides can slowly pick up their lives again and move on. But there is a good chance that won't happen. Leading the way is Al Sharpton – former civil rights leader and current sell-out on MSNBC.

Mr. Sharpton released the following statement after the verdict:

"The acquittal of George Zimmerman is a slap in the face to the American people but it is only the first round in the pursuit of justice. We intend to ask the Department of Justice to move forward as they did in the Rodney King case and we will closely monitor the civil case against Mr. Zimmerman."

He continued: "I will convene an emergency call with preachers tonight to discuss next steps and I intend to head to Florida in the next few days."

Sharpton also said: "I think that this is an atrocity… It is probably one of the worst situations that I have seen."

I guess what Reverend Al is saying is that a properly conducted trial does not meet his ideals if the verdict is not to his liking. That is why we have trials: so decisions are not left to one egotistical individual to throw down his or her version of what is right and wrong. I am not thrilled with some of the recent decisions by the Supreme Court, but such is life.

The thing to do in these cases is that if you really believe that a wrong was committed, then take steps to make sure it does not happen in the future. There are many lessons to be learned from the Trayvon Martin affair for everybody concerned. Instead of rehashing the whole court case, put your time and money into helping to prevent something like this happening again. If certain laws helped bring about this tragedy, work on changing the law. If "citizen patrols" need more screening of participants and training, then make it mandatory. Doing your best to dragging the participants through more court trials does not seem constructive at this point.

There are prominent people on both the left and the right who are good at inciting people, but really stink at doing anything constructive. On the national scene it is like the House of Representatives voting for the umpteenth time to do away with Obamacare. For Heaven's sake, maybe if you come up with a viable alternative, it would be a starting point for coming up with a workable plan that would appeal to everyone.

Life is made up of winners and losers. The only good losers are those who can accept their loss and work hard to make the best of the situation. Losers who whine and cry and do nothing to improve their lot are the ultimate losers. And if you look at our landscape of media figures and supposed leaders, most of them act like losers. Kinda hard for the country to move forward with that attitude, isn't it?

I think it is pretty clear that I have little use for people like Al Sharpton, Rush Limbaugh, Sean Hannity, etc. I think their convictions go as far as whoever is paying them. If they had any fairness in their soul they would at least listen to opposing points of view on their shows instead of steamrolling or ignoring any opinion but their own. And that is what makes up the partisan media outlets today – sarcasm, meanness, and hate.

Obamacare — Illusion or Reality?

July 18, 2013

I think this is the last time I will write about the Affordable Care Act, or Obamacare, for a while. It is time to sit back and see what happens as it becomes sort of fully implemented. I say "sort of" because we have seen portions of the law put on hold because the agencies running it have not been able to get their act together in getting the whole thing off the ground. As a program I will keep quiet about it until I see how it runs. I have a confession to make. My current health insurance plan is to stay healthy. I do not have a health insurance plan. I worked for an employer for over 2 years who thought he was smarter than everyone else and manipulated the system so that there were no benefits. (He has found himself in hot water now.) Working for myself these days, I have decided to wait and see how this all works out and will try to finally get health coverage when the program unfurls here in New Jersey where I live. Using my past history of dealing with government agencies, I cringe at what I am in for, but things are unaffordable right now with health plans I can purchase on the open market.

You see, that is the truth of the issue. Health care is costly and it is not always easy to afford, especially if you do not have it as part of employee benefits. I am thankful I do not have young children anymore. There were many doctor visits and ER stops as they were growing up. Health insurance back then was a life-saver. There are enough stresses in this world without worrying about your options if you get sick. Without health coverage, you have no options.

As far as I am concerned, nobody is really sure how this is going to all shake out. Every day, I can find new articles on the internet proclaiming how Obamacare is going to work and an equal number explaining its downfall. Today, President Obama will brag about how great it is, tomorrow John Boehner will call for the 13, 456th vote in the House of Representatives to cast it into oblivion. (OK, 13, 456 is an exaggeration, but geez, doesn't Congress have productive things it can try to do?)

The implementation of Obamacare has been filled with confusion, uncertainty, and huge projected cost overruns – and that is from the people charged with running it. I pray that once it is under way, our government will have the good sense to try and change pieces that really are not working. One lesson we have from Washington is that they think they can pound a square peg in a round hole by pouring money on the problem. All you get is a battered square peg! This is a huge program and will not start out smoothly. How the Obama administration approaches the issues that come up will make the difference between a sea-worthy vessel and the *Titanic*. Make no mistake, it is the Obama administration that will be judged on getting this to work or not. President Obama is not going to easily plead ignorance on this one if it fails. If Obamacare becomes the best thing since the invention of the GPS, then the president can take credit for accomplishing something. If not, it would be nice if he took that responsibility too.

Like most things in Washington, not enough thought was put into the Affordable Care Act before it became law. The concept is needed in our country, but it got pushed through Congress on party lines. It is not going to be repealed at this time, so it is time to buckle up and see what happens. The unfortunate thing is that it is going to take time before we can separate today's speculation from future facts. Hey, if nothing else I will be able to give you a user's view how it all works.

God help me!

I am curious what this program is going to look like in even five years. I do not think anyone really knows. It can either be a help or implode under its own weight. If the insurance companies start to sink under its rules, they will jettison it faster than Warren Buffett getting rid of a bad stock. The Republicans continue to try and repeal it, but now it is a law that is in effect. We are in the position of having to make the thing work or morphing it into something new.

Tale of Two Commentators

July 23, 2013

You know how Charles Dickens' novel *A Tale of Two Cities* starts out: "It was the best of times, it was the worst of times…" If I started out this column about the media personalities we have to put up with, it would read: "It was the worst of times, and it was getting darker!"

I will probably get both the right and left extremes ticked off at me here, but one of our greatest problems in our country is how certain "news" personalities approach their job with the intention of doing nothing but pouring gasoline on the flames. To wit, let's look at two cases that happened over the weekend. In this corner is Ed Schultz of MSNBC. A man whose show was so bad he was shoved into the weekend. When you are stuck into the weekend slot on MSNBC, that means your following on TV is slightly less than those watching the "Grass Growing" channel. In the other corner is Sean Hannity of Fox. If Sean wasn't doing his thing, he would probably be the smarmy waiter at some high-end restaurant.

Let's start with Ed. On his Saturday show, Schultz argued "Republican policies" led Detroit to become a "conservative utopia" and that is why the city had to declare bankruptcy. He continued by saying, "Detroit, Michigan, used to be really a symbol of industrial strength and manufacturing in this country. But, thanks to a lot of Republican policies, the city is now filing for bankruptcy."

Sorry, Ed, but journalism 101 teaches one to look at the facts. But since you are just a political shrill for the left, you don't care. If you really backed away from the donuts and did some work you would see that Detroit maintains 13,000 government workers but has 22,000 government retirees as part of the financial picture, and their health-care subsidies alone account for nearly $200 million of the city's budget. Pensions alone already account for a quarter of city spending; in three years, they will account for half. Pensions and city workers' health-care subsidies account for $561 per year from every resident of Detroit, which has a very poor population — average monthly income of barely $1,200 before taxes, a fifth of the population in poverty, etc. The official unemployment rate is 30 percent; the real rate is much higher. However, for now, this is all Republicans' fault, despite the fact that the city has been run by Democrats and progressives for decades.

Let's now go to Sean Hannity who has so many followers on the right that drink his Kool-Aid that he is on both radio and television. On last Friday's show, in response to President Obama's speech on the Zimmerman-Martin shooting, Hannity said:

"Now the president's saying Trayvon could've been me thirty-five years ago. This is a particularly helpful comment. Is that the president admitting that—I guess because, what, he was part of the Choom Gang and he smoked pot and he did a little blow? I'm not sure how to interpret that, because we know that Trayvon had been smoking pot that night. I'm not sure what that means."

Look, presidents have had to deal with negative press ever since George Washington first looked around his office and said, "What the hell did I get myself into?" And I have no problem with opposition to the government to help keep it honest. But the pettiness and hate that spills out of people's mouth like Sean Hannity in such a setting as a national radio show is embarrassing and demeaning. As someone told me years ago, you can disagree with someone in government, but respect the office. The George Zimmerman verdict brought to light that racial tensions still exist in our country. Comments like this from Mr. Hannity aren't helpful. It feeds into hate. It feeds into hate that some people have for President Obama. I am no fan of the President, but this continued feeding frenzy that caters to the extreme sharks on both sides of the spectrum is not helpful whatsoever.

As Mr. Schultz and Mr. Hannity showcase, both sides are guilty of this. And I know people on the left and right eat it up. When you become a party of such extremes, it is hurtful and damaging to any progress the country hopes to make. If these mouthpieces weren't making money and attracting ratings, (well, maybe not Ed — I have no idea why he is on TV. MSNBC must be hurting.), they couldn't cause the damage that they do.

I am not saying they should be taken off the air. But I am so concerned that people listen to whatever side they believe in as if it is gospel. We need opposing point of view in the news media. And I know it is difficult to be strictly neutral in reporting and researching the news. But I urge people to take the initiative and listen and research yourselves what is going on in our country. Don't let others brainwash you. You are not giving yourselves enough credit. "Hate" is incredibly evil. As long as we support the ones who make a career of capitalizing on hate, then it is going to be difficult for common sense to win out.

We are in the worst of times. If there is any hope of turning it around, we as voters have to start thinking outside the oppressive box that the news media tries to stick people into.

Anyone pick up on the fact I cannot stand the extremes of the news media? To me it is like brainwashing and the lemmings that follow these idiots are only feeding their habit. I truly believe that is one reason we can't have civil discussions between opposing points of view anymore. And my apologies to Ed Schulz. MSNBC gave him a weekly show again. They must be hurting.

Americans Want to Replace Washington

June 24, 2013

In his 1994 Jack Ryan novel, *Debt of Honor,* author Tom Clancy ended his book with a plane deliberately crashing into the Capitol building during the State of the Union address, effectively wiping out the national government. Unfortunately, this is pretty much what happened on 9/11, but let's not mix up fiction and fact here. I don't know Mr. Clancy, but in reading all of his books over the years, I get a sense he gets frustrated over the garbage that goes on in Washington as much as any of us. He symbolically attempted to show that it was time to start over again from scratch.

In a recent poll, a great many Americans would be up for having everyone in Washington go home and starting over again with new representatives. I have thought for years that what we need is a time out with government and begin again. We keep the Constitution but start over with new people. Nice idea, but not happening. Picture a ship 5 miles long trying to turn around in the ocean. It would take forever. And that explains Washington. It is too big and cumbersome and so entrenched with money and egos and power that it keeps plodding along.

So what do we do? It is like the old saying about how to eat an elephant. The answer is "one bite at a time." If even 50% of the voting public actively did something small – like writing their Congressperson about what they are looking for the government to start doing – the results would be staggering. First, there would be so much sweating in Congress that the Capitol will resemble a sauna. Outside of the 3 months before elections, these elected officials would realize there was a big group of voters they had to listen to. Because, while power and money greatly affect elections, it is still the individual who goes into the booth and votes. It is our fault that we do not hold these adolescents in Washington accountable.

And to effectively communicate with those we put in office, it is important to be aware of what's going on. Too often the Democrat and Republican parties take advantage of leading people around like lemmings, right up to the point of falling off the cliff. Let me give you two stories. One day I was helping a friend with some outside painting. It was near Election Day and we saw people coming down the street. They were "volunteers" working for the Democratic Party and handing out leaflets and encouraging people to vote. My friend, who was current on all things political and liked to debate, engaged one of these people in conversation. In five minutes he had the volunteer's head spinning and we could see the guy had no clue what is going on. Finally, the volunteer said, "I don't know this stuff. We are in a union and the union leaders said to take these flyers and hand them out to people because these are the ones you are going to vote for at the election." And this gentleman and his other friends on the street were blindly following what they were told.

The other story was when I was coming out of church one Sunday. A few people ahead of me were talking about how you just couldn't trust anything you heard on the news. It was biased, distorted and just showcased people's opinions. I tend to be in agreement with that and nodding my head. And then one woman in the group said, "Unless it is Fox News." I wanted to weep.

If we do not start having open minds and using our voice and our votes in the way we are empowered as Americans, then we are just going to keep getting people who couldn't effectively run a hot dog stand as our leaders. If we believe this and are speaking up, then the next best thing we can do is to try and get others to act. As Dante said in the *Divine Comedy*: "The hottest places in hell are reserved for those who, in times of great moral crisis, maintain their neutrality."

I do get disheartened at how many people absorb the rhetoric from whichever side of the aisle they lean on and take all that is said by their party as gospel. What happened to thinking or looking at all sides of an argument? Have we gotten that lazy that we accept what others say without looking into it? I have been part of discussions where people

255

are so closed-minded that it is scary. The one thing I try to do with my writing is that I just want people to start thinking. I don't care if you disagree with me, but think damn it!

People, Not Politics

July 25, 2013

Someone I enjoy listening to and learn a lot from is Ravi Zacharias, a Christian apologist. This, by the way, does not mean he apologizes for being a Christian. Christian apologetics is a field of Christian theology which aims to present a rational basis for the Christian faith, and defending the faith against objections. Yesterday, I heard him say the following:

"People matter more than concepts, and must come first. The worse despotism is the heartless tyranny of ideas."

He was making a point in the matter of spirituality in our lives, but it got me to thinking about the frustrating country we live in. Many of our issues are the result of sticking to "ideals." Liberal Democrats pass a health care plan without taking the time to understand it because it fits their theme. Conservative Republicans want to shoot it down based on their ideology even though something has to be done to give all Americans a shot at semi-affordable health care. Corporate America is raking in record profits while most American's income is 8% lower than 10 years ago. This seems to be the only place we are consistent these days. People do not seem to matter as much as concepts.

In a recent speech, President Obama said something that has made me cringe since Bill Clinton used the line when battling the Monica Lewinsky scandal: "I have to get back to the work the American people elected me for." All politicians use similar language, but I guess I have become so jaded that it makes me gasp when I hear it. I do not believe them. If the line was run through a translator that gave the true meaning of a politician's words, this would read: "I really need you folks to forget that I haven't been very effective. I need to keep my power and prestige so I can continue to feed my ego and make a buck here."

Public Service used to have a purer meaning – people wanted to get into the government to try and make an impact for the folks that elected them. Granted, we all do things for our own reasons. For the most part, you have to see some advantage for yourself to do anything – even get into politics. But it seems the agenda of people has swung heavy to the "what can I get out of it" from "how can I make a difference." And it appears that if anyone gets into government service to make a difference, over time they are seduced by the amazing amounts of money and ego-stroking that goes into it.

I guess this has become my theme of the week: it is up to us voters to put a face on America. We have to remind congressmen/women, senators and the President that they are in office to provide a framework for America to give citizens the chance to have a productive, happy life. That takes into account a lot of things that they have to do. I heard on the news this morning that Congress has passed 19 laws so far this year. I would hate to do the math to figure out how much money that averages into each law when you just factor in all the salaries of Congress and the staff people. If a company had that kind of production, heads would roll and people would be fired.

When things are tough in anything: family, job, a sports team – if you can continue to look up to the leader of the group with confidence, you can hang in there and feel like you are working together to turn things around. We do not have that on the national stage right now. There is way too much wishy-washiness and nobody to look up to. Get out there and remind your reps in the government that they have a responsibility to people first. Ideology should be lower on the list.

If people actually reached out to their various government representatives, there would be a change in how things operate. We all have to be kept accountable one way or the other in life. For our elected officials, it should not only be when election time rolls around. Constantly being reminded that they have to respond to their voters would keep them a little more attentive to their jobs.

President Bush Is Cool

July 26, 2013

Hopefully, everyone has seen the story of how former President George H.W. Bush has shaved his head to show solidarity for the sick child of one of his Secret Service agents. The 89-year-old former president acted earlier this week at his summer home in Kennebunkport, Maine. This was after he saw members of his Secret Service detail with newly shaved heads to show support for the 2-year-old son of an agent. The boy, whose name is Patrick, is undergoing treatment for leukemia and is losing his hair because of it.

There is a delightful picture of President Bush holding the young child on his lap with both of their bald heads gleaming. There is also a photo of about a dozen secret service agents and the President posing with their heads shaved. In another week of watching the news around us, it is nice that there can be such a positive story. I pray the boy's treatment goes well and for his parents to stay strong. Worrying about your child is one of the worst stresses for parents.

I marvel at ex -President Bush. I had the honor to meet him years ago when he was Vice President. For a person who grew up in politics, his humanity and realness always impressed me. Here was a person who showed real dignity in the office of President and has carried that on with him in the 20 years since he left office. Here is an 89 year old guy who had a decent amount of hair for his age, voluntarily shave it off in support of one of his staff. I have a gut feeling that George and Barbara have a family-type of relationship with their Secret Service personnel.

The news also brought up the fact that the Bushes had lost their own daughter, Robin, to leukemia at the age of 4. Though it was 60 years ago, this whole experience had to hit home. I like that George Bush could do something like this that had to be a combination of a loving tribute to his daughter and encouragement for someone who worked for him.

There is a big life lesson here. It helps to take a time-out from the pressures of life and do something for someone else. For some, it is giving money to a cause, and for others it is putting in time to help. And it doesn't even have to be anything big. It could be your neighbor who needs assistance, or your child's friend who needs a shoulder to cry on. I am reminded of the Bible story in Luke 21:1-4:

As Jesus looked up, he saw the rich putting their gifts into the temple treasury. He also saw a poor widow put in two very small copper coins. "Truly I tell you," he said, "this poor widow has put in more than all the others. All these people gave their gifts out of their wealth; but she out of her poverty put in all she had to live on."

I often talk about how in government one really good man or woman can make a difference. The same is true of all of us in life. Take a breath from life's hassles, step back and look around, and see where you can make a difference – no matter how small – this weekend.

We could use more moments of humanity from our leaders like President Bush showed. It helps when all of us are reminded that these are people who are thrust into the limelight. I think in all of the drama played out in front of news cameras these days, we forget that these are real people, not actors in a movie. Sometimes that little glimpse of humanity is enough to bring down the volume of an argument and helps lead to constructive discussions. I always admired George H. Bush. He spent a long time in public service and served honorably. What a nice quality to have.

Obama Administration:
Let's Look at the Numbers

July 29, 2013

I found an eye-opening set of statistics that I thought explained a lot. These numbers showed the percentage of the White House cabinet that was made up of people from the private sector. This pretty much means those folks who accomplished something in the business world and know what it means to move forward in the real world. Have a gander at the list that goes all the way back to the administration of Teddy Roosevelt:

T. Roosevelt.....................38%

Taft.............................. 40%

Wilson 52%

Harding...........................49%

Coolidge.........................48%

Hoover...........................42%

F. Roosevelt....................50%

Truman..........................50%

Eisenhower.............. ....57%

Kennedy.........................30%

Johnson..........................47%

Nixon............................53%

Ford.............................42%

Carter...........................32%

Reagan..........................56%

GH Bush.......................51%

Clinton........................... 39%

GW Bush........................55%

Obama........................... 8%

Less than 10% of President Obama's key people have ever worked in the real world. They mostly come from the avenues of academia and government. There is definitely a place for people who understand the workings of government in theory or by being a part of it their whole life. But there is also a tremendous need for people who know what it is like to succeed and fail in the real world; you know, like most of this country's citizens.

We have checks and balances throughout the government (ok – they seem more like road blocks these days), and in a smart White House you should have the same thing. You would have a mix of people from different backgrounds to interject a mix of theory and realism into making policy. I think how the White House works these days indicates just how one-sided their people are stacked. There is a certain aura of elitism that has surrounded that place for five years now. I have hung around academic-types. They generally feel like they are superior to the mere mortals that work for a living. (This is overall – I also know individuals who are very down-to-earth. But they tend to be the truly smart ones who do not have to hide behind their degrees.) What happens is that they usually just "don't get it." They have no idea how the real world operates or how to adjust when theory goes out the window as the rubber meets the road.

I daresay this statistic is probably also lopsided for Congress and their staffs. What ends up happening is such a big disconnect between the Washington Beltway and the rest of America. How can President Obama go out and do a campaign-type speech of how he has improved the economy and his plans for the future when I read several articles over the weekend of how 15% of Americans are in poverty and a big percentage are close to it? Furthermore, this is the one statistic in our country that is getting balanced as it is now covering all races and ethnic groups more evenly.

The theory behind Communist Russia in the old days is that everyone would be treated equally. Of course this was BS, but the class divisions were drawn up between the government and the common folk.

The government and upper ranks of the military were the elite and the ones who had access to the better things in life. Our country is getting split along the same lines these days. You have the top 1% of wealthy people and the officials who run our government. Then you have everyone else. And the gap between everyone else and the others is getting wider and wider.

Society will never be equal. That will never happen till Heaven comes to earth. But as the gap between the rich and the struggling becomes a chasm, it is going to rock our foundation. There have been enough tremors in Washington the past six years with our elected officials doing the bare minimum to get by. They really need to wake up and see what is going on for the average person to live. And they need to have people on board who understand how to be successful in the real world and are practical and have some common sense. Because if they keep operating on this shaky foundation, the earthquake that is brewing below the surface will destroy us.

I think the most successful leaders in anything are those that have good people working for them. And I don't mean "yes" men. You want people who know their job so you can let them attack their responsibility. It doesn't seem like the White House has had a very successful team the past five years. But President Obama must place great value on who he is comfortable with rather than who is effective since he rarely fires anyone – even those who really screw up. I think that disconnect at the top with how business and the country operates contributes to the chasm that is eating away at America. We are devolving into two classes… and that does not bode well for the future.

Unfinished Stories

July 30, 2013

Thinking back over some things I have written in the past nine months, I realize that there is never any closure in Washington over anything. From the government point of view, I think they figure the longer something goes on that people will just forget about it. On the part of the media, they have the attention span of a gnat and really are only concerned about the newest scandal. For some television news stations, if they cannot make political hay out of a story, they could care less. Whatever happened to those intrepid reporters who kept after a story like a hungry dog going after a bone?

So, what is going on with:

Veteran Administration Backlog: Remember, veterans were waiting well over a year for any progress on their requests for help. Searching for recent stories on this, it may have improved marginally but there are still months and months to wait for a claim to be processed. We honor these brave men and women all over, but can our country get out of their bureaucratic way to actually give them help? The answer is no. Apple can come up with a new iPhone every six months and our government can't get a bunch of computer systems to talk with each other after three years. Incompetence.

Benghazi: We lose an Ambassador who was doing his job. There have been hearings and information put out that confuses everybody. Are there any answers yet? Not to play the blame game here, but has anyone actually taken responsibility for the debacle that happened? Maybe I am old fashioned, but something this prominent means you owe the families involved and the American people a real report on the incident.

NSA Spying: First of all you are putting all of your efforts into getting the guy who spilled the beans. Granted, that has to be done. Or is the government hoping the game of hide-n-seek goes on long enough that we stop asking questions about how far the NSA goes in their spying efforts? Trying to ferret out terrorists is needed, but how far does the boundary go for the NSA, if they even have one?

IRS Cracking Down on Conservative Organizations: Here we have a government department that any American wants to stay on the good side of. Somebody went above their job description to do something that smacked of politics. We like to think the IRS doesn't play favorites. We want them to be morons to everybody. What happens to our faith in the government when even the IRS shows it hates on a bias. So, has anyone heard of any closure to that scandal?

Unemployment: Other than lip service, has the President or Congress done anything to help this situation? It does not count when unemployment numbers go down because people stop looking for jobs. I would like to hear from companies that have started hiring again. Are they doing so because of anything the government has done, or if it is the natural business cycle picking up a little? Because there seems like an awful lot of fear out there with people who do have jobs unsure about how long they will be able to keep them. And most companies do not plan for the future because they have no clue what Washington is going to do next to affect business.

The list goes on. The very real problems facing our country still have more holes in them than Swiss cheese. You used to know the news media would keep the government's feet to the fire, but not anymore. Now politics comes into play for many news outlets as they try to decide if the issue is on the right side of the aisle they favor. I am beginning to think nobody has guts to do the right thing anymore. The truth is, with so many open-ended problems, it is difficult to get anything to work right. And Washington wonders why the majority of Americans are so disappointed in them.

I don't think I exaggerate the scope of problems in my writing. Seven months after originally writing this, these issues are still unresolved but have drifted off the front page of the news. Politics has become more sound bites and getting in the spotlight than anyone actually doing something to bring closure to an issue or to fix an ongoing problem. It's like a book where the chapters never really end…they just sort of drift off.

Congressional Playground

July 31, 2013

It is said we learn everything we need to know in kindergarten. If that is the case, we have some folks in Congress who need to go back to remedial pre-school. Let's look at Senator Ted Cruz from Texas. He has a message for fellow Republicans: It's time to go to the mat to stop Obamacare, even if that means shutting down the government. The Texan's strategy is simple enough. Congress needs to pass a so-called continuing resolution to keep the government running by Sept. 30. Republicans, Cruz argues, should refuse to vote for the measure unless it prohibits spending any federal money on the President's signature legislative accomplishment. If the stance sparks a shutdown, so be it.

In kindergarten if you get mad and run home with the ball all the time, eventually the other kids are not going to play with you. If you do not share your toys, pretty soon you are going to be all alone. In both cases you may have a moment of triumph, but eventually you are going to be pretty lonely and find out that your strategy is a failure. And if you are a smart kid, you can look around at others who tried this same strategy and see how well they made out.

Mr. Cruz has the right to call others out on the carpet from the Republican Party and talk trash about them if they see things differently than he does. After all, the First Amendment allows everyone the freedom of stupidity. It would be nice if the Senator looks at just how this will affect the American people and his own political party.

A government shutdown at this stage of the game would hurt many people. There are enough folks that are reeling from the stupid budget sequestration (or sequester). You remember the automatic spending cuts in the federal budget that went into effect this year because Congress and the President couldn't do one of the basic jobs as outlined by the Constitution: establish a budget! I am all for smaller government, but the fact is that so many people from all walks of life are intertwined with the government that shutting it down will hurt everything. It is time for politicians to stop holding the very reason they are in existence – to run the country – hostage.

A 2010 Congressional Research Service report summarized details of the 1995-1996 government shutdowns, indicating the shutdown impacted all sectors of the economy. Health and welfare services for military veterans were curtailed; the Centers for Disease Control and Prevention stopped disease surveillance; new clinical research patients were not accepted at the National Institutes of Health; and toxic waste clean-up work at 609 sites was halted. Other impacts included: the closure of 368 National Park sites resulted in the loss of some seven million visitors; 200,000 applications for passports and 20,000 to 30,000 applications for visas by foreigners went unprocessed each day; U.S. tourism and airline industries incurred millions of dollars in losses; more than 20% of federal contracts, representing $3.7 billion in spending, were affected adversely

As someone who sides with Republicans 90% of the time, I am sick and tired of the image people like Ted Cruz gives to the Republican Party. Dyed-in-the-wool right wingers are going to cheer Ted Cruz on. It is so much fun when someone can champion your beliefs in such a stubborn display. That is great until election time comes around. How happy are you going to be when you have another Democrat in the White House in 2016? Or to have the jaws of defeat chomp on you when you have a decent chance of winning both houses of Congress in 2014? Because that is what will happen! It is argued that events resulting from the 1995-96 shut down ended up dovetailing toward President Clinton and was a big reason he won re-election. There are extremes of liberals and conservatives in America. But the biggest group of voters are somewhere in the middle. And if the Republican Party continues to be portrayed as a group that constantly wants to take its ball and go home, nobody outside of the core group will want to play with them – or vote- with them anymore.

As I argued two weeks ago, let's see what Obamacare does. It may implode. It may be a true help to lots of people. It may be so frigging expensive that it has to be halted a couple of years down the road. Letting it run may be the best thing to happen to the Republican Party if it totally backfires. But stop having Obamacare being the Moby Dick to the Republican's Captain Ahab. If you remember how that obsession went, the whale won and Ahab died.

Ted Cruz is a puzzle to me. For being so smart, he really bumbles around trying to be a leader of his party. I am not sure but I think he is the first senator in history who waged a filibuster against a bill, and then voted for it! Some Republicans think he is the reincarnation of Ronald Reagan. I think he has the leadership skills and tact of someone else that was deemed brilliant but had no real experience running something...Barack Obama.

Generations Under One Roof

August 2, 2013

I remember how my parents began to spend their life when they were in their mid-40's. As was fairly normal back in the day, they had me and my sister in their early 20's. We were both out of the house at 21. They became world travelers. They went on cruises, two weeks here and there in Europe, trips to Japan and Hong Kong, etc. And they did this with normal, middle of the road jobs. At the same time they kept up a home and did lots of little weekend activities and trips. Figuring out where they were at any given time was like playing "Where's Waldo?"

This was in the 80's and 90's and oh, how life has changed. More than a third of young adults now live at their parents' home in 2012, the highest rate in at least four decades, according to a new study by the Pew Research Center. Thirty-six percent of America's so-called Millennial generation − young adults aged 18 to 31 − lived at home last year, compared with 32 percent in 2007, prior to the Great Recession. In 2009, the year the recession officially ended, 34 percent of Millennials lived at home.

I would bet that many parents charge their kids rent, but it is probably nothing like the kids would pay if they were truly out on their own. The odds may be good that if the child has a job, it is probably in the low-paying range. And I have to imagine it cuts down on the sense of freedom a parent would feel. They raised their kids and still find them around the house. Throw in the fact that the parents' jobs have been stagnant for years and you don't have a lot of disposable income to actually have fun in the last half of life.

I do laugh at how some people do not grasp this problem. I know one couple with teenagers who make their plans figuring the kids will be off to college at 18 and then out of the house after that. Best of luck with that scenario! The two biggest groups where unemployment is the highest are at opposite ends of the spectrum: those who are over 50 and out of work and those young people who graduated college or never did any kind of advanced training. So it is a crap shoot where their kids end up after college – if they stick with it till graduation!

To further compound the problem, people are living longer. And yes, it is a problem if an elderly person outlives their savings (if they had any) and they find they have to move in with one of their kids. Now you have the real possibility of three generations under one roof. No matter how much you love your family, there is such a thing as too much bonding!

I was born at the tail-end of the "baby boomer" generation. Many of us grew up with the idea of how life was going to go. Work and advance with one company all your life, raise a family, get them out and successful on their own, and enjoy life when the financial pressures ease off as the nest is emptied.

That applecart tipped over long ago. Some of us are adaptable and re-invent our careers. Others hit a wall when they cannot immediately find a job and sink into a depression. Some have kids who majored in theatre in college and work at Wal-Mart or didn't train for any type of career and are really floundering. Some of these are bad choices, but a lot of it is where America is today. There are many economic and governmental decisions over the past 30 years that have gotten us here. I have written about them before and probably will again. The point for today is that I just do not think our government leaders or the top of the food chain in corporate America have any clue how bad it is for the average family who is struggling. If they did, maybe their focus would be sharpened on how to get people feeling confident that things would get better. They would take real action instead of a lot of empty talk and posturing. Let's face it, if a politician asked today what Ronald Reagan asked in the 1980 election with particularly devastating effect: "Are you better off now than you were four years ago?"; most Americans would give a resounding "NO!"

I guess in one way our current economy is helpful with the problem of multiple generations in one house. With many available jobs being offered on a part-time basis, it means that grandparents, parents, and kids would have such a staggered work schedule that everybody would never be home at once. What planning!

I do think the foundation of family life has been ripped apart in so many ways. The scariest is when you look into the future and it is very gray and uncertain. It's very stressful to live that way and worry about your future and your kid's future. And often it is people with a good education who find themselves in this state, not just those who never got through school. It is just another sign of the huge reality check that Washington DC needs to periodically have.

Do as I Say, Not as I Do

August 5, 2013

As if the country doesn't distrust what goes on in our nation's capital enough now we have questions all over the place about how Obamacare is going to affect people's health insurance and coverage. This uneasiness extended all the way to the halls of Congress where members of Congress and their staffs were especially panicked, because it appeared that the Affordable Care Act required them to purchase coverage on the law's new insurance exchanges, but without the generous subsidy they receive for their current coverage.

So what happened? President Obama personally became involved in the controversy over whether or not Congressmen and Hill staffers should retain access to their insurance subsidies. This came about because some lawmakers had privately threatened to push through a legislative fix—possibly attached to a must-pass spending bill—that would require the government to continue its contributions for health care premiums for Hill employees. But the White House feared that such a legislative change would open a door for Obamacare opponents to try to unwind other parts of the 2010 legislation, and senior administration officials want to avoid that step. After all, the President had already stepped in to slow down some implementation points of the law to lessen its chance of being a tangled mess coming out of the chute.

Because most Congressional staffers are poorly paid, but are paid enough to not have eligibility for the Obamacare subsidies that low-income Americans will receive, losing their current health insurance subsidies would be a big financial blow. Many members fear that their staffers would leave for better-paying jobs in response. Some in Congress have categorized this as a "brain drain." With the minutia that has come out of Congress for the past several years, I think it is ok if some of the brains drained away.

At least members of Congress and their staffs will have to shop for coverage on the exchanges. It will give the people writing our laws some insight into the health-care system they have foisted upon the rest of us. But the subsidies they will receive—however justified—will partially insulate them from the degree to which Obamacare drives up the cost of individually-purchased health insurance.

Employees of the IRS and the Department of Health and Human Services should also be required to join Obamacare's exchanges. Not surprisingly, federal employees are unhappy about that prospect. The labor union representing IRS agents has urged its members to tell Congress that they are "very concerned" about such an outcome. Incidentally, these are the two departments tasked with running the damn thing.

There is such disconnect between Washington and the country it is supposed to administer. When the government passes laws that affects all Americans to some extent, and then manufactures loopholes for those in government, isn't that a conflict of interest…if not outright wrong? We all know about the elitism of the 1% - the very rich and wealthy – but our government is becoming more elite in their own way. They are a legend in their own minds and put themselves up on such a pedestal it is difficult to have any idea what the masses – that's us – are going through.

As I said the other week, let's get Obamacare going and see where the chips fall. But it should apply to everybody. I believe the line in the Declaration of Independence is "all men are created equal." I don't think it says "all men are created equal unless they work in the government and are thus above others!" Because that is how the elite of Washington act and why we have so many confusing, screwed-up laws.

I really believe Congress should not be allowed to pass a law that they can excuse themselves from. That is just wrong. Since so many laws seem to add another degree of stress to the average citizen, then let Congress experience what they have wrought. That may actually do something when they pass laws – like take the time to actually think them through. What a concept!

Baseball Did Good But Took Forever

August 6, 2013

The decision yesterday by Major League Baseball to suspend a bunch of players for taking performance enhancing drugs is to be applauded. Any sport's league needs to take pains that the games and players are honest and that there isn't any cheating going on. Especially with their high salaries, players are always looking for an edge – legal or otherwise. Cheating has been involved in sports since the first foot race. For a league to be above reproach, they have to make sure their sport is clean. Even players are glad it is happening. You wouldn't want to be the one who works out hard and do your best to excel at your position, only to lose your spot to someone who gained an edge by injecting something into their body.

There will be ongoing ramifications, especially with Alex Rodriguez of the Yankees who finally surpassed others in his sport – he received a longer suspension than anyone else. I guess the only thing that bothered me about the entire event is the speed in which baseball tackled performance enhancing drugs. It seems that unlike the three other major sports (the NFL, NBA, and NHL) baseball worked on this problem with all the speed of one of their baseball games.

First of all, it took baseball forever to acknowledge the impact drugs were having on their sport. We went through the era of home runs records falling with the likes of Barry Bonds and Mark McGuire. Everyone loves watching a ball sail out of the field of play. Highlights on Sports Center on ESPN during this time of year are mostly home runs or players snagging the ball and stealing a homer away from some hitter. Pitching duels have their own drama, but home runs are where the money and prestige is. No sport honors statistics as much as baseball and now there are some in the books that shouldn't have asterisk next to them, but rather a skull and crossbones symbol to show performance enhancing drugs were involved in achieving the record.

I understand that baseball wanted to makes sure their investigation was thorough, but this announcement was strung out longer than a presidential election. Rumors and the promise of an impending announcement on whom baseball was going to punish and how long their penalties would be went on forever. Baseball has a richly deserved reputation for not making snap decisions. The other leagues definitely act quickly when some type of wrong-doing comes to light. The way Commissioner Bud Selig and the rest of baseball took their own meandering time on getting the news out makes President Obama appear to be the most decisive president we ever had. I guess they had their reasons, but from the outside looking in, it appeared that baseball is still plagued by an inability to get out of its own way.

Still, doing the right thing at any time is better than not doing it at all. Cheating will still go on. At this very instant someone is trying to figure out how to get an edge in a way that it will not be detected. It would be nice to think that players tempted to take the dark side to success will see their colleagues who are going to lose a lot of money because they cheated, and learn from it. The biggest mistake baseball can take is to think that it solved the problem and it no longer has to be vigilant. Let's hope what we see on the field are athletes who are naturally the best at what they do.

As America's past time, baseball has had a rough 20 -30 years. Player strikes that actually cancelled the World Series, a long history of the performance enhancing substances, and a slowness to respond to these problems have plagued the sport. I actually remember reading the sports section of the newspaper (remember them?) and you read about the performance on the field. It wasn't filled with lawyers and investigations and drug tests. Yes, I do yearn for simpler times!

Common Courtesy

August 12, 2013

I have seen a couple of things in the past week that distresses me. I do not know if it is the technical world we live in where people are constantly cut off from real personal contact, or just a reflection of the cynical, distrustful civilization we seem to be evolving into.

First case in point is a very good friend who has a gift for keeping calendar dates. She knows all the anniversaries and birthdays of all her family and friends. This comes in handy because she is really good at sending out birthday cards and monetary gifts to all of her nieces and nephews as well as gifts for milestones like graduations. She commented to me the other day how she has sent a bunch of cards out over the past several months with not one acknowledgement or thank you for the gifts. In some cases there are issues with even having the checks getting cashed. It is not that she is looking for a thank you letter (God forbid that kids would actually have to learn how the mail works). She would be happy to get a "thank you" text on the phone.

Some of the nieces and nephews are teens who should know better. The others are younger kids whose parents should know better. Is this where we are in this day and age where we are so totally self-absorbed we cannot literally take 10 seconds to thank someone with a text message? Are parents so fricking busy that they forget how to teach their kids to say "thank you?" I had that drummed into my head as a kid so much that it is natural today. I look at some people like waitresses and the guy who can barely speak English pumping my gas when I say "thank you." I am surprised by the look of wonder I get, and there is almost always a grateful smile.

I also wonder if we give our kids such a sense of entitlement that they just expect the birthday and Christmas gifts to keep coming. No matter if the person sending it may have to carefully budget to give them something. This is definitely where a parent needs to take a moment and give some valuable life lessons here. Gifts are to be appreciated. They are not a requirement of the giver. So many of our root problems come down to selfishness. And this is a problem that I will lay at the parent's feet. If you cannot instill in your kids or teens the proper courtesies of "please" and "thank you," they damn sure are going to have problems getting it as adults.

The other thing that is starting to get to me is how many people are like zombies when they are out and about. Maybe it is all of the zombie movies and TV shows these days. I am a walker. I write from home and as long as the weather is nice I go out one to three times a day for a three mile walk. I do it for exercise, to take a break from work, and to help myself from going bonkers. I have a 3 mile route around my neighborhood, or I drive 5 minutes to a park for the same thing. I live in the suburbs so when I am out walking, you can count on one hand the number of people I pass. I make a point to try and say "hello" and give a smile to everyone I pass. It makes me feel good and I like when it is returned. But I am surprised at how many keep such a focus on the ground: no eye contact, no smile, no acknowledgment of another human being. It is not like I want to engage in conversation. I am cruising and like to keep a certain pace. It is almost like the idea of any personal contact, no matter how superfluous, is foreign to some.

I wrote this to make a point to certain families that their kids need training. Since that didn't work, I will highlight this chapter when the book comes out and hit them in the head with it. Who said words can't hurt?!

Wisdom from Newt

August 15, 2013

That is a headline I didn't think I would ever write. As a stalwart of the Republican Party for decades, Newt Gingrich has sometimes been a voice of reason, and at other times a cartoon. Yesterday at the Republican National Committee's annual summer meeting in Boston Newt said, "We have to get beyond being anti-Obama. We are caught right now in a culture, and you see it every single day, where as long as we're negative and as long as we're vicious and as long as we can tear down our opponent, we don't have to learn anything. And so we don't," Gingrich said. "This is a very deep problem."

Gingrich said congressional Republicans would have "zero answer" for how to replace the president's health care overhaul when asked, despite their having voted repeatedly to repeal the measure. This has been a problem for Republicans ever since President Obama came into office. Their rhetoric has been loud and negative, but rarely with any good alternative solutions to solving the problems that the nation is faced with.

Since hardly anyone seems to put a value in history, I'd like to point out that we are going through a period that is very reminiscent of 1994. That was a mid-term election where Republicans gained control of the House of Representatives in the middle of President Clinton's first term and Newt became Speaker of the House. This is exactly what happened in 2010. The exception in this scenario is that back in the 90's the Republicans always had clear alternatives to what President Clinton wanted. Neither side always had the right answer, but it gave a clear starting point to working together in coming up with bills and laws that were passed and enacted.

Now we have such a "my way or the highway" mentality nothing gets done. I work from the premise that the great majority of Americans are somewhere in the middle of the two extremes that dominate government today. Unless you are a news and political junkie, many Americans just want to put their hands over their ears and say, "la-la-la" very loud to drown out the consistent BS coming from both sides these days. They are worn out from politics as a contact sport. They are tired of hearing nothing but negatives. I believe people are much more open to hearing about why something will not work when given an option of what will work better. It's like being told your car is broke and you should get rid of it. If there is not a viable option of how to get a better car, the feeling that is left is one of frustration and depression.

I think America will elect whoever can show a promise of real leadership in 2016. It is a vacuum that desperately needs to be filled. I already am not crazy about all the talk for the next presidential election, but the Republicans need those three years to rebuild their message and be a party that can attract the many in the middle. I think people will flock to a strong, coherent message that is balanced in how it addresses economy, business, taxes, health, people's struggles, etc. I really do not know if there is a Republican with the guts to ignore the extreme fringes of the party in order to pull it off.

I hope the people who have been mentioned as possible Republican presidential candidates listen to Newt. Any Republican candidate cannot run on a campaign of "change" unless they give firm information on what the change will be. That was one of the biggest frustrations in 2012 for me. Both sides seemed to campaign on the fact they weren't the other guy without much more than that. And when you vote for style and personality and party over substance, you get exactly what we have today: no leadership, no direction, and many unanswered questions.

The Republican Party is so full of factions that nobody, including the Republicans, knows what their message is. A house divided against itself will fall and the Republican Party has to get their act together. If they continue to fight among themselves and do not present a united front, the White House should just be painted blue. Because to be President you have to bring in more of the country then the other guy and the Republicans are not doing a good job of that.

Wal-Mart and McDonald's Are the Barometers

August 16, 2013

It looks like President Obama is patting himself on the back again. The U.S. employment data on Thursday showed that the number of jobless claims fell to a near six-year low last week. What his administration always appears to reluctantly acknowledge is that many of the people who do find work are finding it in low-paying and, often, part-time jobs. And they always seem to forget about the ones who just gave up looking for work.

One constant scale to show how the country is really doing is to look at the performance of Wal-Mart and McDonald's. Also on Thursday, Wal-Mart, the world's biggest retailer, posted disappointing quarterly sales of $116.9 billion, from a projected $118.5 billion, as shoppers pinched by higher payroll taxes and gas prices made fewer trips to its stores. The world's biggest restaurant chain McDonald's, meanwhile, reported quarterly profit below expectations in July, and said sales for the rest of the year are expected to remain "challenged."

Whatever your feelings about these two companies, they are the "go to place" of the masses. Fueled by ok quality and ok prices, these are traditional areas for the middle-class and struggling segments of Americans to go to for shopping and eating out. When they are struggling and not doing well, it is a snapshot of the economic reality in this country.

A recent survey by the Associated Press illustrates a widening gap between rich and poor, with the loss of good-paying manufacturing jobs as reasons for the trend. While the low end of the economic scale is doing very, very poorly, the top 20 percent is thriving. In the long run this does not bode well for any nation. Just look at history where countries were thrown in turmoil when the rich keep getting richer and the poor get poorer.

It is distressing that the hiring practices of so many companies took advantage of our recent economic spiral and the uncertain business climate that the government encourages. The recent great recession allowed many businesses to reset their mindset. They were able to bank on the concept of "you are lucky to have a job and if you squawk for more, you are out of here!" Unfortunately, the economic needs of the average American did not get set at a lower amount; in fact the cost of living continues to rise. Likewise, worrying about Obamacare and the very real problem of not knowing what the government is going to do next regarding business have caused companies not to stick their neck out. It is safer and cheaper to hire part-timers. If this becomes the new normal for business, we are in for some long term trouble.

I am getting more and more distressed at all of the talk by both parties and total lack of action. I don't think we are close at all to people rising up and demonstrating against the government, but 10-20 years down the line things may be very interesting if we keep on our current trends. Tell the king and his court (President and Congress) that the emperor has no clothes. Maybe if they actually see where people are, they will have the motivation to start governing the country for people and not the Party.

Our leaders really do not get it. Working two part-time crappy jobs is not the same as one decent job. It takes that person off the unemployment tally sheet, but he is not making good money and it is a struggle. The heartlessness that comes out in some of the things our politicians say is appalling. We should have swap day in Congress. All House and Senate members are replaced by one of their constituents for a week, and in turn the politicians take that person's place in the real world. A week of working a low-paying job, trying to pay the bills, or maybe spending the entire week looking for a job would change some attitudes.

Field of Dreams Exist

August 19, 2013

There is something so American about baseball. I do not mean the A-Rod version of the big leagues where scandals make the headlines, millionaires are playing a kid's game, and you have to take out a small loan to afford taking the family out to a game. Throw in obnoxious fans and traffic (depending where the game is) and the experience can be more ordeal than fun.

I am talking about minor league baseball. I had the opportunity to attend a minor league game for the first time in about 5 years over the weekend and it was so much fun. A last minute purchase got tickets about 6 rows away from first base for the same cost as going to a movie. Food and drinks were the same price as going to any restaurant or eatery. There was not a $9.00 beer in site. The game was spirited and fun to watch and the whole evening was capped off with fireworks that were as good as any 4th of July celebration.

While the game was not a sellout, there were plenty of people in the stands. The Girl Scouts and the local hospital were honored at the event as well as announcements recognizing other groups, birthdays, anniversaries, and the like happening throughout the game. When teams changed sides, there was always something going on the field for entertainment from a sack race with kids to adults doing the "spinning around the bat dance" and then trying to run a straight path to a finish line. It was fun, wholesome, and everybody seemed to have a great time. The home team happened to win but I do not think it would have crushed the spirits of any of the fans if they happened to lose. This did not seem like a group who would have an unhealthy fanaticism to their team like you see people have with the upper levels of pro sports.

I write about this as a celebration of the simple things in life. Too often we get hung up with how complicated and jaded things are. Sometimes technology and circumstances have brought that on and sometimes we are our own worst enemy with not being able to get pass what bothers us. I write with a touch of cynicism of the inability of our nation's leaders to effectively govern the country. It was a nice reminder this weekend that some things that seem so darn American keep moving along if you know where to look.

Summer is almost over (boo, hiss). In some areas of the country school has already started up. If you have not already done so this summer, I urge everyone to get out and do something fun. Go to a ballgame, hit the beach, or visit one of the many beautiful local or national parks we have in this country. America is a truly diverse, beautiful place. It is a tonic to go somewhere where people are having fun and taking a break from life. It can even be contagious. Yes, sooner or later we have to get back to reality, but the lingering effects from some relaxation and enjoying what we have in this country are a good thing.

You can pursue your own little field of dreams in the place of relaxation you yearn for. You know what they say: when you are dying you are not going to regret that you didn't spend more hours at the office; you will regret not doing more of the things you really wanted to do. Labor Day is two weeks away from today. Take the timeout you need to breathe and feel refreshed. You will be pleasantly surprised how you can then tackle the important issues in your life.

Lesson here: we all need to have fun!

Benghazi Baffles Me

August 20, 2013

To refresh everyone's memory the American diplomatic mission at Benghazi, in Libya, was attacked on September 11, 2012 by a heavily armed group. The attack began at night in a compound meant to protect the main diplomatic building. A second assault in the early morning of the next day targeted a nearby CIA annex in a different compound. Four people were killed, including U.S. Ambassador J. Christopher Stevens. Ten others were injured. The attack was strongly condemned by the governments of Libya, the United States, and many other countries throughout the world.

In the aftermath of the attack, then Secretary of State Hillary Clinton told four mid-level officials to clean out their desks and hand in their badges after the release of the report of its own internal investigation. This was compiled by the Administrative Review Board led by former State Department official Tom Pickering and former Joint Chiefs Chairman Ret. Adm. Mike Mullen. Those four officials have been in legal and professional limbo, not fired but unable to return to their jobs for eight months, until yesterday.

Secretary of State John Kerry has determined that these four State Department officials placed on administrative leave by Hillary Clinton after the terrorist attack on the U.S. mission in Benghazi do not deserve any formal disciplinary action and has asked them to come back to work at the State Department starting Tuesday.

All four officials placed on administrative leave will return to regular duty and not face any formal disciplinary action. It seems that Kerry reaffirmed the ARB's finding that no employee breached their duty or should be fired, but rather that some should be reassigned. This mirrored the concern in Congress that only mid-level officials with little direct responsibility for the Benghazi attack had been taken out of their jobs following the ARB report release.

Here's the confusing part for me. This was a tragedy. Somewhere the process or people broke down that enabled the events to happen. It is great that the State Department has taken steps in Benghazi's aftermath to strengthen embassies around the world, but it still does not answer the question: What happened?

I am not necessarily looking for a scapegoat. That never solves anything in the end, but if specific people did (or did not) do explicit actions that led to Benghazi, it should be known. I have a big concern how this has been handled by the government and the press. wTo the government I wonder why getting answers about something that happened a year ago is so hard? There seems to be more sleight-of-hand and misdirection in anything I have read on the subject that has come from the different investigations. Does the current administration just want this to go away? Does former Secretary of State Clinton want to distance herself from this so it does not have a negative bearing on a potential presidential run? Is the American government just incapable of doing anything in a professional matter?

As for the media, is this story not sexy enough for you? Are there only ratings or interest when you can show clear-cut animosity between the two parties on an issue? Or is a lot of the news media truly left-wing and they do not want to cast a shadow on the administration they support?

If the four people who were let go and now back in the State Department really had no effect on the attack happening at the embassy, then it is good they were given their jobs back. But this is not a kid's game where when something goes wrong you just get a "do over." Since politicians have the historic perspective of a sea slug, they probably forgot that while anything that goes wrong in government is bad, it is the cover-up that makes things worse. We have a case here of something being hidden or pure total ineptness of the administration. And to fix something that is broken, we first need clear-cut answers.

I am still very much in the dark with this terrible event. For something so bad, there has never been any definitive explanation given to the American public. It seems to come out in bits and pieces with no real conclusion. That is not usually a good sign. It would be nice if a truthful narrative was presented. If nothing else, the families of those that were killed deserve that respect.

Rich College, Poor Student

August 23, 2013

Yesterday while speaking before the University of Buffalo, President Obama rolled out a plan to tame the rising cost of college. Like many Obama initiatives, the concept was big in talk and concept, but lacked any real teeth. The idea was that Washington should fund the colleges that get the best results while keeping tuition reasonable. By 2015, the Department of Education would begin grading institutions based on factors like average price, student debt loads, graduation rates, employment, and the number of low-income students enrolled. Then, starting in 2018, the government would start directing federal aid to schools with the highest grades compared to their peer institutions. As colleges try to shape up to meet Washington's standards and attract students, tuition prices should theoretically drop, or at least level off.

Up to this point, Washington has tried to improve access to higher education by acting as a source of no-strings-attached cash for college students by freely handing out loans and grants to help them cover the rising price of a degree. The results have been decidedly mixed. Tuition has kept marching up. Americans are now shouldering more than $1 trillion in student debt. Millions have defaulted on their education loans. And the free-flow of government money has helped guide colleges towards an overwhelming desire for more money from the national money tree.

The White House calls this "pay for performance." And like so many ideas that come out of the White House these days, some of the details are still vague. It's unclear whether troubled colleges would actually lose aid as a punishment for a bad score, or if high-performing schools would simply be rewarded with more funds. The White House summary states only that that students "attending high-performing colleges could receive larger Pell Grants," which generally go to low-income and working class students, "and more affordable student loans." But on a broad philosophical level, the proposal would fundamentally rewire the relationship between the federal government and the world of higher education, by introducing at least somewhat meaningful accountability measures for the first time across all sectors of the industry, from the Ivy League to the University of Phoenix.

The key to the whole plan, though, really lies in government's power to dole out aid dollars based on results. Without that, you just have a government-sponsored college guide that the least sophisticated, most at-risk students probably won't bother to use. And sadly, accountability is the one thing the White House needs Congress for. The Department of Education is free to start grading colleges as it sees fit, but it can't use its rankings to decide aid eligibility without legislation. And Congress is in charge of that legislation. At this point there is no great leap on the President's bandwagon to move forward with this.

This whole issue showcases two big problems. The first is our colleges. They know they are in the catbird's seat. With the supply of jobs much lower than the pool of people seeking them, education becomes a bargaining chip. Jobs that used to go to high school graduates are now going to those who went to college. It is not that the jobs have gotten more complex, it is that an employer now has the luxury of pooling from young people who have more education. Thus the state of our country has given a marketing boost to universities. But just as many companies hold employees and customers in disdain for the sake of increasing their corporate earnings, colleges show the same attitude to their students. The sad truth is that underneath all of the lofty words carved out on university buildings, the bottom line for colleges is MONEY!

The other problem is that anything out of the White House are "feel good" ideals that will come into being only if my two favorite sports teams, the New York Mets and Minnesota Vikings, win their championships in the same year. (By the way, those odds are greater than you winning the Powerball Lottery three times in a row.) President Obama is like the absentee father who promises his kids he will come and take them to Disney World and then never shows up. Kids are resilient because you know what happens: they stop believing in Dad and pretty much disregard what he says. That is where we are as a country. With a five-year track record, it is hard to take anything President Obama says seriously. I think the country as a whole, and this includes both parties, has taken on the attitude of a kid waiting to turn 18. We will put up with him, but are looking forward to not having to deal with him anymore when we become adults.

Colleges and tuition is a huge issue that will only get worse. I certainly do not have an answer. Our national institutions and corporations have a poor track record of working towards the greater good. And having government bureaucracy heavily insert itself into another facet of life is disheartening. But at the least, let's have a national call for the president's office to stop pretending it is going to fix problems. That Gift of Silence may help some smart people to actually come up with solutions that have the potential of working.

As I reread this column it struck me how political the entire plan could become. I have also reflected that anything the government usually gets involved in usually becomes worse. There is a movement starting to create new solid colleges that provide a great education at a much cheaper price. They may not have the prestige of a Harvard, but that is not where the average student is going anyway. I think the only thing that will help the college situation is if the established institutions are truly challenged with viable cost-effective alternatives.

In a Nation of Hypocrites, the NCAA Is the Biggest

August 29, 2013

If you have any interest in sports you probably saw the news yesterday that Heisman Trophy-winning quarterback Johnny Manziel of No. 7 Texas A&M has been suspended for the first half of Saturday's season opener against the Rice Owls. This was announced by Texas A&M and the NCAA (the National Collegiate Athletic Association which governs college sports).

Johnny Manziel was under investigation for receiving money for signing autographs. The statement released yesterday said that there was no evidence that Manziel received payment for this. The NCAA and A&M agreed on the one-half suspension because Manziel violated NCAA bylaw 12.5.2.1, an NCAA representative confirmed. The rule says student-athletes cannot permit their names or likenesses to be used for commercial purposes, including advertising, recommending, or promoting sales of commercial products, or accept payment for the use of their names or likenesses.

The flip side of this story is that former UCLA basketball star Ed O'Bannon is the lead plaintiff among 16 former college athletes in a long-running legal battle consisting of a high-profile anti-trust lawsuit that claims the NCAA owes billions of dollars to former players for allowing their likenesses to be used without compensation.

The staff of the NCAA has to rank right up there with used car salesmen and lawyers for the bottom rung of the integrity ladder. The NCAA makes scads of money, mainly on men's football and basketball, and rule over their kingdom with the wisdom of a hamster lost in a maze. Time and again, they bring penalties down on college athletes and schools for the mildest of infractions. Indeed, they make their money on the backs of athletes who give up a significant portion of their young lives to be the best they can in their sport of choice. If anything, the NCAA

289

is more concerned about what is in their best interests than they are in the student's. And whenever an organization pays more attention to making themselves viable and needed, then their original mission goes down the tubes.

Let's take two examples. The first is the Johnny Manziel situation. He came upon the college football scene a year ago like a lightning bolt and came out of nowhere to win the award for best player. This is heady stuff for a freshman and he made some mistakes in his offseason. A college does make quite an investment by giving a player a scholarship and it is hoped an athlete will take advantage of it to get an actual education, but sports is fickle. Very few players make it to the pro level in which to earn some money, and one injury can ruin a career. If someone can make money on his talent, then isn't that what we are about in this country? It seems like capitalistic principles are ok sometimes, but not others. In cases like this it does not seem like the NCAA is protecting the student-athlete or the member schools, but itself. It cannot seem to bear the idea that money is being made on a college sport and they do not get a piece of it. As a side note – a half game suspension? Why didn't they just make Johnny write "I will not sell my autograph" 500 times on a blackboard?

The second example is one that has bothered me for years. Many times a kid goes to a college and finds it is not for them or the coach who recruited him left, and they want to transfer somewhere else. If he or she does, then they very often have to sit out of their sport for a year before they can play for their new school. This is ridiculous. Many non-student-athletes do the same thing. My daughter decided her first school was not for her and transferred to another in the middle of her freshman year. It wasn't like she had to sit out biology for a semester. But any coach who gets millions more than the millions he is already paid by his current school can take his ball and go play with the new suitor. It does not matter that he promised his recruits he would be around for the long haul. After all, they are just kids and will learn to adjust. Forget about teaching values like honor and the meaning of giving your word. The truth is that the NCAA and coaches can be bought – lock, stock, and barrel!

I nominate the NCAA for the Hypocrites Hall of Fame. By the way, factor in all of the money that changes hands due to college athletics and try to fit that into the equation of the outrageous tuition that many colleges charge. It may take a little shine off when rooting for your favorite school team.

I stand by this article. The NCAA needs to be disbanded and a new organization formed that really does look out for the student-athlete. What a concept – colleges concentrate on the student. Not the boosters, or the coaches, or the big payday from bowls...you get the idea. The NCAA is like Congress: most members of either group couldn't work in a real job if they had to!

So What Was Celebrated Yesterday?

September 3, 2013

Labor Day in the United States is a holiday celebrated on the first Monday in September. It is a celebration of the American labor movement and is dedicated to the social and economic achievements of workers. It constitutes a yearly national tribute to the contributions workers have made to the strength, prosperity, and well-being of their country.

As with so many national holidays, we like having the day off, but we often forget about what the day is all about. I have to wonder how many people yesterday wish they had a job to have a day off from. Or how many had to go to their part-time jobs because that is all they were able to find? And when you have a part-time job you almost always have to go in when you are told. That is because those employers know they have you by the nape of the neck and you can be easily replaced. There are an awful lot of people out there who need a job who can be fitted into the slot.

And that is the real shame of yesterday's celebration of Labor Day. There was not a lot to celebrate. Unions are looked at as the enemy of business instead of a way for workers to be able to band together and work towards having a good work environment and a living wage. It is true that the pendulum swung in the unions favor for many years to the detriment of business. But now it has gone the other way as the rallying cry is for business to make every last penny for the benefit of its stockholders or owners and to hell with the employees. This is a generalization I know, but look at where we are. Relatively speaking, many families aren't bringing the same amount of income into the home as they were able to do twenty years ago. The unemployment figures given to us every week do not reflect the underemployed and those who have given up looking for a job. Unemployed youth and those over 50 have a hard time finding anything.

I don't know who we are trying to fool anymore. It seems all of the speeches about creating jobs are just that: talk. I know President Obama has been completely distracted by what to do in Syria this weekend and it got him out of any major addresses on labor in America. You know we had all of the talk this time last year on strengthening the middle class during the Presidential election; that got forgotten on November 7 – the day after the election.

Employees, unions, and management have to work together to keep the balance in our economic system. And that balance is necessary to give our country a solid foundation to do anything well. That has always been true in our history and I see no reason why that will change in the future. It comes down to a common sense approach to planning for the future by everyone involved – and not driven by immediate gratification or downright greed. Unfortunately, our recent track record of being motivated by cool-headed planning for the future has not been great.

The government is going to be greatly distracted for the next several months as it deals with Syria, another debt-ceiling crisis, implementation of Obamacare, etc. Haven't we seen this movie before? Let's hope as we limp along to the end of the year that some things actually get accomplished that will set the nation on a positive course. It would be nice if more people can actually enjoy and celebrate Labor Day next year for what it is.

This seems like an appropriate place to end this book. I continue to write everyday so feel to visit the "Common Sense" section at www. authormax.com . One of the biggest themes over the past year in my writing is how the employment situation is worse than the numbers show and our leaders seem not to care. But since the industrial revolution in America, jobs have forged our growth. Aside from our Constitution, it is a main pillar the United States has been built on. That foundation is crumbling and shaky and until the government and business wipe the selfish scales from their eyes, we are in trouble.

About The Author

JJ McKeever is a writer who has worked in the government, business, and nonprofit worlds, traveled around a lot, and never gets tired of watching people and figuring out how life works. Making the transition to full-time writer, JJ launched "Common Sense," a daily column that looks at everything from government to the church and everything in between like school, sports, and family life. Started as a way of disciplining himself to write something original every day and helping people find his website (www.authormax.com), "Common Sense" took off! People liked to read his commentary and suggestions on practical approaches to some of the most vexing problems facing life in America today.

Born in New Jersey and living back there again, he is an admirer of other writers like Ben Franklin and Art Buchwald and loves how they could make a real point using short compositions riddled with observations, practical solutions, and humor. These influences, along with a varied life, taught JJ to look at issues from all sides. It is that insight that he brings to his writings. He figures if people do not agree with him, at least he hopes he can help make them think! And in that thinking, the American Dream just may be attainable for all Americans.

36297701R00172

Made in the USA
Charleston, SC
29 November 2014